Hangchow, My Home

Growing up in Heaven Below

=====

Eugenia Barnett Schultheis

LOST
COAST
PRESS
Fort Bragg
California

Hangchow, My Home
Copyright © 2000 by Eugenia B. Schultheis

Lost Coast Press
155 Cypress Street
Fort Bragg, CA 95437
1-800-773-7782

Cover concept by Graphic Results
Cover production by Mendocino Graphics

Library of Congress Cataloging-in-Publication Data

Schultheis, Eugenia Barnett, 1913-
    Hangchow, my home : growing up in heaven below / Eugenia Barnett Schultheis.
        p. cm.
    ISBN 1-882897-46-3
        1.Schultheis, Eugenia Barnett, 1913--Journeys--China--Hangzhou. 2. Hangzhou (China)--Description and travel. 3. Hangzhou (China)--Social life and customs. I. Title.

DS796.H25 S38 2000
951'.242--dc21   99-054123

Manufactured in the United States

Contents

Foreword

When I look at a full moon, I always see the Rabbit—not the smiling face of the Man in the Moon.

This is an instance of the way I've looked at almost everything in my life because of having grown up in China.

In many ways it was a typical American childhood. My parents made no effort to be 'Chinese' or to 'live' Chinese. But they entered into life in the city of Hangchow (Hangzhou) with respect and admiration for its history and character; and though their children were taught to appreciate what was best in the home country of America, they caught the enthusiasm (and love) of our parents for China—its people—and the richness of its culture.

Every American child growing up in pre-Communist China was affected by its differentness from the West. Those who were children in a traditional Chinese city absorbed from everything about them a different way of experiencing and reacting to the world—a way that would persist wherever they might be in future years.

It wasn't taught them; it was simply there in everyday scenes, the ways of life, the actions and interactions of people, the customs, the snippets of regional folklore.

Nobody told me, as a formal lesson in folklore, why to look for the Rabbit in the Moon. It was pointed out as a matter of course on nights when the moon was large enough and then the story might be referred to of how the Rabbit came to be up there forever grinding powder for the Elixir of Immortality... and so I have always seen it.

How we learned and absorbed the more profound philosophies and values of the culture and people would be harder to explain.

For most of us—even those whose parents were determined their children would grow up fully 'American'—the Chinese way would always be part of us, whether or not recognized as such.

It was wonderful—this dual vision we received. Confusing sometimes—often difficult; but I've wanted others to know something of what it was like in the receiving of it—especially in a city of such distinction and charm and so ideally Chinese in character as Hangchow, my home.

Author's Note

I confess to some inconsistency in my choices of how to present the Chinese language, which was my first along with English. In writing about Hangchow life, I found that I had to 'think' in Hangchow dialect, and I have tried to replicate Hangchow dialect (a southern Mandarin) in my phoneticization and spelling of local names, dialogue, phrases, and words.

Hangchow dialect as spoken is very different from northern Mandarin and to my knowledge, there is no official phoneticization for it. Therefore, for names of many places and persons I write about, I have drawn on the spellings (varied in themselves) found in the writings of the early Western residents of Hangchow—including my father's. Perhaps I should mention that in the old-timer's spelling of words beginning with gy, like gyao for 'bridge' and gya for 'street', the initial g is soft as in the English word 'gem'. Gyao is pronounced 'gee-ow' spoken as a single sylable.

When I have had no texts to go by, I have invented my own ways of phoneticizing words, phrases, and bits of speech and doggerel as I have remembered the sounds. I am not sure how well I have done, but I think they are close.

For transliterations of Chinese words that I do not associate with Hangchow dialect, I have chosen the Wade-Giles form of romanization which was used in the teaching of northern Mandarin when I was studying it in my post-college years.

Finally I am using the names by which cities and provinces in China were commonly called at the time by English-speaking Westerners: e.g. HANGCHOW for Hangzhou, SOOCHOW for Suzhou, PEKING for Beijing, NANKING for Nanjing and CHEKIANG for Zhejiang Province as the places are currently spelled when using the standard northern Mandarin dialect.

I have been a long time in producing this book. My parents—particularly my father—would be pleased at its completion, as would other relatives and friends from long ago.

I am grateful to the many who have encouraged and helped through the years—especially members of my family and most especially my sons William and Rob, who have been my star editors, advisors, designers and enablers. For absolutely essential help, I thank my friends Marjie Mayer and Francis (Mike) Hugo and my skilled and gifted consultant Martha Jolkovski, who is also my friend.

Hangchow, My Home

Growing up in Heaven Below

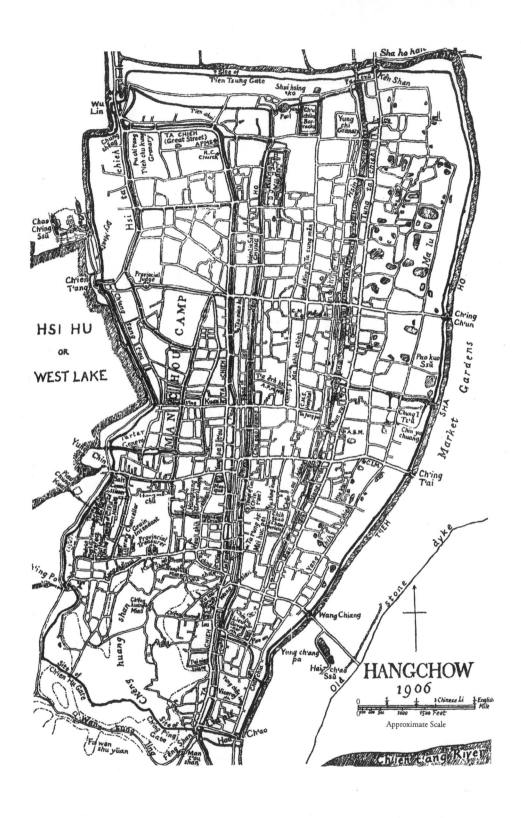

HANGCHOW
1906

Approximate Scale

First Impressions

When my parents set out for the Far East in the fall of 1910, the Dragon Flag still flew over China, and the last of the Manchu emperors—a small boy only four years old—was still in possession of the Dragon Throne and with it the awesome title Son of Heaven. For the past several decades, the outside world had been encroaching more and more upon the long-cherished privacy—and the sovereignty—of the Celestial Kingdom; the dynasty was on the verge of total disintegration; the coming of great changes seemed an imminent promise—or threat. But in spite of all this, the old look prevailed over most of China and the old ways continued across most of its countryside and in most of its towns and cities . . . By the time I was born, the dynasty had fallen. But it was this "old China" that I first knew; its scenes and sounds and manner of living constituted the world of my early childhood.

It was in the Chinese New Year season, the coldest time of year, when the young couple packed their suitcases in Shanghai and boarded the train for Hangchow. January 1911.

The train stopped outside the city wall at the Wu-lin Gate.

The newcomers got off and looked about them, waiting to be greeted and welcomed. But apparently no one was there to meet them.

"Are you sure they knew we were coming today?" my mother asked.

"Yes, they knew . . . I don't understand it." My father was puzzled, and (though he had been here once before) unsure of what to do next.

Through the hubbub and confusion they saw a Chinese making his way towards them. By means of sign language and a few words and phrases vaguely recognizable to them, he indicated that he was a servant sent to meet them and take them to the mission compound which was to be their first (and temporary) home. They stood by while he checked on all their baggage and commandeered a small corps of coolies to carry it; and

1

then he led the way and they set out on foot followed by a procession of chanting coolies.

Through the massive archway of the city gate they walked and into the eddy and flow of life and movement on the Great Street, my mother holding up her long skirts with one gloved hand as she picked her way carefully over the uneven surface of stone paving and cobblestone.

"It's really not far," my father assured his bride of a few months, while privately more than a little indignant that a sedan chair hadn't been provided for her entrance into her new home city.

Actually it was only a few hundred yards (no distance at all for the old-time missionaries accustomed to getting about on foot . . . the idea of a sedan chair to carry a healthy young lady that short a distance probably hadn't occurred to them!) The servant motioned them around a corner into a quiet little lane and soon they found themselves at the gateway of the Southern Presbyterian Compound, where they were greeted with such warmth and genuine welcome that they instantly felt almost like kinfolk—not strangers at all.

———

I asked my mother in her 80s about her first impressions of Hangchow.

She didn't say anything, but smiled the same fond smile that always came with the recollecting of Hangchow days (the same happy look I've seen appear on the faces of friends of the same generation when Hangchow is remembered).

"What did it look like to you when you and Dad first came there?" I persisted.

"It was different," she finally said earnestly. "Everything was different."

I was disappointed. But actually that is probably as good an answer as any she might have given—perhaps truer than if she had tried to give a more detailed description.

Still hoping to learn a little more about her specific reactions, I asked, "How did it make you feel? Did you feel uncomfortable? Was China frightening to you?"

"I think it was for some people [she meant Westerners] at first," she

told me, "but you see [her eyes brightened] we were living with the Stuarts*
and they helped explain things for us and made us feel at home."

But I remember stories that suggest the strangeness she and my father
must have experienced—shocks of surprise or dismay that came to them
those first months . . . and continued to come every now and then for
years thereafter.

One story was about my mother's sedan chair being separated from the
others on their way to another mission compound for their "first dinner
party" in Hangchow—how she felt herself carried off alone into the dark,
silent city along narrow deserted streets and alleys. No lights except the
flicker of a lamp hanging from the shaft of the sedan chair. No sounds
except for the occasional hoarse grunts and cries of the bearers. Where
were they taking her? And for what . . . ? She couldn't understand them or
speak to them. You could still hear the relief in her voice years later when
she told of arriving at the open gate of their hosts' compound just as the
other sedan chairs arrived after coming by a different way.

Another: the afternoon of an outing to the site of the new Hangchow
College campus on the bluffs overlooking the Ch'ien-t'ang River southwest of the city—how the group of hikers lost track of the time and suddenly noticed that the sun was dropping low in the sky. Would there be
time for them to reach the city gate and go through before it was closed
exactly at sundown, not to be re-opened for any reason until the following dawn? My mother, with her infant son Robert there in the city waiting for his next feeding, was in utter panic. But they made it—just barely.

There's my father's sedan chair story—about riding to an appointment
across the city, going most of the way by the Great Street. He was so tall
that his head hit the 'ceiling' of the chair; and he asked his bearers to
remove the top. They were reluctant, but did so. As he was carried through
the city, pedestrians stared and pointed and burst into laughter. He didn't
know till later that a convicted criminal was always taken to his execu-
tion, riding in a sedan chair with his head exposed to the public view.

---

* John Linton Stuart came to Hangchow in 1868 a bachelor. He lived "native-style"
(over an opium den), had health problems, was sent home, came back with a wife
(Mary Horton, "Belle of Mobile Alabama"). They had four sons. The eldest, John
Leighton, was U.S. Ambassador to China after the end of World War II.

Yet, however much they later felt at home there, China never lost its novelty for them—its difference from their native America where they'd lived till early adulthood. They never stopped feeling surprised—at things that would seem perfectly natural to me; and they were always able to talk about China to people in the West in a way that I never could. What they remembered as interesting was interesting to their listeners, and their voices still had a ring of discovery and excitement that was infectious. Their hearers invariably hung on every word. (This never seemed to happen to me. Most of my life, I've been very dull talking about China—especially Hangchow. What could I say that was entertaining about a place that was simply my frame of reference for everything else?)

During my growing up years, there hadn't seemed to be anything extraordinary or mysterious about my American parents being in China, and when I was a small child it didn't occur to me to wonder why they were there. Living in China seemed so inevitable and normal that I couldn't imagine anything else. All small children, I suppose, accept their whereabouts as natural; they have no choice in the matter—and the world is equally familiar and at the same time fresh and new to them or deprived and fearful wherever they are.

All the same, I have to admit that I couldn't help knowing there was something unusual about our living in China, though I preferred not to dwell on it. I remember the times when my older brother and I were oohed and aahed over by American visitors in our home—or when we were on family furlough back in the States . . . "So here are our little Chinese children! . . . How does it feel to be a little 'Chinese'?"

Robert, being more socially responsive than I, would reply brightly, "It feels fine." I would stare back and say nothing. For both of us, the question fell in the category of silly things grownups say to children (like "How you have grown!" spoken in great astonishment, when it would have been more surprising if we hadn't). At the same time it bothered me because it forced me to wonder for the instant how I would "feel" if I hadn't been born in China but rather in America where my parents and all my other relatives had been born. It seemed to me that if this had been the case and if I'd always lived in that strange, bright, but unreal country, I would be an entirely different person. And this was a truly frightening thought, for it threatened my very identity.

Later on when I was of school age, I never gave much thought to the fact that my parents had left their homeland to live and work in China. It seemed unremarkable—partly, I suppose, because I was just one of my many China-born Western schoolmates and friends—none of whom, I imagine, were any more curious about their parents' reasons for coming to China to live than I was about mine.

But now I'm interested; I want to know why—why choose to leave America in the early 1900s—a happy time of peace and plenty at home? Why go abroad when almost any place 'abroad' was almost sure to be less clean and comfortable, less safe, and not necessarily more interesting? And why China, which was so far from home and not (at that time) thought to be a glamorous or agreeable place to live—or even attractive to visit? The answers are to some degree implied in the questions.

Among the Americans in China at that time were representatives of American businesses (like Standard Oil and Singer Sewing Machine) who were challenged by the opportunities and difficulties of opening up markets in that vast, populous—and poor—land, only recently accessible to them. There were also Americans posted in diplomatic, consular, or military assignments in China—most of them transients, but a few of whom became lastingly involved with its language and culture and development.

But by far the greatest number of the Americans living in China at this time had come as missionaries or in some form of Christian work. The enthusiasm for foreign missions and other Christian enterprises abroad was at a flood tide in the first decade of the 20th century; and it seems to me that it was partly inspired and certainly encouraged by the confidence and optimism and zest that prevailed in the climate at home.

The early 1900s have been called America's "Good . . ." and "Innocent" years. The nation had been reunited after its terrible civil war—had engaged successfully in a war against Spain—and was now enjoying a period of peace and prosperity. The continent had been explored and settled and now stretched from "sea to shining sea" with the Pacific Ocean as its last frontier. Americans were proud of their beautiful land. They loved their flag as a symbol of freedom and democracy. Most of them believed quite simply but profoundly that we were a nation peculiarly blest—a sort of Chosen People who had been led to our Promised Land for a

5

divine purpose—and that our government and way of life and institutions (and the faith that was felt to be their foundation) were to be the hope and salvation of the world. Good times—pride in the nation—the native energy and generosity and pioneer spirit of the American people, along with this hopefulness and faith, found expression in Christian enterprises abroad (and it's not surprising that there were Americans of that era both at home and abroad who tended to feel that Christianity and American democracy were very nearly synonymous).

The idea of going off to serve—for life—in a foreign land was tremendously exciting to the idealistic young person of that day. The Student Volunteer Movement (recruiting for Christian work abroad) was active in college and university communities all over the country. Its appeal to the youthful imagination has been compared to that of the Peace Corps after World War Two, but my impression is that it was more pervasive and inclusive—taking into account that in most colleges the student population then was predominantly White Anglo-Saxon Protestant. According to my father, there was hardly a college student—even among the most frivolous—who didn't at least consider becoming a Student Volunteer, which meant asking himself or herself, "Shall I choose to leave home to spend my life in service in some other more needy part of the world, wherever it might be?"

The majority of young people who decided in the affirmative were (I believe) among the cream of the crop—the more imaginative, the more independent and daring, and the more seriously committed.

Some, of course, were not well-equipped for the difficulties, physical and psychological, of life on the mission field. There were missionaries in China who should have never gone there in the first place. Some were romanticists. Some (perhaps unknowingly) had come to escape problems at home or their own unresolved emotional perplexities. Some were too rigid and inflexible of mind and belief, and China itself proved to be too much for them: they were overwhelmed by the rich complexity and the many admirable qualities of what they had thought of simply as a godless ("heathen") nation and people.

I remember hearing of a good many 'breakdowns' among the China missionaries—of men and women sent home because their "health had failed" in ways that were not reported as dysentery, tuberculosis, malaria or any of the recognized physical illnesses, but were left mysteriously un-named.

But the missionaries who were my parents' best friends in our part of China, and especially in Hangchow, were whole, happy, spirited individu-als—gifted and bright, not saints perhaps though some were close. They were among the most delightful and effective human beings I have known.

An Assignment to China

I suppose at this point I should say that I never felt like a Missionary Child and I never thought of my parents as Missionaries.

But both of them—quite independently of each other, I believe—be-came Student Volunteers as undergraduates in college.

Neither one, as far as I've been able to find out, felt any special pull in the direction of China.

I keep thinking that their story (and mine) would be more romantic if I could discover some portent—some far-off link with China in either of the families . . . a sea-faring ancestor who had sailed on a Clipper ship, a pioneer missionary relative or friend who had brought back stories to fire the imagination—even an early and unusually strong curiosity about the Orient.

I've tried in my own mind to make something of my father's descrip-tions of Sunday afternoons in his boyhood outside his father's parsonage in the little town of Leesburg, Florida, when the whole family—with Jessie the cow gently chewing her cud near by—sat on the grass talking together or reading (inspirational literature) under the shade of a china-berry tree. But it's hard, even for me, to attach much significance to that.

When I think of Leesburg in the early 1900s and of the slightly larger town of Jasper (my mother's home) in north Florida, both seem a far cry indeed from the centuries-old city of Hangchow, provincial capital and one-time imperial capital of China! too far for there to be any easy com-patibility between my parents and their adopted city . . . and yet there was, almost from the beginning. Perhaps the true romance lies in this unforced, appreciative, yes—and loving rapport between the ancient, so-phisticated Chinese city and two young, hitherto untraveled individuals from the recently wilderness state of Florida.

Families seem to have been large when my parents were children—at least in the deep south. My father, Eugene, was next to the youngest of eight children—seven boys and one girl. One brother died in infancy—another, the eldest, of typhoid fever when sixteen. And my mother, Bertha, was one of ten brothers and sisters, one of whom, the first-born—a boy, died as a baby. She had an older brother, to whom she was devoted, and was the adored big sister to all the others.

When my father was about fourteen, the Rev. R. H. Barnett (his father) was assigned to serve for a brief period as pastor of the Methodist Church in the town of Jasper in the piney woods section of northern Florida. The most active and whole-hearted member and supporter of the little church was a Mr. C. W. Smith, an enterprising and prosperous business man and a leading citizen of the town . . . also himself a lay preacher, who often conducted services for the men in his logging camps or in tiny out-of-the-way churches with no resident ministers of their own.

The Smiths made ready to welcome the new minister and his family and to help them settle in—and invited them for their first meal in Jasper. When I was little, I used to love to hear my father tell about when he first saw the Smith home—a great rambling white frame house set far back in a lawn shaded by live-oak trees. There on the white-pillared veranda that fronted the whole house, he saw "a beautiful girl with long golden curls hanging down her back." The "beautiful girl" was, of course, my mother-to-be.

The families became fast friends; the teenagers, (my father, my mother and her older brother Austin) were together in school, did their homework together, took part in social activities at school and church together. The following year, the Barnett family moved to Tampa.

My father graduated from Hillsboro High School in Tampa. He was a straight A student and participated enthusiastically in many extracurricular activities. He had been a star debater since grade school—debating was almost as important and exciting as competitive sports at the time; and this probably had something to do with his intending to prepare for the law when he went to college. But soon after entering Emory College in Oxford, Georgia (now Emory University in Atlanta), he became active in the campus YMCA and in the Student Volunteer Movement, and his legal ambitions were forgotten.

When my father joined the Student Volunteer Movement, it was with the intention of service abroad with the YMCA. I'm not sure he would have considered signing up as a would-be missionary—partly because none of the three main categories of missionary work (evangelistic, educational, medical) suited him. But I have a feeling that even then he had his doubts about working as an American among the people of another land for an enterprise (however noble and helpful) that was directed and entirely supported from back in the United States of America.

After graduating from Emory, he entered Divinity School at Vanderbilt University (Tennessee), where he studied Hebrew and Greek and Homiletics and other courses that would give him a solid grounding in the history and theology and expression of the Christian faith. He wasn't going to be a preacher, but he had chosen a religious vocation, and knowledge and understanding of the basics of that religion (Christianity) were essential.

When my father filled out his application for YMCA work, it was for a lifetime career of service in the foreign field.

His first assignment, however—given him after his year at Vanderbilt— was as general secretary of the campus YMCA at the University of North Carolina at Chapel Hill. It was here while serving as student secretary and taking graduate courses on the side that he received a letter from the International Committee in New York City offering him a post abroad— possibly in Brazil. Would he consider it?

He promptly sent back his answer: Yes.

Then he wrote the news to the eldest Smith daughter in Jasper, Florida, and asked if she would go with him; and she promptly sent back her answer—and it was also Yes.

"That was really brave!" I told my mother when as a widow she was reminiscing fondly (with my encouragement) about "Eugene's letter of proposal" and her quick—not to say eager—reply. "Didn't you have qualms later—about going off to spend your life in another country?"

My mother was never one to dramatize herself. She didn't answer immediately—and then it was in an off-hand way. "Oh no," she said. "You see, I'd always wanted to be a missionary—ever since I was a little girl."

That was news to me—even though I knew that being a "foreign missionary" had been a favorite dream of little Protestant girls of my mother's generation.

I was curious. "Where did you want to go as a missionary? China?"

"No, I never thought of going to China. I wanted to go to Africa."

My mother was twenty-two when she accepted my father's proposal.

After graduating from high school, she had attended a school—a sort of junior college—in Mississippi and then entered and graduated from Virginia College (now defunct) in Roanoke. (In the college annual, her picture is included among the superlatives—Most Popular, Best Dancer, Cutest, etc.—as Best Student. In my childhood this seemed a little dull to me.) She had chosen Virginia College for its excellent music department and had majored in music. She had studied for two summers at the Cincinnati Conservatory of Music.

Now she was back home in Jasper, giving music lessens (piano) and helping provide programs for church, school and community.

Life was never dull in the Smith household with its large tribe of lively, talented, and individualistic children, their buoyant, energetic father and quiet, large-hearted mother, plus the numerous friends and strangers always welcome in the home.

My mother had her admirers, among whom was a seminary student soon to be a minister, and another a young lawyer. My father used to tell us with unbecoming glee about coming to visit and sitting on the front porch helping himself liberally from a crate of peaches sent to Bertha by one of her would-be suitors. Mother never encouraged any of them; she was too candid and kind-hearted to be the traditional southern coquette. She couldn't even enjoy years later hearing her husband tell about eating those peaches given her by his unsuccessful rival.

The visits to Jasper were part of the courting. Before that, the Barnett and Smith families had kept in touch. The young people had seen each other at church-sponsored youth meetings during high school and at student conferences in the college years. At a summer conference at Blue Ridge, North Carolina, the courting, chaperoned with loving approval by my father's older sister Loulie, developed into what used to be called an understanding, but no formal engagement.

Since then, letters had been going back and forth regularly and often between Chapel Hill and Jasper. But my mother has told me that she was beginning to wonder if she was included in my father's hopes for a foreign assignment which he had been discussing in almost every letter without any specific reference to her.

(This was the way he was and would always be whenever possible: to know and explore all the factors of a situation to be dealt with before plunging ahead into it—or asking anyone to plunge with him . . . My mother—like most of the Smiths—was more of a spur-of-the-moment person. She actually enjoyed unexpected challenges, though in her own way she also liked to be prepared for the coping . . .)

The wedding was set for midsummer.

The flow of letters between Jasper and Chapel Hill became more copious. There was no long distance phoning in those days. Letters were how you communicated. The only sample of the correspondence I ever saw was a postcard my mother smilingly showed me many, many years later. On it was a comic picture of a handyman staggering under the weight of an enormous grandfather clock, with the accompanying caption, "Time hangs heavy when we are apart!"

Eventually one of his letters brought the news that it had been decided they would be going to China . . . China! . . . This caused great excitement in Jasper and would have brought a certain degree of apprehension if not secret pangs of dismay to the typical bride-to-be of the time. I imagine that my mother was both excited and calm—and began to wonder what kinds of clothing and household supplies she should begin gathering together. The problem was that she didn't know where in China they were to be.

It wasn't till early summer that they knew. My father was called in to a personal meeting with the great man himself—Dr. John R. Mott. Dr. Mott told him at great length and in much detail of urgent requests he had been receiving for someone to organize and open up YMCA work in the city of Hangchow, capital of Chekiang Province. He asked my father if he would consider this assignment. Such was the power of Dr. Mott's personality that my father said (later) it would never have occurred to him to refuse or even ask for time to think it over—even though until that hour he had never heard of Hangchow.

Immediately after the meeting he looked it up and wrote what he'd learned to Jasper ... where I'm sure there was a lot of further "looking up." ("Looking up" was compulsive in both the Smith and Barnett families.)

I don't know what their sources of information were. I can quote from a volume published in 1908 (*Richard's Comprehensive Geography of the Chinese Empire*) which says, first of all, of Chekiang Province: "Area— 36,680 square miles. It is the smallest of the eighteen Provinces ... Population—1,580,000 inhabitants, or 310 to the square mile ... Name— Chekiang (the name) signifies crooked river Province. This name has been given it on account of the bore or tidal wave of its Northern river, which drives back, and as it were bends its waters ... Boundaries— Chekiang is bounded on the N. by Kiangsu, W. by Nganhwei (Anhui), Kiangsi, and Fokien (Fukien). S.—by Fokien (Fukien) E. by the Eastern China Sea ... Capital city: Hangchow Fu."

Of "Hangchow Fu" it says (in part): "Population, 350,000 inhabitants. Situated 150 miles S.W. of Shanghai, and 80 from Ningpo, it is a treaty port and one of the finest and most famous cities of China. 'Above is Heaven,' says the Chinese proverb, 'and below, Soochow and Hangchow.' It is built on the left bank of the Ts'ient'ang-kiang (Ch'ien-t'ang River), and at the southern terminus of the Grand Canal. Its site is most beautiful, beside the river with its great tidal wave, while to the rear of the city rises a graceful hill crowned with pagodas and kiosks, and in the distance is a range of mountains furrowed with deep valleys. One of the sights of Hangchow is the famous Si-hu or West Lake, celebrated by poets, covered with elegant boats, dotted with islets upon which are numerous kiosks and villas, while in Summer the surface of its water is decked with thousands of water lilies [actually lotus]. Hangchow is still noted as a pleasure-resort. It is also a silk manufacturing center, but it no longer enjoys its former celebrity, for practically speaking, it has but one long street bordered with rich warehouses, the rest of the city being a vast desert since its devastation by the T'aip'ings ... " (1860s)

Looking elsewhere, other facts about Hangchow could be found: Served as Southern Sung dynasty capital (1127-1279 A.D.) ... Marco Polo (13th century) called it "beyond dispute, the finest and noblest (city) in the

12

world" . . . Renowned as a cultural, religious, commercial (as well as) silk-producing center . . . Dialect—Mandarin (southern) . . . climate—winters cold with some snow; summers oppressively hot.

The population estimate would vary probably in different accounts. By 1910 it was closer to 600,000, and the city itself grown back out of the ruins of the T'aip'ing violence. It was still a walled city and still with almost no modern amenities.

———

A few years ago, I found an account of my parents' wedding. It was in the July issue of a periodical called the *Florida Christian Advocate*. It begins: "A beautiful wedding was that which took place in the Methodist Church in Jasper, Fla. on the evening of July 20, when Mr. Eugene Barnett and Miss Bertha May Smith were united in the holy bonds of matrimony. The church was tastily (sic) decorated for the occasion with southern smilax, cut flowers, pot plants, and over the chancel hung the letters S B (for Smith Barnett) made of white carnations . . . " I am tempted to quote the whole story, but it is long and is at once fulsome and stilted in the style of the times—a style which I find evocative and touching, but could seem affected (and tiresome) to others.

Most of the members of both families were at the wedding. My grandfather Barnett and "Brother" Scott (the church's regular minister) conducted the service. My grandfather Smith did not walk down the aisle but watched with others of his large family from their pew in the little church. He had always said he would never "give away" any of his daughters, refusing both the notion that they were commodities to be exchanged and the idea that he would be "losing" them from the family. By no means did he object to this marriage. On the contrary, he and his good friend, my grandfather Barnett, always claimed to have thought of this match years before, and (like proper old-fashioned Chinese fathers) would have tried to promote it—or at least prod along the courtship—if it had been necessary.

After an informal reception at the bride's home, the young couple left for Jacksonville to board a small steamer for New York City. "The bride's going-away gown [I quote again from the *Florida Christian Advocate*]

13

was of Rajah silk in Copenhagen blue and she wore a becoming hat of Milan straw trimmed in shades of blue to match the suit . . . " Quite a cosmopolitan outfit if you think about it—and the bride must have been bewitchingly pretty in it.

The whole town of Jasper had shared vicariously and happily in the heady excitement of the wedding and seeing one of its number about to go off to live in China! All, that is, except for the bride's ten-year-old sister Lillian* who hid herself away during the festivities and cried her heart out. But after it was all over and the bride and groom had left, there was a general sense of gloom as others in Jasper also realized what a long goodbye they had just said to one of their favorite fellow townspeople. When would they see her again? Would they ever see her again? Would she be swallowed up by a China which to most of them was dark, dangerous and impossibly remote?

———

It was to be a number of weeks before the honeymooners actually left for China. First they were at Silver Bay, the YMCA summer conference grounds at Lake George (N.Y.). Then they went up to Northampton, Massachusetts to join with others who were also about to go abroad for the YMCA and had gathered there for final counseling and inspiration before setting off for their respective posts in various parts of the world.

After that, there was a week in New York City which they spent mostly in shopping for household equipment they would need in China—my father trailing along unhappily while his bride considered at length what was absolutely necessary and what they could afford that was not. She had been brought up in a rather lavish household, but knew she would have to be thrifty on the income of a YMCA secretary—which was roughly that of the average Protestant missionary.

And then, one day in September, they boarded a train bound west and were on their way to San Francisco, in those days a five-day journey. This must have seemed the real beginning of their Big Adventure—their trip

---

* Lillian was to go to China herself in 1922 to teach music for three years in a mission school in Huchow. Her first novel (never published) was about China. Her second was the bestseller *Strange Fruit*.

14

to a life in China.

In San Francisco they were at the farthest shores of the American continent with the Pacific Ocean and Asia on beyond. It was an exciting city.

But their sense of excitement and anticipation must have reached a peak when they found themselves walking up the gangplank of the ship that was to carry them across the Pacific Ocean.

After stowing their hand luggage in their stateroom (which was small and rather stark), they hurried back up to the main deck to take their places at the railing that faced the shore. Suddenly there was a hoarse blast from the ship's funnel—and a frantic flutter of wings overhead of sea gulls frightened out of their peaceful flight over and around the ship. Late-arriving passengers pushed their anxious way up the gangplank past visitors hurrying to leave the ship.

Slowly the gangplank was pulled up. The passengers standing at the railing exchanged startled glances as they felt the vibration of the deck beneath their feet—and then there was a shout from the crowd on the pier below as they saw the ship beginning to move. A slit of water appeared between ship and dock—and handkerchiefs waved wildly while people called to each other across the broadening gap.

The young honeymooners from Florida, caught up in the excitement, raised their arms to wave and began to call out—then let their hands fall back to the railing and were silent; for there were no familiar faces in the crowd on the gradually receding shore—no eyes straining for a last glimpse of their faces—no lips moving to call out to them, "Goodbye . . . Goodbye . . . Have a safe voyage . . ." In that instant they realized how far they had already gone from home, family, and friends—and how much farther behind they would leave them.

Yet, oddly, they were to keep closer to their relatives and friends than many Americans who have moved only a town or county away from each other. And, though they may not have known it, they were not leaving "home" and America entirely, but taking the essence of both along to China as invisible and ever-present luggage.

This was the "America" that we children would first know (secondhand, it is true)—the one that was cherished in our parents' hearts and perhaps idealized in their rememberings. What they passed on to us when they spoke fondly of Leesburg, Jasper, Blue Ridge, Chapel Hill, Silver

Bay were pictures of a land that glowed in good fortune, good will, and near-perfection. Later on, of course, we would hear of its flaws and failings, since our father always kept up with what was going on in China, "at home," and all over the world and would discuss and deplore such unfortunate developments and events as the failure of the United States to join the League of Nations—the Teapot Dome Scandals and the like. Our first 'view' of America, however, was the one that stayed with us; it was one we saw blurred "as through a glass"—not darkly, but suffused with brightness. Perhaps this made it harder for us later—for how could we easily reconcile that early vision with the reality which we encountered and had to live with when we came "home" to America as adolescents?

In 1910 it took four weeks to cross the Pacific from San Francisco to Shanghai, with stops en route at Honolulu and Japan.

My parents' ship, the Asia (not to be confused with the Empress of Asia, the splendid Canadian Pacific liner of a later date) was medium-small, rather grubby, strictly utilitarian. Fresh water was in short supply; and unappetizing food became progressively less palatable as the days went by—refrigeration being inadequate (no deep-freezes in 1910—or even electric refrigerators).

But the days passed agreeably. There were the stops in Honolulu and then in Japan. The long days in between were spent mostly on deck reading—walking—gazing with awe at the vastness of ocean and sky—talking or playing shuffleboard with the other passengers, among whom were two young bachelor YMCA secretaries also bound for China. There were also several missionaries, including one couple, like my parents, just married and going to China for the first time. (The young wife died of smallpox only a few months later: out of some personal religious scruple, she had refused to be vaccinated.)

Not long after the last port of call in Japan, the passengers could see the waters of the Pacific growing dull and dingy and then becoming yellowish-brown in color. The Asia was now in the Yellow Sea, passing an occasional slow-moving, square-sailed Chinese junk. Finally it turned into the mouth of the Whangpoo River and anchored, the river being too low for steamers to go all the way to the landing piers. The passengers climbed down a ladder and into a small launch which had pulled alongside the ship. After the usual delays, the motor began to sputter; the little launch chugged purposefully inland up the river; and in just a short while, the passengers were clambering onto the pier.

Shanghai

Shanghai in 1910 was not a "Chinese" city though its population was predominantly Chinese. It was an international port city where East and West met and mingled in colorful but largely superficial ways. It had the bustle and busyness of the West but the slower pace of Asia. Except in the old walled Chinese City, streets were wide and paved, allowing for street cars (called trams there), motor cars, horse-drawn carriages in addition to rickshaws, other man powered vehicles, and pedestrians. There were department stores, solid and very British. There were streets of row houses, brick—each with its own little front yard—that might have been transplanted from London or Glasgow. The city had a strong British-colonial flavor which somehow prevailed even in those sections that were more European or Japanese in population.

In Shanghai, there was electricity, running water, modern plumbing—"all the comforts of home" as my father might have put it . . . in fact, as I believe others have noted, maybe more comforts than some Westerners in 1910 were used to, if they had come from out-of-the-way rural places back home.

Shanghai provided an interval of transition from West to East for the young couple from Florida. They were warmly welcomed by Americans in the YMCA and missionary community. The Southern Methodists in particular were delighted with the arrival of such an attractive bride and groom with such impressive Southern Methodist credentials, and they made much of them. My mother's trousseau—all those pretty wasp-waisted, puffy-sleeved dresses and wide-brimmed hats (feathered or flowered) in the latest style were joyfully admired and studied by the missionary ladies.

During this interval in Shanghai, my parents stayed in the home of the Fletcher Brockmans. (He was senior secretary of the National Committee of the YMCA, headquarters of which were in Shanghai.) Language study arrangements were made for them there in the home; and the Chinese lessons began almost immediately with a teacher who spoke the Hangchow dialect—and not one word of English.

If either my father or mother felt any misgivings over their arrival at Shanghai—or, for that matter, any trepidation over the prospect of living in China, I never caught a hint of it in their reminiscences of their early days.

They were both not only idealistic but sanguine by nature. Both were outgoing and friendly—expecting to like and be liked. They were young; they were healthy and happy and very much in love; they were eager for whatever the future offered them.

Pictures of my father at age twenty-two show him as a tall, thin, hollow-cheeked young man with deep-set eyes and a serious, almost somber expression. But photographs can be misleading. He was earnest and serious-minded, but he also had a quality of alert responsiveness and a sense of fun and mischief that the pictures do not reveal. These characteristics—the quick and genuinely friendly responsiveness and the almost puckish humor—made it easy for him to establish a rapport with almost anyone, but were especially appealing, I believe, to the Chinese—particularly those in this area of China where people tended to be more volatile and spirited than in the North. In addition, he had an inexhaustible curiosity about the world and its peoples and deeply probing interest in places, politics, and ideas. From the first, China stimulated his curiosity and interest, and he reacted with zest to everything he saw and learned that was different and new to him.

My mother, on the other hand, instinctively looked for likenesses rather than differences wherever she happened to be—and therefore could make herself feel at home anywhere. To her, all nice, normal people—of whatever nationality or race—were basically the same. As to her physical surroundings, she had the happy and sometimes surprising faculty of finding familiarity in the most unlikely scenes. How often when we were children she would excitedly call our attention to a Chinese hillside, exclaiming that it was "just like" a spot in the Blue Ridge Mountains of Georgia or North Carolina! Or a stretch of bank alongside a canal in Chekiang province could remind her happily of the Suwanee River or of some Florida creek where she had often gone picnicking in her girlhood with her family and friends.

Moreover, as was true of many typically southern women of her generation, underneath her gentle femininity she had a mind and will of her own and a generous store of good hard common sense. Her whole look and manner—the fluffy golden-brown hair, English tea rose complexion, sea-blue eyes, winsome expression, pretty clothes, and the sweet eager tone of voice when she spoke—might have given the impression that she was too tender and vulnerable for any unusual stresses and strains of life. But in fact she was practical, resourceful, and serenely confident that she could cope with almost any situation. Should there come times of extreme difficulty and crisis, she knew she could call on the Lord for help; otherwise, she felt she could probably manage pretty well without having to bother Him.

First Family Home

Abounding Joy Bridge

About six months after coming to Hangchow—and well over a year since their wedding in Jasper, Florida—my parents moved into a place of their own, the Fong Leh Gyao (Abounding Joy Bridge) house.

Most of the widely scattered mission compounds or residences were referred to by the Chinese name of something in their vicinity. Often—since Hangchow was a city of many canals and bridges—it would be the name of an ancient and well-known bridge. The Southern Presbyterian Mission compound, where my parents had been living with the Stuarts, was T'ienh Sway Gyao (Heavenly Water Bridge). Across the city the Northern Presbyterian Mission was to have a large compound always called Tsoo Jia Gyao, the Tsoo Family Bridge.

Fong Leh Gyao was my parents' first home.

(My first home too, though I don't remember it.)

It must have been a peculiar place to start housekeeping in. Its history as mission property went back to 1870 when the lot with its dilapidated buildings was bought by the Northern Presbyterian Mission. Maybe the original Chinese main residence was kept and built onto by its first missionary occupant. Many early mission homes were built without benefit of architect; they just grew like Topsy. My father has described the Fong Leh Gyao home as "labyrinthine" with many large rooms bewilderingly placed. They used only a few of them.

There are a few family snapshots of the place—taken both inside and outside. One indoors is of my mother at the piano, looking very young and pretty but petulant at having her picture snapped. A front view of the outside shows a large building of indeterminate architectural style almost filling the space across the farther end of a rectangular lot (length three times its width) enclosed by high walls. There must have been separate servants' quarters—and surely a well—behind the large building, but they are not visible. On either side of the rectangle of grass are a few well-grown trees, but I can see no plantings of flower beds or ornamental shrubbery. I may be too imaginative about this place, but it seems to have a somewhat angular and Spartan look, as if its occupants during the years had no time, in their pursuing of Christian duty, for grace and charm in their daily lives at home.

My mother was a born homemaker, but it couldn't have been easy in this first home, where in addition to not having any of the usual comforts and conveniences she was suddenly immersed in problems of language, servants, food . . . and strange customs in dealing with every area of homemaking and daily life. Also—and this has just occurred to me—she was expecting her first child (she was well along in pregnancy when they moved). Dauntless as she was, sometimes it was too much for her and she succumbed to tears. (All new American brides in Hangchow did . . . and laughed together about it years later.) She did have someone to take her troubles and perplexities to (and never ceased being grateful): Miss Rebecca Wilson (later "Aunt Becky" to us Barnett children), a spinster missionary from South Carolina who was a sort of cheerful, commonsensical fairy-godmother-guardian-angel to all young couples newly arrived in Hangchow from America . . . particularly (I think) those from the American south.

Rumors of revolution against the increasingly weak and ineffectual Manchu dynasty had been growing louder and more insistent. On October 10, 1911, word came that the cities of Hankow and Wuchang, up on the Yangtze River, had successfully revolted. Hangchow was sure to follow suit, though no one knew how or when.

On November 6, 1911, Hangchow revolted against the dynasty and declared its independence from Manchu rule.

On that same day, my brother Robert was born in Shanghai, a true Son of the (Chinese) Revolution (eligible also to be a Son of the American Revolution—though that's beside the point). This timing of the firstborn son gave a certain amount of unexpected and agreeable 'face' to my father in his Hangchow contacts.

A cablegram was sent home to the families announcing Robert's birth on November 6. It arrived in Florida on November 5—the day before— an anomaly due (don't ask me exactly how) to differences in time and the International Dateline.

My father had brought my mother up to Shanghai and stayed until Robert was born and mother and child were obviously doing well. Then he went back to Hangchow (they would return later) to find the city still celebrating its overthrow of Manchu domination. But he wondered about the white banners he saw flying everywhere—in every street, from every gateway, every shop front (many banners improvised or simply strips of white cloth). He knew that white was for mourning. He learned that the city was paying its final respects to the last Emperor of the (native) Ming dynasty. The Manchus had forbidden all the traditional rites of mourning at his death 267 years before.

I had always believed that it was because of political unrest and possible violence and danger in the event of revolution that my mother was in Shanghai for the birth of her first child. She had been persuaded (I thought) by friends concerned for her safety in these uncertain times to come to Shanghai, where she would be in the home of the Fearns (both of them missionary doctors) and Dr. Anne Walter Fearn would deliver the child. Otherwise she would have stayed in Hangchow, and Robert (and later I) would have been born there with Dr. D. Duncan Main, old-time Scottish medical missionary, in attendance.

Not so—said my mother with some vehemence when we were talking one day about the event of Robert's birth. "I wasn't going to have my first baby with Dr. Main in charge. I was going to have a good American doctor!" I was somewhat taken aback, never having realized my mother was prejudiced against the British medical profession—and almost hurt on dear old Dr. Main's account.

On consideration, however, I realize that my mother was following her sensible and natural instincts. Dr. Anne Walter Fearn was a trained obstetrician and a woman (and a southerner); she knew how to bring babies safely into the world and always with the utmost solicitude for the mothers.

It was all so eminently satisfactory that it was natural to follow the same procedure the next time; and in about sixteen months there was another trip to Shanghai to the Fearns' home on Rue Palikou in the French

Concession. And on February 21, 1913, Mrs. Dr. Fearn helped bring another Barnett baby into the world. This time it was a girl, but that was all right since the first born was a son.

February 21 was my father's birthday. A daughter's name had been chosen: Elizabeth Anne after the two grandmothers. Instead, I was named for my father—Eugenia, the feminine form of his first name Eugene . . . and my middle name was Mother's before she was married, except that mine was spelled Mae which she thought looked prettier than her May . . . I always felt that with such a name, Eugenia Mae, I was expected to grow up to be tall, handsome and intellectual. That didn't happen, but I still think it is a nice name—even if too distinguished for the bearer—and I like being named for both my parents. The birth date has always been memorable too—particularly after my granddaughter Alexandra was born also on a 21st of February.

I still regret not being able to claim Hangchow for my birthplace—though sometimes I fudge a bit on the facts and do. The actual birth was in Shanghai, but before and after, my life really began in Hangchow.

I don't believe my parents sent a cable announcing my birth (or, for that matter, those of my two younger brothers). And they forgot to register me at the Consulate—until two and a half years later when applying for a family passport to go 'home' on furlough.

I sometimes tell people that perhaps one reason for my feeling so 'Chinese' is that I wasn't an American citizen till I was going on three years old. I was Chinese.

First Family Furlough

In 1914, instead of going to Mokanshan, the hill resort in Chekiang province, my parents had decided that our summer vacation would be in Karuizawa—a beautiful mountain resort in Japan frequented in those days by American missionaries from all over the Far East. This was my first visit to another country, but was probably wasted as such on me—and on my brother Robert too. I'm not sure at what age international travel begins to be "broadening" and culturally enriching for children, but I rather doubt that it does much for those as young as we were then (I was a year and a few months old, Robert not yet three).

In August, war broke out in Europe. The news—which came to my parents in Japan—was shocking. It also complicated the return to China, the German ship which was to take us back being suddenly ordered to sail (or steam) home to Germany to be available for sterner duties.

The Great War in Europe was to have an impact on us in remote Hangchow. (I didn't know till recently that when America joined the Allies, my father seriously considered volunteering for service in France.) But it did not interfere with the scheduled furlough in 1915 . . . four and a half years after my parents had left America.

Later furloughs came after six or seven years abroad and each one was for a year; this first one was for only six months—an exciting and somewhat hectic period spent in travel (extra trips for my father for meetings and speaking), visiting relatives and friends, and showing off two small children—a lively rosy-cheeked three-year-old boy whose bright blue eyes and curls of spun gold made him look like a Botticelli cherub, and a plump two-year-old daughter with dark straight hair cut in bangs ("A real little Chinese girl!" people exclaimed).

People don't quite believe me, but I still have a few flickering but vivid memories of that first visit in America and the journey home to China. They may be mixed in with pictures I've seen or stories I've heard, but I know they are true memories because nobody but a child (and maybe this particular one) would remember things so inconsequential—so irrelevant to what an older person would consider important or worthy of notice.

I can't claim to remember the voyage across the Pacific from China—or my first glimpse of America—or visiting the Barnett relatives in Florida; but I do have one specific memory from the time we were with the Smith relatives in north Georgia close to the end of the furlough. (My grandparents and my mother's younger siblings had moved from Jasper to live in what had been their "summer place" in the Blue Ridge Mountains of Rabun County.)

I remember everyone in a circle around a log fire. The littlest person (not yet three) doesn't see all the faces. (When you're little, grownups' faces are way up there, so that you don't look at them much except from a distance.) But my youngest aunt—Esther—is in a chair across the circle where I can see and admire her. She is such a pretty lady (actually she was all of sixteen then, but she was tall and seemed grownup to me). She has wavy chestnut-colored hair, soft around her face, caught with a ribbon at the nape of her neck, and pouring down her back. She has on a white blouse with a high neck and a small-waisted skirt reaching almost to the floor. Suddenly I notice there's only one foot on the floor underneath the ankle-length skirt. Oh—this is too bad—for such a pretty young lady to have only one leg! How did she lose the other one? . . . While I ponder, there comes a sound of someone at the door—the hearty voice of my grandfather on the front porch. He is back from cutting down a fir tree (still covered with snow) for Christmas. Everyone gets up to go and exclaim—and I see my aunt Esther walking on two feet—she hasn't lost a leg after all!

I have three memories of the journey back to China—one in the American Southwest, one on shipboard, one in Japan.

On our way to the West Coast at the end of the furlough, we stopped off to visit relatives in Colorado Springs. One day we were taken to see an Indian dance. We are on a sort of high place—the Indians in paint and feathers down below on the floor of a canyon. Everything is bright and dry and golden. Now this memory may have derived something from pictures of Indian war dances (black and white photographs) seen later in the *National Geographic* magazine, source of so much of our learning about the larger world, including America. But it is basically true, because I remember that Robert was holding by its handle a child-sized suitcase someone had recently given him for a special present; and after we had been standing and watching the dance for a while, he laid his little suitcase flat on its side and sat down on it. "Get up, Robert! Get up!" someone (probably our mother) said. "That's not very strong. You'll smash it and ruin it!" . . . Why do I remember this? Probably because of the combination of unusual circumstances. And partly I was beguiled, I think, by the suitcase as a diminutive version of what was ordinarily a large grownup sort of thing. And I felt sorry for Robert for not being allowed to do what he wanted with something that had been given him. It was *his*, wasn't it?

The voyage. I doubt that I saw the Pacific Ocean much in all its vastness on the first crossings; I was just too small. What I remember is being perched up on a chair (on books? or what? It wasn't a regular high chair) in the dining salon about to have my breakfast. On the table in front of me is a large, flat soup plate (not a proper cereal *bowl*) filled with Cream of Wheat. I don't like Cream of Wheat. (I don't *hate* it; I just don't like it.)

The ship is pitching and rolling. The soup plate slides towards the center of the table—pauses and begins to slide back—closer and closer to the edge. Maybe it will topple over and fall upside down onto the floor! But no . . . just at the edge it stops—and I see there's a protective rim all around the table that keeps the dishes and everything else from going onto the floor in stormy weather. This is so interesting that eating my cereal doesn't seem so bad, after all. Maybe this tiny episode helped teach me very early in life that "wishing" (or wishful thinking) doesn't necessarily "make it so." I had wished—*expected*—that bowl to go over the edge, but it didn't.

Japan. Some time or other—maybe it was after we had moved to Shanghai—I saw a picture (I think a Japanese print) of a rural scene with rain slanting down, and walking single file on a foot path, two or three farmers wearing wide-brimmed flat woven bamboo hats and thatched straw shoulder capes. And I knew I'd seen something like this before—only not in the Japanese countryside. I remembered being in a rickshaw going up the incline of a little cobbled street. The rain is coming down. On either side I see pretty little one-story buildings . . . varnished light-colored wood, lattice work, papered windows . . . everything small, everything clean. And the rickshaw puller has on the same kind of large, flat hat that was in the picture and a straw cape sticking out almost horizontally from his shoulders like a sort of personal thatched roof to keep off the rain. Chinese farmers and coolies wore similar rain gear, but the scene I've recalled—and that I can 'see' now—is, I'm sure, a remembered glimpse of Japan in 1916 when I was three.

Finally the *homecoming* . . . I don't remember but I can imagine the bewilderment and confusion of the arrival in Shanghai and the hours-long train ride to Hangchow with all the strange-looking, strange-sounding people in the train and at the stations . . . Then we are in a room filled with people who are laughing and talking excitedly. The room has high ceilings and a somewhat bare, dull look—different from what we've been used to. My mother seems to be the center—or a center—of joyful attention. (My father may have been encircled in another part of the room.) I'm standing by her chair (my head about knee level with all the standing-up grownups). I see my mother looking over to where someone is standing in an open doorway. She leans down and says to me in a low voice, "Go with Amah now." "Amah" must be the person in the doorway. She has black hair smoothed back from her face and over her head. She's wearing different-looking clothes with a large sort of apron over the front, and she has tiny feet bunched up into black cloth shoes with pointed toes. She has black eyes. She looks very—safe. Obediently I go to her and take her hand—or we take each other's. She says something to me, but I don't know what it is; maybe she's simply making reassuring sounds . . . We go out into a dimly lit hallway and up some stairs. Near the head of the stairs is a small room. We go in. "Hsi-hsi shou," she says to me—and immediately I reach both hands up to be washed. I knew what she was telling me to do; the strange-sounding words are not strange after all . . . This is when I knew that I wasn't in a new or different place. Everything was the way it was supposed to be and this was where I belonged. I didn't consciously think (at age three), "I'm home"—but I knew that I was . . .

House on Horse Market Street

The house at Fong Leh Gyao had been reclaimed by the Northern Presbyterian Mission for some of its own people. Our home now (again temporarily) was in another missionary residence—this one rented from the C.M.S. (Church Missionary Society—British). The C.M.S. had been the first Protestant mission to settle in Hangchow following the T'ai P'ing hostilities (1850-1864) . . . [The American Presbyterians were very soon after . . .] and this property must have been purchased at a modest price while the city was still largely in ruins, for it was in a choice location, just around the corner from the Great Street in the heart of the business district.

We always called it "our Ma Zse Gya house." The front gate opened on a street called Ma Zse Gya (in Peking dialect Ma Shih Chieh)—or Horse Market Street, a name probably given it back in Sung dynasty days, or even earlier, when streets were wider and horses were a familiar part of the city scene.

After we had moved away to our next home—about a year and a half later—we always spoke of Ma Zse Gya with a kind of fond nostalgia. I don't believe I ever saw it again, either while we were still living in Hangchow or visiting there later, but I know from snapshots, my parents' references, and my own hazy recollections that it was not so insistently plain and utilitarian as some missionary homes, and in fact had a sort of unassuming character and grace of its own.

There was a deep lawn (*not* narrow like that at Fong Leh Gyao) between the front gate and the house; and alongside the enclosing compound walls and close around the building were shrubs and perennials that had been planted and nurtured into growth many years before by some missionary and/or his wife who loved to garden. The two-story family house (the servants' quarters were in a separate building behind it) was large and pleasantly proportioned—with generous-sized, airy rooms and wide comfortable porches. Ma Zse Gya was friendly yet reserved. It had a faintly storybook quality (for some reason I think of Kipling when I remember it). Perhaps it was because of the surprise of coming out of the clamor and dirt and busyness of a Chinese midcity and entering another little world—quiet, private, uncluttered—a bit of Victorian Britain surrounded by Asia, still seeming to belong to the late 1800s and the British missionary family who had first made it home.

I don't remember much about the interior of the house except for the downstairs hallway, dark and cavernous—the wide stairway leading to the upper floor, and a small "moon window" high above my head, overlooking the halfway landing. I have no idea what a taller person might have been able to see through this window. I saw a circle of sky. Nothing else; but it fascinated me. Sometimes it was a clear blue; sometimes there were clouds wandering across the picture, slowly changing shape as they went. On overcast days it could be an off-shade of white—or else dark grey and heavy with rain; and at night it was a background for a sprinkle of stars and (once in a long while) the sliver of a crescent moon. And sometimes it was not a picture of the sky at all, but an ominous round of total blackness. On those nights, I hurried past the landing on my way up to bed—out from under that frail transparent barrier against which a whole ocean of darkness threatened to burst through.

After we moved, I often thought of the moon window at Ma Zse Gya and wished (unrealistically) that we could have brought it along with us. But then, we had a moon *door* at the new home. It wasn't the same . . . it didn't frame the sky or anything else interesting, but it was round and so was a partial substitute.

Why this simple but deeply-felt pleasure in being able to see a part of nature or the world through a circular opening? I suppose I could attempt some profound psychological or philosophical explanation, tying it in perhaps with the fact that the Chinese symbol for the complementary elements that make up the harmony of all things (the Yin-Yang symbol) is enclosed in a perfect circle. I could ask questions: Is the response of satisfaction to the symmetry, balance, and never-ending completion of a circle an instinctive and primitive reaction?—or is it a sophisticated esthetic response developed through systematic thought and philosophy? Is it universal?—or more natural to the East than to the West? In my particular case, is it an indication of my *Chinese-ness*, or at least of how early in life my tastes were influenced by Chinese culture?

But this sort of speculation verges on the precious. As a matter of fact, I think any child, anywhere, would be intrigued by a moon window or a moon door simply because of its difference from the usual kind of window or door.

And I must admit that our enjoyment of the moon door at the new house turned out to be less esthetic than athletic; for Robert and I used to try to see how far we could walk or run up its smooth inner curve (sneakers were best for this), and after we were old enough to have heard about something called centripetal force, we believed that if only we could go fast enough, we would be able to go all the way around without falling on our heads at the half-way point.

I have only dim memories of the Ma Zse Gya lawn and gardens, except for a lushly grown space at one side of the house, cut through by a pathway that was pebbled in a pretty design and bordered by ornamental grass. I remember the translucent berries, like beads of white jade, that bejeweled the clumps of grass at a certain season of the year. But I don't remember the day my mother found me busily pulling off the berries and cramming them into my mouth. Instantly she thrust a finger into my mouth and forced out the half-chewed morsels. But how many had I already swallowed? And were they *poisonous*? If so, how deadly might they be? The servants did not know. No one seemed to know.

Send for Dr. Main! And hurry!

Off went a messenger on flying feet. It shouldn't take Dr. Main too long to come from the mission hospital in the city . . . but the minutes passed. What if he were out visiting patients at his T.B. Rest Home on

29

Needle Pagoda Hill, or (even worse) looking over the grounds of the new Leper Hospital in the valley beyond? . . . It seemed that hours had dragged by, but at length the doctor arrived, my mother rushing to the gate to meet him, her face drawn with anxiety—for to see her child (or any child) threatened by danger was the one thing that shattered her basic calm.

Dr. Main (looking as usual like a jovial Santa Claus in mufti and minus the beard) gazed thoughtfully at the little white berries she held out to him. Yes, he had seen them often enough, but never in all his years in China had he heard of anyone *eating* them.

"Does that mean they're poisonous?"

Instead of answering, he asked, "How long ago did she eat them?"

On being told, he shook his head. "Too late to take her to the hospital and pump her out."

My mother turned a shade whiter, but the doctor seemed relatively unperturbed as he leaned over to take a good look at the small patient (or culprit) standing by her side.

"She doesn't seem to be paining. Any signs of a belly ache?" (Dr. Main had always taken a boyish delight in using words that might shock or surprise his more staid and proper fellow-missionaries—and sometimes a word like "belly" would crop out.)

"No, I don't believe so."

"Well then, I don't think we need to wor-r-ry. But she had better have a good cleaning out. So give her a big dose of castor oil r-r-right away."

Happy the generations of children who have not had to gag down the nastiness of castor oil whenever they seemed to need "cleaning out"!

It is not surprising that I have conveniently forgotten an episode that had such a disagreeable aftermath. But—come to think of it—it is surprising that every child (foreign or Chinese) who knew Dr. Main adored him in spite of the fact that his visits were so often followed by a "big dose of castor oil"!

There was another crisis at Ma Zse Gya that I only remember hearing about when I was older—more frightening than the episode of the Questionable Berries and with more poignant connotations.

We had a servant (I think he was the gateman who also ran errands and performed other services) named Tsong Dah—a gentle man of unusual sweetness and sensitivity. He was devoted to the family and especially to Robert and me.

Tsong Dah was ordinarily eager and conscientious in his work and outwardly cheerful, but every now and then was seized by sudden and unaccountable fits of deep melancholy. He had attempted suicide more than once, and on several occasions while he was working for us, the other servants had come posthaste to tell my parents that Tsong Dah was threatening to do away with himself . . . and my father had spent hours talking him out of the depths of his depression.

One day my mother was in the house writing letters when she heard a sudden clamor of alarm from out in the yard and cries of "The well! The well!" She glanced frantically about her. There was Robert on the floor playing energetically with building blocks. But where was his little sister? . . . Instantly she concluded that I had ventured out and fallen into the well.

She ran outside in time to see the servants dragging a body out of the well. It was Tsong Dah. Water poured in streams from his clothes and hair, but he was obviously alive and unharmed. This should have been a relief, but all my mother could think of was that he had jumped into the well to try to save her small daughter—and had failed. The servants tried to reassure her, but she was much too overwrought to understand what they were saying. When she caught sight of the amah hobbling towards her as fast as bound feet could run, her one thought was, "What now? Has something happened to Robert too?" Panting breathlessly, the amah announced that she had found hsiao mei-mei (little sister) napping peacefully in the crib upstairs.

Tsong Dah was penitent, and all was well for the time being; but when might the black mood come back again to make him desperate?—and what if he succeeded in trying to kill himself? What effect would it have on the impressionable minds of the two small children who were so fond of him, if it happened there on the premises?

It was a sorrowful dilemma. This was long before the days of mood-controlling drugs—or of psychiatric therapy of any kind (available maybe in Vienna, but not in Hangchow). My parents reluctantly decided that Tsong Dah would have to leave us. My father found a job for him at the then-temporary headquarters of the YMCA. Perhaps feeling a useful part

31

of the newly developing enterprise with its lively activity and enthusiasm was the kind of therapy Tsong Dah needed. He worked as a YMCA employee for many years. He was always a family friend—and of the servants we had in our home during my parents' twenty-six years in China, he was the one they always spoke of most tenderly.

In our early years, our mother always kept us aware of the needs and distress of people not as fortunate as we—those who were cold and hungry or sick. She was so successful that, though she and our father enjoyed life in its various blessings and bounty as much as any individuals I've known, I have never felt completely at ease with comforts and luxuries when so many others in the world do not have—may never have them . . . indeed are desperate for the basic necessities. Their deprivation is not my fault—but neither is it *theirs*. As a child, I learned somehow—mostly from my mother—*not* to equate or confuse "fortunate" (or "rich") with "deserving," and I can't till this day—which accounts for many of my personal, social—and political—attitudes.

But though she kept our sympathies sensitive, sometimes almost to the point of rawness, she managed at the same time to deflect or soften the personal blows of fate that might shock or hurt us too deeply.

This is why I can remember Tsong Dah but not his attempted suicide or his moods of despair—and why I can remember our little dog Zip and that he "got lost," but not the actual day of his disappearance. One day he was with us as usual—a warm, active, loving little companion—and then when we looked for him to play with us in the garden, he just didn't seem to be around. Our mother explained to us after a while that he must have wandered away—but he would probably be coming back, maybe next week, maybe even tomorrow.

Whether he was stolen or slipped unseen out of the front gate when it was open and then was lost in the labyrinth of the Hangchow streets, we never knew. But we never gave up hope.

Even on our visits back to Hangchow years after, I found myself looking for him down every side street and dark alley, and my heart would give a leap of hope if ever I caught sight of a small, white dog, however mud-splattered, mangy and forlorn.

"Zip! Zip! *Here* Zip!" Robert and I used to call when we were younger.

"If it's Zip, he'll know us," we assured each other—and when there was no response or if the poor creature we were calling only turned dull eyes upon us, we would sigh in disappointment and try to console each other. "I guess Zip is looking for us somewhere else. Some day he'll find us."

The loss of our little dog was a continuing sorrow, but our greater grief was for him—lonely and bewildered, forever searching for his home and the family who had loved and cared for him.

In the excitement of moving to the Tartar City, we temporarily forgot Zip, but afterwards Robert and I continued to hope that we would find him or somehow (as it happened in stories) he would find us in our new home.

The Tartar City

The "Tartar City" is what Westerners called the area close to the lakeshore that had been the special reserve of the Manchus. It was also sometimes referred to as the Manchu City or Manchu Camp or Manchu Village . . . these latter two names probably being the more accurately descriptive. "Tartar City," however, has a finer, more romantic ring to it. And it was, indeed, like a small city inside the big one . . . with its own walls and its own "city gates" that were closed at nightfall. Non-Manchus could not enter, day or night, without permission.

The Manchu garrison had been stationed within the walls, and military and other Manchu families had their homes there. They were the privileged class—and foreigners at that—and their presence had been resented for over two hundred and fifty years. When the dynasty fell and Hangchow freed itself of Manchu domination in 1911, the city took back for itself this very choice property near West Lake. The surrounding walls were torn down, the inhabitants evicted and all the buildings razed. None of the structures, I believe, were especially grand or pretentious. (My impression is of a rather large village with low-lying, single-story dwellings fairly close together, and wandering streets, wider than in the crowded city.)

The Hangchow authorities decided to "modernize" the area, which involved laying it out in a spacious and orderly pattern—and to make it accessible to West Lake, which meant taking down the western section of the city wall. This latter was done without benefit of modern tools of machinery . . . by hundreds of men, women, and children swarming over the old wall and taking it apart, brick and masonry, bit by bit.

Meanwhile the Tartar City was laid out in large blocks, intersected with straight, wide streets with sidewalks (an authentic modern touch). The streets were dug deep, laid with a foundation of solid slabs of rock, filled in with dirt and clay, and finally surfaced with gravel consisting of broken bits from the city wall that had been torn down . . . I never realized in later years, when we used to dribble a small stone ahead of us while strolling the street near our house, that we were kicking along a chunk of the old city wall.

I wish I could have seen Hangchow when it was a totally enclosed city—with the old walls intact. Old-timers fondly remembered walking along the top (a wide, grassy promenade) of the western section at sunset. It must have been an experience particularly contemplative and satisfying and the Lake as seen from this elevation must have been particularly enchanting . . . But now the Lake was there for everyone to enjoy at any time. Public walks were being built and public gardens had been planned along the shore. And no more worrying about being caught outside the city wall at sundown! As Dr. Main wrote in one of his little booklets about Hangchow: "We were sorry to see the fine old wall and its massive gateways go, but the improvement is great and has proved a boon and a blessing to the people. So we have to let our sentiment go."

What of the former residents of the Tartar City?—the Manchus who had been living a life of privilege and indolence at the expense of their Chinese subjects? In some cities, the occupants of the Manchu garrisons had been massacred at the time of the Revolution. In Hangchow they were driven out of their homes with their belongings and expected to fend for themselves.

(My father told me once of at least one exception to this. An elderly Manchu widow, childless and with no close relatives, refused to be evicted from her home. "You will have to kill me first," was her ultimatum. Out of respect for her age, she was allowed to stay; and long after other homes were demolished and the area around her was leveled, one small house and one large tree and one old lady remained . . . and so it was until she died.)

A few of the evicted Manchus had enough drive and initiative to cope and make their own way, but most of them—having no skills or training or practical knowledge of the workaday world—kept themselves going by selling off their fine clothing, jewelry and household treasures. When this source of income was used up, they were destitute. They might have died homeless and starving. But the city of Hangchow had a long tradition of taking care of its indigent and helpless, and the civic authorities adopted the Manchu families as "wards of the city," constructed housing for them on a lot in the Tartar City and provided them with regular allotments of food and clothing.

The two-story buildings of the Manchu Compound enclosed a large square unpaved courtyard. Rows of identical rooms—hardly more than cubicles—opened onto narrow balconies facing the central open space of the courtyard. Each family, however large or small, was assigned one room for its sleeping and living quarters.

The compound was only a couple of blocks from our "new house"; and later on, when I was a little older, I remember passing by on walks and seeing it through the bars of its wrought iron gate. It had a crowded and yet curiously empty look. People drifted in and out of the cubicle doors like shabby ghosts. In the courtyard—walking about, standing, seated on benches—they were listless and vacant-eyed. Even the children were unnaturally subdued.

The atmosphere livened after the children began going to a school organized and conducted for them by what might seem an unlikely assortment of patrons and supporters. The priests in a nearby Buddhist temple donated the use of one of its buildings for classroom space; furniture was given by some of the Protestant missionaries in Hangchow; the city government provided funds for textbooks and supplies; and the volunteer teaching staff was recruited by the YMCA from among its members.

"Ecumenical" cooperation in public service wasn't exactly new to Hangchow. As an example, the first public hospital in the city (maybe in China)—founded in c. 1090 A.D.—was supported by government funds and private donation (by the poet Su Tung-po) and was administered by a Buddhist priest.

A talent for organizing and instinct for cooperating were not recognized as parts of the Chinese character by many of the Western missionaries, coming as they did at a low ebb in Chinese history and serving for the most part among the poorest of the poor ... American business men, I believe, did in many cases accept and respect these qualities in the men they did business with. But the early missionaries in general seemed to feel that they had only native ignorance, incompetence, and inefficiency to deal with. They saw the Chinese also as having little or no social conscience or care for any besides themselves and family . . . and no "patriotism." If they had known more about the historic workings of Chinese society and what these had had to do with the achieving and sustaining of a great, continuing civilization for thousands of years, they might have wondered at their impressions and questioned their assumptions about Chinese characteristics. (As some did, over a period of time)

My Father's Office

Missionaries in Hangchow had been among those eager for YMCA work to be opened up in the city, and they had welcomed the arrival of my parents. But the months had passed by and nothing seemed to be happening. Why didn't that young Mr. Barnett hurry up and do something? have himself an office? get a program started?

My father has written in his memoirs about his concentrated language study with a teacher who was a true Chinese scholar and gentleman and introduced him to the subtleties and appropriate courtesies of Chinese politesse—and about meeting and becoming acquainted with people of all walks of life, among whom were scholars, students, officials, members of the gentry. It is intriguing to me, when I think about it, to imagine this very young American talking—in his newly learned language—to these citizens of Hangchow about an organization he believed they would want to help bring into being and support—a Christian organization in its spirit, but not a "foreign" one. When it seemed that its purpose and what it could do were understood and really wanted and its work could be financed by a local membership and its programs could be initiated, planned, and carried out by members of the community (with the help and cooperation of its Western fraternal secretary—or maybe secretaries), then it was time to get started. This happened about two years after my parents came to Hangchow. The first membership drive overshot its campaign goal—and its subscribers were many and varied: they included a Hanlin scholar (the very topmost rank) and a rickshaw puller.

The temporary headquarters for the new YMCA were in a small yamen in the Tartar City, loaned rent-free by a local official. The permanent plant was also to be in the Tartar City. Before the first furlough, the military governor of Chekiang province (at this time, every province had both a civil and a military governor) had donated a large lot, which was also in the Tartar City, for the YMCA to build on . . . The building costs were to be funded by contributions from America . . . The leaders of the ancient and prestigious Hangchow Silk Guild had bought the adjoining property and presented it to the YMCA for an athletic field. There's a wonderful photograph of the Silk Guild in our oldest album. Posed in an elegant traditional courtyard, these gentlemen, dressed in the richest of dark satin and figured silk robes and brocaded jackets, are "old China" at its most dignified and impressive. I can't imagine any of them moving in anything but the most measured and stately manner. Their generous gift to the YMCA seems both incongruous and touching. They must have been looking at the future in a new way.

The yamen used by the YMCA as its first building was new, I believe, but not modern. The architecture was old-fashioned and picturesque—long, low buildings with latticed fronts and tiled, curving roofs, flanking stone-paved courtyards. I liked going there—seeing the double doors of the entrance flung open invitingly—stepping over the wooden threshold onto the clean stone paving of the front court. My father's "office" was off beyond a rear corner in what must have been another complex of single-story buildings, for I seem to remember his desk was near a door or window opening onto an inner and smaller courtyard. I remember this room as being rather long and narrow, with a bare floor, exposed ceiling beams, and a good deal of dark brown varnished woodwork. The real reason I liked to visit this room was because of the two stuffed birds that had been presented to him or to the Y—an owl that stared down at me from the top of a bookcase behind his desk and a stork, much taller than I, that stood on the floor nearby and gazed thoughtfully off into the upper distance.

The activities of the newly-organized YMCA were soon overcrowding its charming, but anachronistic headquarters—and it would be at least a couple of years before the new and permanent building was ready to move into . . . I was a little sad at the move when it came about and I always thought that the owl and the stork, who went along with the move, looked somewhat lost and unnoticed and maybe disgruntled in their new and modern setting.

The House on Law Court Street

With the loan of the temporary quarters in the Tartar City and the plans for the new building on its choice site also in the area, my father had begun to search for a place for us to live that would be close to his work. It was time anyway for us to stop depending on the missions for our housing.

Our new house was close to the northeastern corner of the Tartar City . . . just outside it, in fact, for the property was on the "Chinese city" side of where the Manchu (or Tartar) City wall had stood. It probably had belonged to someone fairly well-to-do and there must have been a home there, because the place was surrounded by eighteen-foot high residential walls—not new—and contained an obviously old and used stone well.

When my father found the place, the original buildings were gone, and construction on the new residence was about halfway towards completion. The location was fine. Arrangements were made for renting—and we would move into the house as soon as it was built.

One day, my father triumphantly announced to the family that the landlord had sent him an important message: except for some minor carpentry, the house was finished. The other workers had all cleared out. Tomorrow afternoon (my father said) we would all go for an inspection tour.

From his tone of voice, I knew that this was to be a momentous occasion, and by the time we set forth the following afternoon, the feeling of suspense had reached as high a pitch of intensity as if we were on our way to open an extraordinary Christmas package.

It was quite a distance from Ma Sze Gya to the Tartar City—too far to walk—and so we went by rickshaw. Rickshaws had recently come into use in Hangchow (the rickshaw, incidentally, was one of the few importations from Japan into China—instead of the other way around; and the Chinese—maybe typically—had developed a version that was not so trim and neat as the original, but was larger and more comfortable . . . at least, for the rider or riders. It was wide enough for two not-too-large passengers to sit side-by-side).

I remember bumping and jostling over a hump-backed little stone bridge that crossed a canal and then suddenly breaking out of a narrow noisy street filled with pedestrians, into the sudden space and quiet of the Tartar City. There was no one in sight on the wide, straight street ahead of us.

"We're almost there now!" my father called back from his rickshaw that was leading the way. "This is Fa Yuanh Gya."

Fa Yuanh Gya—or Law Court Street—took its name from buildings at its further end, near the Lake, where the Provincial Magistrate tried cases and transacted legal business for Chekiang Province.

"Kau dah! Kau dah! (Turn right! Turn right!)" we heard him tell his puller—and our rickshaws followed his into a residential alley, on either side of which were walls, punctuated at intervals by modest wooden doorways, all discreetly closed. Across the end of the alley was a higher wall with larger, more impressive entrance gates—also closed. There must have been a fine old garden just inside, because we could see the full, leafy branches of trees cresting the wall.

For an instant I thought we were bound for this rather grand-looking place, but my father's rickshaw suddenly turned left and dived into another, very small alleyway. It seemed at first to be an empty cul-de-sac, blocked off at the end, but then we caught sight of a freshly-varnished doorway in the wall to our right (to the north). We came to a halt, and in our eagerness Robert and I tumbled out of our rickshaw almost before the shafts had reached the ground.

Our father opened the door and, one by one, we stepped over the wooden threshold. And here was our first surprise—for we found ourselves in a kind of vestibule . . . a dark little high-ceilinged cave of a room. What it was for (except, perhaps, for added security against uninvited visitors), I still don't know; but it always seemed to me that it should have had in it the images of a pair of scowling guardian gods like those in the entranceways of temples.

Opposite the door we had entered was another just like it. We stepped over its threshold (a high, laborious step for a four-year-old) and paused for a moment on the stone paving just inside.

There seemed to be no one else on the premises, but the workmen might have just gone, leaving evidence of their recent activity in an exciting medley of smells—the acrid tang of damp plaster, the aromatic fragrance of newly-sawed lumber, the bright sticky pungency of

Ningpo varnish (which anyone who ever lived in this part of China would recognize).

To our left was the door to the usual "gateman's room," which was built onto the inner side of the wall enclosing the lot—and beyond it, a space roofed over but with no front wall, which we called a "shed." Its purpose, I believe, was as a shelter for the resident's private sedan chairs . . . Straight ahead was a stone path cutting through the center of four rectangular grassy courtyards, separated from each other and the rest of the grounds by ornamental walls about seven feet high. The lower section of each of these walls was solid and plastered white; the upper half was an open filigree made of curving roof tiles fitted together in a geometric pattern. Through it you could see little bits of scenery on the other side.

At the end of the path, we saw a long, low building with latticed windows and entrances and a tiled roof that overhung a front porch and was held up by varnished posts.

"Is that our house?" Robert demanded.

"No. That's the east wing."

"What's a wing?—and what's it for?"

"A wing is a building attached onto another building . . . This one is a reception hall."

"What's a reception . . . ?"

"Come on," my father interrupted. "We'll see the main building first." And my mother caught hold of Robert, who was about to dash off to inspect the "wing."

We turned left on a path that took us through an opening in the ornamental wall and paused again. From here we could see the rest of the front yard all the way to the enclosing wall at the further end. To our right was a large grey-brick building with a front porch and side porch (to the east), at both the first and second floor levels. Beyond it was another wing, two stories high, with a moon door in the white plastered facade that connected it with the main building. To our left—opposite the big house—was another shed (like the one next to the gateman's room, only longer) with an open front and a slanting tiled roof built out from the compound wall about two thirds of the way up to its top.

Perhaps, before describing our new home in more detail, it would be helpful to explain who built it and for what purpose.

I don't remember ever seeing the landlord who was owner of the property and had built upon it—although I recall hearing my parents refer on occasion to "our landlord."

What I do know is that he had built it with the intention of offering it for rent to one of the many officials who came to serve their localities or the provincial government in Hangchow, capital of Chekiang Province. He also had decided to build a modern-style—and that meant Western-style—residence . . . and I don't know what knowledge he had of "modern" (or "Western") other than what he'd seen in pictures—and possibly from visiting missionaries' homes, most of which at that time had been built without benefit of expert planning or 20th century refinements.

What he and his contractors and carpenters had produced was a mixture of Western look and traditional Chinese features—particularly those tied in with officialdom and its demands. The result was more curious than picturesque or distinguished. Our house and its grounds and complex of buildings would never have rated a tour of "Interesting Homes" or an article in an architectural digest—but never mind. This was the point from which I saw and experienced Hangchow in the most impressionable and aware years of childhood. Beyond that, it is also interesting as a modest example of old China trying out the new without quite understanding it or being ready to relinquish elements of an old life style that were becoming out of date.

The "Western-style" family house on the outside looked like a blown-up version of a doll's house built by a Chinese carpenter for a foreign child. Inside, the rooms were high-ceilinged and not Chinesey—except for the one in the center where one entered from the porch: this room was shallower than the one on either side (which became—on the east—our dining room, on the west—our parlor) and was obviously designed to be an official reception area, where visitors would present calling cards or credentials and be invited to wait for a formal welcome. We never used this central room for anything except an entrance and a way to go elsewhere on the first floor.

The east wing, with its predominantly Chinese architecture, was to be used by our hypothetical official for his large formal receptions. If I remember correctly, it had been given an appropriate name for such a hall— something like the Eastern Flowery Pavilion. It became for us a sort of family room—not to be cozy in (there was no central heating!), but put to many uses. At one end was our school (one teacher, two pupils—which I'll tell about later) and at the other end was my father's "study" where he had his daily sessions at a large table with Mr. Dzen, his elderly Chinese language teacher. It was also a play room, where some of our larger toys and playthings were kept and used. To give an idea of its size—it was in the reception wing that I learned to ride a bicycle at age six, when my Shanghai best friend, Ruth Black, came for a visit bringing her new bicycle with her . . . It was the setting also for certain memorable occasions—like the Hangchow Red Cross unit's Halloween party, and Robert's and my Graduation from second grade.

Between the family house and the west wing was an odd little concrete courtyard with a large area of sunken floor in the middle, a skylight in the roof high overhead, and the moon door opening into the front yard. The sunken area was only a couple of inches deep—too shallow for a pool and, in spite of the skylight, too dark for potted plants or any growing things—so what was it for? The west wing itself, with its six identical rooms (three up and three down) had been planned with the objective of providing sleeping accommodations for relatives or the out-of-town guests an official was sure to have.

In the back yard, not quite against the compound wall, was a smallish white-washed building, joined to the rear of the family house by a covered walk. It was two-story, with four modest-sized rooms—the servants' quarters. Over to one side was a stone well, set in a stone platform.

Altogether, our home at the edge of the Tartar City contained about twenty rooms, most of them fairly large. It sounds impressive—maybe pretentious for a family like ours, but it really wasn't. The buildings were flimsily constructed (how the floor shook when my father did his setting-up exercises in the morning!). The window frames didn't fit. There were no closets or built-in shelves, heating or plumbing facilities (no running water), no phones, no power (gas or electric) for any possible use of modern appliances. It did receive enough electricity from Hangchow's one small power station to provide dim lighting in each room from a single bulb hanging from the ceiling. Those in the three front rooms downstairs each wore a small porcelain shade like an inverted saucer. I can't recall the others.

There was little of convenience or of elegance here, but I was impressed that first afternoon. I thought it was all perfectly splendid, and my wonder increased as I followed my father from room to room, sniffing the delightful smell of newness and listening to the echo of our voices in the empty spaces and to the hollow sound of our footsteps on the bare floors. I admired the chalky white of the walls with their fresh coating of plaster; I noted with awe the lofty height of the ceilings; I was thrilled by the expanse of the grounds outside, bare as they were except for the squares of sodding that had just been laid down in the front yard and the curls of wood shavings that still were strewn about in the back. My only disappointment had to do with the trees—one tall and skinny, another quite small—it was an ornamental peach tree—an unhappy palm, and another so unobtrusive as to be almost invisible. None were proper trees either for shade or for climbing. But I accepted this disappointment; for I think I knew then, as I do now—but forgot for a while in between—not to expect anything in this world to be quite perfect.

My recollection of Fa Yuanh Gya (our name for this home ever afterward) the day we first saw it blends quickly into the way—or ways—it looked when we were living there, for there are few fixed pictures of its various parts.

The garden changed according to season, from the time the first snowdrops appeared in the flower bed below the front porch to the beginning of winter when the blaze of the last chrysanthemums had been quenched and the lawn was brown and dry; and it changed from year to year, as my mother added to it and transplanted for new effects and enlarged the beds of annuals. In the back yard, near the well, in the growing months there would be a few neat rows planted with leaf lettuce, strawberries and the like, which if they survived and thrived, we could eat fresh and uncooked . . . We had a chicken coop back there too one year with baby chicks, but when they were let out to run, one by one they were picked off by an enterprising hawk. (How I hated seeing him circling overhead!)

The interior of the house changed also from time to time, either to adapt to the season or to satisfy my mother's creative instincts. "I wonder how it would look if the piano were over here," she would muse—referring to the parlor. And so the piano (the British-made tropicalized Moutrie upright, bought in Shanghai with a wedding check from her father) would be moved and everything else would have to be shifted and re-shifted till it "looked right" in relation to the new position of the piano . . . the wicker chairs with their prettily covered cushions, the Chinese carved end tables and benches and, of course, the portraits of four Great Masters—Beethoven, Brahms, Handel and Mendelssohn that always hung above the piano. Other wall decorations might be moved—the large framed and tinted photograph of Nikko, Japan, showing the avenue of cryptomeria trees—which was fascinating, because wherever you were when you looked at it, you seemed to be gazing straight down the aisle of trees . . . or the sepia-tinted picture of Peter and John hurrying to Christ's Tomb. But the red satin embroidered scroll was always hanging on the wall near the doorway to the back hall. It pictured a bearded Sage holding the peach of Longevity with a fawn standing nearby. The embroidery was so fine that I often stopped to stroke the fawn gently or even (most respectfully and with one finger) the old man's beard.

Upstairs, in the spring, chests of drawers and wardrobes in the family bedrooms were rearranged when beds were moved out into the fresh air—though actually the air inside was already pretty fresh, thanks to leaky windows. The children's beds went out on the front upstairs porch, our parents' to the porch at the east end of the house, overlooking one of the grassy courtyards.

As summer approached, mosquito nets were installed—hung on bamboo poles attached to the four corners of each bed (this was always interesting to watch, as each bed and set of poles seemed to present their own special problems). This was the time also for the parlor rug (bought in Peking for fifty dollars and used in every one of my parents' subsequent homes) and all the smaller wool rugs to be rolled up with mothballs and stored away, to be replaced by cool matting covering, made of bamboo or rushes.

In the fall, the summer carpeting was exchanged for the woolen rugs; and when the nights grew cool, the beds were moved indoors again and the mosquito netting and poles were put away. Then, just before the winter cold began, the big iron-bellied stove was set up at the farther side of the dining room and the drum in the bedroom above. Holes had been made (with the landlord's permission) in the wall to the outside and the ceiling above for tin pipes to carry the smoke to the outer air and the residual warm air to the drum in the upstairs room. I'm not quite sure how the smoke and the hot 'knew' which pipe to travel, but it seemed to work. I can remember, in the coldest days of winter, getting dressed in the morning huddled against the faint warmth of the drum—a large, square, box-like contraption of lead (I believe) coated with tin, which tended after time to curl off the surface like sunburn and tempted one to peel it off the rest of the way. (We must have taken a long time to dress in the winter—especially when we were putting on double of most of our clothes—from union suits on out!). In these coldest weeks of winter, the three front rooms downstairs were closed off by thin partitions—theoretically to seal off the bitter chill that poured in whenever the front door was opened; and we had school at the table in the dining room, the only warm place in the house.

Of all the rooms in the family house, the bathroom was the only one that was always the same. The washstand, with its porcelain basin, pitcher, soap dish and other appurtenances, was just inside the door. On the floor beside it was a water k'ang (crockery container) and a long-handled tin dipper. Across the room was the commode—and I was secretly rather proud of it, because it was not like those found in most missionary homes (made by a local carpenter—and quite uncomfortably square and sharp-edged). Ours was imported and had a nice smooth oval seat and an enamel (rather than tin) bucket beneath. On the floor nearby was the inevitable can of Jeyes' Fluid—that indispensable brown liquid with its powerful smell of benzine and other nameless antiseptics.

The glory of our bathroom was our Soochow Tub. It was magnificent—a giant oval bowl made of heavy pottery. The exterior was an olive-brown—rather nubbly and rough—and was decorated with a huge yellow dragon in relief; there was a green glaze on the inner surface. The tub was almost an "old swimming hole" for us children; when full, it was deep enough for us to float in, and we could climb on the edge and slide down the slippery sides with a satisfying splash. In the warmer seasons, it could be filled with cool or lukewarm water from the well; in the winter, wooden buckets of hot water were brought by coolies from the nearest hot-water shop, and the steam rose in great clouds as one by one the water was emptied into the tub. Almost the only time we felt thoroughly comfortable during the six weeks of the Great Cold was when soaking blissfully in the genial depths of the Soochow tub on Saturday night.

The tub was set on a wooden platform lined with tin. When the cork at the base of the tub was pulled, the water drained onto the platform and out through a pipe that joined the rain spout outside. The tin that lined the platform came from ten-gallon Standard Oil cans—which were put to use in many remarkable ways all over China—by the Chinese even more than foreigners. My father's shower fixture was a whole ten-gallon Standard Oil can, one end of which was pierced with small holes. It hung on a sort of scaffolding over the Soochow tub and was filled with cold water every day by one of the servants. In the morning, my father pulled a string which up-ended the can—and presto, a cold shower!

Looking back, I realize how uncomfortable our house was in many ways (though not exceptionally so for Hangchow at that time)—how unwieldy and inconvenient to manage and what a succession of challenges it must have presented to my mother . . . I think she enjoyed them . . . But however far it fell short of what most of us demand in a home nowadays, it offered us two luxuries: space and privacy.

There in our own home, we children had the scope for an almost endless variety of activities—which helped compensate for the lack of daily companionship of others our own age, and for other possible advantages we might have enjoyed if we had been living in America.

I can remember times—usually rainy days—when Robert and I ran to Mother, demanding plaintively, "What is there to do?" But this was not often; there were all sorts of things we could do if we used our imaginations and exercised a little initiative.

We might decide to play with certain of the toys that were kept in the east wing—and often took them somewhere else (on a porch or outdoors) that offered a more favorable or interesting setting for their use. Or we could play out in the larger of the open-fronted "sheds," where we had our own playground facilities—a fine, large sandbox, a swing and a wooden slide (most of these made to order locally)—protected both from the wet of rain and the heat of sun. On the sunken floor of the concrete courtyard, we could build houses of old packing boxes—or ride the scooter and the Irish Mail wagon brought on two successive Christmases by Santa Claus (via Montgomery Ward). The three upper rooms of the west wing were off limits for us: we visited them only when invited by whatever guests—transient or longer-term—were occupying them. But we could explore the three lower rooms, which were used for storage. One was partially filled with old magazines and periodicals—and we spent many hours digging through the piles like pirates searching for treasure, looking for special kinds of pictures to cut out. We could rummage through the trunks in the third-story attic of the big house for "dress-up" clothes. And of course, we could race and romp on the front lawn.

We even staged a series of full-fledged track meets here, using bamboo sticks and poles of varying sizes (what a useful plant—the bamboo!) for the hurdles, high jump, pole vault, and javelin throw. This particular project was instigated by Robert after he had attended a city-wide track meet organized by the YMCA. I was a less than eager participant—partly because I was physically lazier (less energetic sounds better) than he and partly because there were only two contestants for all the events and the same one of them (Robert) always won. I was much more enthusiastic about our tennis practise in the smaller of the covered sheds. As soon as we were big enough to hold racquets (halfway up the handle), both Robert and I wanted to learn how to play tennis—so he drew a line across the back wall of the shed at the proper height of a net and we used to take turns hitting an old tennis ball against the white-plastered wall.

Robert was the initiator, the doer—the restless and gregarious one; and as he grew older, he began to go out more and more on his own. By the time he was seven or eight, he was able to take over as tourist-guide for out-of-town visitors when neither of our parents could spare the time. I remember that for a while he went by himself into the city for carpentry lessons at one of the mission schools. But most often he walked over to the YMCA, where he was always gladly welcomed by the older boys and young men who were playing volleyball or basketball or were engaged in other sports activities.

I didn't mind being left alone. I could always find an empty room, where I could read quietly and without interruption—or a part of the garden to wander in, looking at Mother's flowers and thinking long thoughts. I had my special places outside. One was the narrow space between the end of the west wing and the compound wall, where violets grew at the foot of the building and overhead there was a magical slit of sky. Another was a corner of one of the front courtyards; hidden from view by the ornamental walls, I could lie in the long grass and gaze up at the changing clouds—and if the trumpet vine was in bloom its honeysuckle fragrance would pour down from the wall above and seem almost to float me nearer to the sky.

I was never lonely, because I knew there were always others not far away—and if I listened from my most secret place I could always hear the sound of someone busy at a familiar task or activity. The swish of broom as the houseboy did the daily sweeping. My mother's voice as she consulted with the gardener about the roses or the flower beds over in the farther end of the front yard or her little vegetable garden in back. The creak of the rope when water was being hauled from the well. The sound of the amah scrubbing clothes (with a bar of yellow soap) on a wooden washboard (on fine days, she sat on a low stool outside near the well—with her flat wooden washtub on the ground before her). Then—unexpectedly—the cheerful brassy clang of the small bell that hung outside the front gate, announcing someone's arrival.

Who would it be? Someone in the family coming home? The cook back from his daily marketing on the great Street, bearing a basket loaded with eggs, fresh vegetables and fruits—and maybe a couple of live chickens squawking furiously? A peddler? A friend? Or someone different from anyone I had ever seen before?

This was a good place to live. Every day had its easy familiar rhythms, but also its variations—with their quickening tempos—of the new, different, and surprising. Outside was a world full of wonderful things, but here within the four high walls was where I felt secure and where I knew I belonged.

When I think of home in Hangchow, Ma Sze Gya comes briefly to mind like the memory of a dream. The first home I remember as reality is this hybrid, slightly absurd, not always comfortable, but much lived-in place at the edge of the Tartar City.

Our Extended Family

In our new home we had a cook, a houseboy, an amah, and a gateman who doubled as gardener. Four servants—or five, if I count the cook's wife who helped him in the kitchen and lent a hand to the amah with the washing and the ironing. This may seem an overabundance of household help, but was about the usual complement for a foreign family in Hangchow—except that the several households in a larger compound usually shared the services of a gateman and one or more gardeners and coolies to keep up the grounds and run the errands.

When a newly-arrived American couple took up housekeeping—probably after boarding for a few months in the home of older missionaries, as my parents did—they might 'inherit' the servants of a family leaving Hangchow. Or the young housewife—in many cases still a bride with no experience in keeping house—might have to undertake her domestic responsibilities with servants who were untrained and completely ignorant of what their tasks should be. She had to learn and teach simultaneously.

This initial period during which the neophyte Western mistress was engaged in training neophyte Oriental servants must have been awkward for all concerned, particularly since communication by language was limited. Sign language was a necessity—and I have sometimes wondered if my mother's habit of "talking with her hands" (a seeming inability to explain anything without the use of large gestures) was acquired when she was a young housewife in Hangchow. Most of the servant stories told later by old-time missionaries had to do with the unexpected results of misunderstandings due to the use of the wrong word or a faulty pronunciation by the foreign lady who had not yet mastered her household Chinese—like the time one of our friends kept telling her horrified cook that she wanted roasted veal for dinner and then found out that she had been ordering roast *girl-child* . . . Fortunately, the confusion was cleared up by

50

an interpreter called in by the cook (of course, the cook would never have taken the order literally! But he did have to know what he was supposed to cook; hence the interpreter).

In general, however, these servants—no matter how green they were at the beginning—learned quickly. They were cheerful, adaptable, and possessed of an innate courtesy—and that intuitive sensitivity to the feelings of others that seems to have been bred into the Chinese at all levels of society by the traditions of the centuries.

But this sensitivity worked two ways, as the foreigners soon discovered . . . so that while the cook, houseboy, and amah were trying to understand such puzzling matters as to how they were to wage constant combat against germs (which they didn't quite believe in, since they had never seen any), their employers were having to learn the even more subtle lessons of 'face' in all its ramifications—whether in regard to the individual servants or their relationships with each other in the household. In this little hierarchy, the loss of 'face' by one member in the eyes of the others could completely upset the equilibrium of the entire household.

The learning all took time; but usually after certain adjustments and changes—and perhaps an unhappy experience or two—the missionary couple had in their home a small corps of devoted servants who lived in harmony with each other and were loyal members of the household as long as they were able to serve the family. Usually also, the servants became Christians—out of conviction, or in some cases perhaps out of respect and affection for their employers.

Inexpendable as servants were, they were an added responsibility—like extra dependents in the family. The missionary could not afford to give them a great deal in the way of money or worldly goods, but took care of them when they were sick, shared their troubles, and helped in planning the future for themselves and their children. Oddly—or perhaps naturally—it was often the servant whose needs were greatest who also evoked the deepest affection—just as the frail or troubled child holds a special place of concern in the hearts of his parents.

When a servant retired (usually to the native village), he or she would come back for visits. But when a missionary left China for the last time, this was a final parting, though everyone tried to pretend otherwise. The servants, eyes red with weeping, brought in their farewell gifts; and their

employers tried to smile as they expressed their appreciation of the offer-
ings (the silver loving cup—the silver shield with its engraved message—
the rather gaudy tea set) but often found it difficult to finish what they
had begun to say. The ties of mutual loyalty, tolerance, and interdepen-
dence had grown strong over the years; and the irrevocable breaking of
those ties was too painful to deny and to hide—though the Westerner
usually tried to camouflage his emotion . . . The Chinese—so often called
"impassive" and "inscrutable"—were not ashamed to show their grief, or
perhaps they felt it more deeply. Parting, I think, is more sorrowful for
those who are left behind.

There were various changes in our household staff during the Hangchow
years. A servant on loan while a missionary family was on furlough returned to them when they came back; others had found satisfactory employment while we were away on the first furlough; some turned out to
be unacceptable for one reason or another.

I don't know what happened to Ah Hung, my parents' first "houseboy."
He was one of their favorite servants—a stalwart, good-humored young
man, devoted to the family and especially to my brother Robert and me.
At that time, there were still no rickshaws in Hangchow; and when Robert and I were too small to walk very far, it was something of a problem to
take us anywhere outside the home compound . . . Ah Hung solved the
problem in a rather novel manner. He would transport us coolie-fash-
ion—each of us seated comfortably in a shallow basket suspended by ropes
from the end of a bamboo carrying pole. Since we were so nearly of the
same size, the cargo at each end balanced nicely—and Ah Hung enjoyed
the joke (relished by all passers-by in the city streets) of carrying the foreign children as if they were vegetables bound for the market.

I don't remember hearing much about our other early servants, except
for Tsong Dah (whose story I have already told) and the first family amah.

The choice of an amah was considered extremely important by both
my parents—and especially Mother. We children were never "turned over
to the amah," as some foreign children were, but we were left in her care
at such times as when Mother was busy with guests or household duties,
or was out teaching a class of Chinese mothers in baby care, or leading a
Bible class or (later) training the choir in our Chinese church. The amah
therefore had to be, first of all, responsible and of good character. Also

she should be clean, healthy, intelligent (though not necessarily educated)—and *she must not spoil the children.*

Robert's first amah was a fine, intelligent woman, who more than fulfilled the necessary qualifications—or seemed to. She had a son of her own—a few years older than the infant Robert; and to my parents this seemed an added recommendation, because he would be a companion for their son, and the two children (one Chinese and the other American) would have the opportunity of growing up together as brothers. As soon as Robert grew out of infancy, the two little boys became constant companions under Amah's watchful eye; but no matter how firmly my mother insisted there should be the normal give-and-take between the two children, Amah was determined that her son should not overstep certain bounds which she considered proper. Robert soon learned that all he had to do was to wave a chubby hand and the older boy would hasten to do his bidding. This was hardly the relationship of equality and fraternity expected by my parents, and it seemed undesirable both for their son and Amah's. Sending the boy away from his mother was an unthinkable option, and so, with her consent, they found employment for her elsewhere . . . I have often regretted that we didn't have servants' children to play with and to learn from about the childhood games and songs and folklore of China. I believe it was 'on purpose'—that my parents, because of their upbringing in the deep south, were unusually sensitive to the possibility of their children developing attitudes of racial superiority (it sometimes happened—more often, I think, with children of southerners than of missionaries from other parts of America).

Our new amah, Tsong Dah Sau, who was with us when we moved to the Tartar City house, was a little bit of a woman. She was never sick or ailing, but she was so tiny and seemed so frail, that after my brother DeWitt was born, my mother wondered how in the world she could keep up with all the extra work—or even lift and carry the baby, a robust little boy who grew huskier and heavier almost by the hour. But how Tsong Dah Sau doted on that baby! In fact, on all three of us. We were her children.

It must have been when DeWitt was still in his first year that there was a major shakeup in our household staff. My parents said later they had sensed something was brewing, but couldn't be sure what was wrong . . . And they never did know exactly.

The explosion came one evening when they were out at an early supper meeting at the YMCA—and as a special treat Robert and I were to have our supper in the dining room instead of upstairs in our bedroom.

After Tsong Dah Sau had put the baby to bed, she helped us wash our hands and followed us to the dining room, where places were set for us opposite each other at one end of the long table. Robert and I sat down, feeling grownup and important. The houseboy came in from the kitchen and began to serve us.

We were too busy enjoying our moment of glory to notice any unusual tension in the air—although towards the end of the meal, the houseboy seemed more elaborately attentive to our wishes than even this special occasion demanded. Time came for dessert. He swept in and set a dish of prunes in front of each of us. This was a frequent supper dessert—being one of those dull foods, like oatmeal-for-breakfast, that our mother considered good for us; and ordinarily we might have wrinkled our noses unappreciatively and exclaimed, "Prunes *again?*"

Tonight we ate them without comment.

"Would you like some more?" the houseboy asked us in a way that made a second helping of prunes one of the privileges of the evening.

We nodded.

He picked up our bowls and bore them with a flourish back to the kitchen.

"The children want more dessert," we heard him announce loudly to the cook.

"They shouldn't have any more!" the cook shouted back angrily.

Robert and I looked at each other and giggled. What a funny thing to argue about—a second helping of prunes, when usually we didn't particularly want a first!

As we sat waiting at the table, the voices in the kitchen grew louder and angrier. We glanced at Tsong Dah Sau; she seemed frightened and uncertain as to what to do. We slipped down from our chairs and before she could stop us, darted back to the kitchen and took our stand just inside the door. We were vaguely aware that the amah had hurried after us and was begging us to come away, but we paid no attention.

The kitchen was a large rectangular room, equipped with plain but sturdy furniture. Wooden cupboards, unpainted but varnished, lined most of the walls; the coal-burning iron stove was over in the corner; and in front of it, in the center of the floor, stood a long heavy wooden work table. The cook—a stocky, middle-aged man with round close-cropped head—was standing near the farther end of the table glaring at the houseboy, a much younger man who pranced like a boxer before him, shouting incoherently . . . Robert and I had stopped giggling by now.

The cook's face darkened with rage, and the veins on his neck and forehead swelled. His wife rushed in between the two men and fluttered back and forth trying to pacify them. Tsong Dah Sau tried again to take Robert and me out of the kitchen, but we were rooted to the floor. On the streets of Hangchow we had seen noisy quarrels, but we had never seen any at such close quarters—nor one as furious as this.

The houseboy seemed to be having the better of the verbal battle, when suddenly the cook leaned forward and spat out an insult which I couldn't understand. The younger man leapt for him, grabbed him by the shoulders close to his neck, and shook him violently back and forth, beating his round head against the wall at the end of the kitchen. The sounds were dreadful—whack, thud, whack. We were horrified.

Just then our parents appeared, hurrying through the door from the dining room. My father said something in a commanding tone. The houseboy let go his hold on the cook, and the whole scene froze.

I still don't know how my parents happened to arrive just at that crucial moment. The gateman must have hurried to their meeting to call them home.

Robert and I were hustled upstairs. For once, no one had to tell me not to dawdle. Bed that night seemed a welcome refuge.

Next morning, while I was getting dressed, I could hear my parents discussing the events of the evening before and what should be done now.

Some of what they said was indistinguishable, but now and then a phrase or sentence came clearly through the thin wall between the rooms, and I heard enough to learn—with a slight shock—that all our servants would have to leave us.

My mother sounded distressed, and her voice rose a little.

"If we knew for sure whose fault it was . . . It doesn't seem right to have to let them all go just because of one . . . " Mother never "fired" a servant; she always—more gently—"let him go."

Then my father's voice: " . . . it's customary to make a clean sweep . . . doesn't do to fix the blame on any one individual . . . too much loss of 'face' . . . "

After a brief silence, I heard Mother speak in a brighter tone.

"I think I can find a good place for Tsong Dah Sau. Young Mrs. Duncan Main is going to need a baby amah soon." . . . Duncan Main was Dr. Main's son. He was an administrative assistant to his father in his many medical mission enterprises—and had married a missionary's daughter who had finished her schooling in England and come back to China a young lady.

There was another pause. Then my mother again: "What about Spring Cow? I suppose he goes too."

"Spring Cow" was the code name my parents used for our gateman-gardener when they had to speak of him in the presence of any of the other servants (who were likewise mentioned by their own "English names"). The characters for his Chinese name, Juin Niu, meant something entirely different, but the sounds were the same as for the words, "Spring" and "cow."

"No," said my father. "The landlord hired him; he comes with the house—so I guess he's the only one who will stay."

"Oh well—that's good," my mother spoke doubtfully. "Of course, I have worried about his (her voice dropped and I couldn't hear the word) . . . and I'd hate to have the children" and her voice became faint again. "But he's very faithful, poor fellow—and he's awfully good with the flowers."

Except, then, for the gateman, we had a complete turnover in the household staff. How it was managed so smoothly, I don't know. I don't recall any awkwardness or inconvenience during the transition. . . . It's possible that Robert and I were sent over to play for a day with our young friends at T'ienh Sway Gyao . . . At our house, the old force left and a new one came—and that was that.

I don't remember much about the new cook or his wife. Like our old cook, he preferred not to have children bothering him in the kitchen.

Our new houseboy, Yienh San or Yienh the Third (indicating that he was the third son in his family), was a slim bright-eyed youth, happy of disposition and entirely without guile. New to his duties in a foreign house, he was diffident at first, but when his strangeness wore off, he became an interested member of the household, always eager to take a helpful part in any of our family activities and to give Robert and me a hand in our special projects . . .

When kite season came around and the blowy March sky was full of flying centipedes and giant paper butterflies and birds, Yienh San made us a kite—though not such a fancy one. In pleasurable impatience we watched it take shape under his nimble fingers out of a small heap of bamboo strips, paper, and string. And then came the excitement of trying it out and taking turns to fly it . . . the suspense while racing down the lawn holding the kite aloft, wondering would it fly, letting it go—seeing it dive and falter—and then the joy of feeling it tug the string as it soared higher and higher into the sky . . . I've forgotten whether it was Robert's turn or mine that first spring when our kite was caught in the top of the tall skinny tree in the front yard. It was a peculiar tree—like an oversized beanpole crowned with a ridiculous tuft of branches. Robert and I gazed dolefully up at our kite, which was unharmed but seemed irrevocably lost to us. But Yienh San, who had been standing by, took a calculating glance at the smooth tree trunk and, without saying a work, shinnied up agile as a monkey, retrieved the kite gently from the branch where it was caught, slid down, and handed it to us. We had liked Yienh San from the first, but this feat—so impressive, but performed so modestly—won from us a lasting admiration and respect.

We had not been at all enthusiastic over having a new amah to take the place of Tsong Dah Sau . . . Saying goodbye to her had been a sad little ceremony. Robert and I had been playing in the front garden when Mother called us to come—Tsong Dah Sau was about to leave. Dressed in her best clothes, Tsong Dah Sau was standing in the gateway that led into the outer courtyard. She pressed my cheeks lovingly between the palms of her little hands. Tears welled in her eyes. Then she turned to Robert and held his face for a few seconds in the same way. She would never forget us, she told us. We looked at her mournfully.

"I shall come to see you often," she promised, and turned away along the path to the front gate.

We met the new amah for the first time at almost the same spot where we had bade farewell to Tsong Dah Sau.

"Children, this is Tsong Ma," our mother said. For a single instant, we saw a stranger—round-faced, dressed in clean but faded blue cotton. Immediately after that, it seemed as if we had known her always. She was that kind of person—as real and natural and inevitable as earth and food and water.

Tsong Ma was as sturdy and solid as Tsong Dah Sau was delicate. Where the latter had tottered precariously on her bound feet, Tsong Ma stumped about firmly and resolutely on hers.

She seemed middle-aged to us, but was probably in her early thirties. Long ago, when she was sixteen or seventeen, her parents and a go-between had married her off according to custom—to a young man whose family lived in a village neighboring hers near Ningpo. Her husband had long since deserted her. They had one son, by now almost grown, who was apparently following in his father's footsteps, for he was a gambler and ne'er-do-well. The only times she ever saw either of them was when they appeared unannounced, asking for money.

Tsong Ma wore her hair in the usual fashion of the ordinary woman of that time—skinned back tight from her forehead and face and wound into a smooth knot at the nape of her neck. Her ear lobes had been pierced, and a tiny circlet of gold hung through one of them. She wore this earring, it seemed, more from habit or for insurance than out of feminine vanity. If she had ever had a mate to it, it had probably been pawned or sold.

She was scrupulously clean; and there was about her always a faint smell reminiscent of strong yellow soap and starched clothes under a hot iron—and, sometimes, when she had just hurried from her meal with the other servants, a whiff of garlic and oil. Her habitual expression was one of preoccupied—but pleasant—seriousness . . . a sort of cheerful severity. When she smiled her cheeks rounded up as firm and red as ripe pomegranates.

Tsong Ma was always busy. Some amahs might spend hours out of the day gossiping with the other servants or sitting on a porch step cutting pieces of paper into marvelous, useless things for the children to stare at and then toss away. Not she. When she took time to sit down, she usually had a basket of mending beside her. Over her finger she would slip her thimble—a brass band, like a wide ring with indentations all over the outer surface. Then she would take up a shirt with buttons missing—or fit a worn sock over a wooden darning-egg—and stitch away busily while keeping a sharp eye on her charges.

We accepted Tsong Ma immediately and without reservations. In a way, she was more comfortable than little Tsong Dah Sau. Tsong Ma laid upon us no burden of sentiment. We were her family and she loved us; and there is no doubt in my mind that she would have given her life for us if necessary—but she would have been as matter-of-fact about it as she was in her everyday care of us. We children were to be looked after constantly but not bothered when we were happy and behaving properly. If we did misbehave, she promptly expressed the disapproval we deserved. Frowning and pursing her lips, she would reprimand us in a tone of gruff authority, but there was never any outrage or personal pique in her scolding.

All these servants—the new cook and his wife, Yienh San, Tsong Ma, and Juin Niu ("Spring Cow")—who was the one holdover from before—stayed with us during the remainder of the Hangchow years and were part and parcel, in varying degrees of importance, of our daily family life.

"Spring Cow" always was somewhat of an enigma to us children. Small children in China were made much of by their elders; and I suppose, as foreign children, we received an extra lagniappe of attention, amused and friendly, both from the people we knew and from strangers. But our gateman-gardener never spoke to us. He hardly ever even *looked* at us, though we might be playing almost at his elbow when he was working in the garden. He left us strictly alone, and somehow made us realize that we were to leave him alone. It was a family rule—and one which we faithfully observed—that we were not to encroach on the servants' privacy by going into any of their rooms—although we often watched them at their work or visited with them companionably when they were eating or taking their ease on sunshiny days in the back yard. But Spring Cow wouldn't even let us stand in the doorway of his little room by the front gate. Usually the door was closed when he was gardening; when he was being "gateman" it was often ajar, but we were discouraged from looking in . . . and we didn't see why we shouldn't. He was a silent, unlaughing man, but not frightening. On some days he was more morose than usual, and sometimes I noticed that his eyes were painfully red and bloodshot. I brought this to my mother's attention on more than one occasion, but she always changed the subject.

Mother, Robert, and I had gone on foot one afternoon to visit friends in the Tartar City; and on our return, as we rounded the corner from the long alley into our small one, we caught sight of something lying in a heap against the wall not too far from our outer gateway. A cold pang struck me and my hair seemed to prickle at my scalp when I saw it was a man, huddled oddly on the ground, limp and completely senseless. I glanced at Robert; his eyes were as round as mine must have been.

"Is he . . . dead?" we whispered.

"No—no, he's not dead. Don't look, children." My mother spoke in some agitation—and we hurried fearfully through the entrance and into the normalcy of our own garden.

It was years later that I realized the hulk of a man we had seen in our alley must have been our gateman-gardener. All the little things that had puzzled me about him suddenly came clear. It was very simple: he drank.

As far as I can remember, he was the only completely intoxicated person I ever saw in Hangchow—which is interesting when you consider that Hangchow was the chief distributing center for the much-esteemed and very potent Shaoshing rice wine . . . and, more important, had for centuries been noted as a place of conviviality and pleasure. Drinking had been a part of that, but the drinking was usually done along with feasting (not for itself alone)—or in an esthetic context—as the poets liked to do when they were boating on the Lake or sitting in contemplation on a monastery terrace composing verses between fiery sips of wine out of tiny cups.

What is ironic is that we had as a permanent member of our household someone who drank too much, for if my mother had any phobias at all, the most intense and unreasoning was her dread—almost paranoic—of alcohol. My father, who had come from a much stricter Southern Methodist environment, never took wine at the Chinese feasts he so heartily enjoyed, but accepted it in others as part of their custom and culture. He had never—like my mother—seen a charming, dearly beloved relative die at an early age of alcoholism.

Tsong Ma was the only one of our Hangchow servants to follow us to Shanghai—and who could blame the others? why should any sensible person choose to leave Hangchow for any other city?

Actually, Tsong Ma didn't have much choice in the matter: she knew she would be needed when the new baby was born; and then, when it was suddenly decided that we were to stay in Shanghai, she was needed more than ever—not just to help with the baby but with all the family adjustments that came with the move. Those first months in Shanghai turned out to be a period of desperate crises—and my mother often said later that she couldn't think how we would have gotten through them without Tsong Ma.

She was waiting for us when we came back (1924) from the second family furlough, and was with us at the new YMCA compound in the French Concession.

I remember her trying to corral the two younger boys every late afternoon, hobbling after them on her bound feet calling "Bah-foo dong! Bah-foo dong!"—which meant "Bath time! Bath time!" and was the only English she ever learned.

Then the youngest—hurrying to "catch up" to the three older ones—became too self-reliant to require the attention of an amah. Here in Shanghai there were many conveniences, including a laundry where most of the wash could be sent. And Robert and I—in preparation for the college years in America—were expected to make our beds and keep our own rooms tidy and do certain other small household chores. Tsong Ma wasn't needed any more, but it was quite a while before the day Mother told us Tsong Ma was going. We were shocked. We had come to take her very much for granted—tossing her a greeting as we passed her on our way to this or that of our important activities. But she was a member of the family and not to have her around was unthinkable. How could our parents cast out someone who was like our own kin? Mother tried to explain that it wasn't just that we couldn't afford an amah; Tsong Ma herself was uneasy and unhappy with not enough work to keep her busy. My mother was right, of course. Tsong Ma had in her nature the kind of basic integrity that made it impossible for her to be paid for sitting idle in someone else's home—even one in which she had worked so hard for so many years.

I'm not sure when Tsong Ma went back to her native village. The last time we saw her was when she had been to the small hospital near us in the French Concession and had been told she had cancer. It was far advanced. She came to say goodbye. She was hardly recognizable—so terribly thin, her once rosy, firm cheeks now pale and fallen away.

When word came from her native village that she had died, I was genuinely sad, but briefly and in a once-removed, sentimental way. Rural Chekiang province seemed distant; and at this point, I was more interested in people who were clever, talented, amusing, or "with lots of personality."

It was a long time before I came to recognize the value of simple human goodness and to realize how much glory is due—but seldom given—to the plain, unspectacular, honorable people of the world . . . Tsong Ma was pure gold. I wish that I had been less offhand with her during my self-centered teens and could have shown her more of the affection I felt for her then and the appreciation I feel now—but I am quite sure that this was more than she ever expected and she probably would have puzzled over why it should have been in any way owed her.

Our Star Boarder

Our West Wing was never as fully used by guests and kin as it would have been if a Hangchow official had been master of house and household; but the upper story was occupied most of the time.

Two of the rooms were guest rooms; the third had been converted into a bathroom of sorts. There was rarely a time when we didn't have guests temporary or longer term, or perhaps some of each—staying in the West Wing.

Our first long-term guest (my father called her our "star boarder") was Aunt Becky.

Miss Rebecca Wilson of the Southern Presbyterian Mission had 'family' of her own elsewhere in China—two sisters who were missionary wives; but she was aunt by courtesy to any number of young couples like my parents . . . and to their children. Our little Southern Presbyterian friends in Hangchow called her "Aunt Beppie" in a proprietary tone and manner that Robert and I secretly resented, though we pretended to consider it only babyish. We felt we had as much claim on her as they did—maybe more, since she lived with us.

At about the time we moved to the Fa Yuanh Gya house, she had been assigned to teach in a boys' school near by; and my parents had urged her to come and board with us. We had space to spare, and it was a convenient location for her; so she settled into one of the upstairs rooms in the West Wing—had her meals with us—and became as much a member of the family as if we were truly kin.

It may seem incongruous, but I tend to associate my early memories of Aunt Becky with the "Great War"—which was what everybody called World War I before there was a World War II.

Hangchow, thousands of miles from the trenches and not really involved in the grim conflict, may have seemed a little oasis of tranquillity during the war years; but I remember a sort of hushed gravity in the atmosphere, an undercurrent of anxious waiting, a darkening of the sun when my parents talked of it—especially in conversation with their Western friends. I think the War came closer and became a reality sooner to the handful of Americans in Hangchow than to most of their fellow-countrymen back home, because they saw it through the eyes of their British friends and experienced vicariously their anxieties and griefs. As the War moved into its latter stages, I doubt that there was a single Britisher in Hangchow who had not heard of some relative or beloved friend wounded—missing—or (with tragic finality) "killed in action" on the fighting front.

The British and Americans in Hangchow formed their own Red Cross Society unit and met once a month to roll bandages; and in between meetings, all the wives were constantly knitting olive-drab woolen socks and "helmets" for the boys at the front. Some of the men even—inspired by the example of the Prince of Wales—learned or tried to learn to knit, and were teased for their awkwardness by the ladies. But there was always a note of deep concern underlying the laughter.

When America entered the war and President Wilson announced that we were going to help "make the world safe for Democracy," most of the Americans in Hangchow had a sudden sense of relief and pride. This is when my father, believing so strongly in his country's responsibility to the world in its crisis, thought seriously about leaving his work in China and volunteering for war service in Europe. He wrote to the Committee (YMCA) in New York explaining how he felt but was persuaded that in the long run he would be serving the world better by continuing his work in Hangchow.

To make up for not being direct participants in America's war effort, my parents tried in every way possible—in their thoughts and habits—to share in whatever their people back home were going through. For example, when they heard of shortages of certain foods back in the States, we "cut down" on them at our table whether or not there was any real or helpful reason for it. One of the family rulings was: either butter or jam on a piece of bread, hot biscuit, or muffin—but not both. We were also stringently rationed in our use of sugar, even though there was plenty of native sugar in the local markets. I remember at one meal Robert and I were trying to make the agonizing choice between butter or strawberry jam on our bread, when Aunt Becky suddenly couldn't stand it any longer.

"It's all very noble of us grownups to make sacrifices 'out of sympathy'," she said to my surprised parents, "but it's nonsense for the children." So saying, she pushed her chair back, came over and took the slices of bread from our hands and spread each piece lavishly with butter, then with a thick layer of jam, and finally sprinkled them over with several spoonfuls of sugar. Robert and I were amazed and delighted, but before we took a first bite, paused to steal a look at our parents. We saw them exchange a somewhat sheepish glance—but they never said a word!

Mother smiled when I told her of writing about this little episode. She didn't remember it, but it was in character and obviously had been accepted as such.

"But you know," she added, "Aunt Becky never interfered in anything that was really important to us in regard to you children—like our way of talking about the Bible."

"Would she have disagreed?" I asked in some astonishment.

"Oh, yes. Aunt Becky was born and bred a Fundamentalist; and so, of course, believed that every word in the Bible was literally true."

A Fundamentalist? Aunt Becky? Amazing when I remember our daily "morning prayers" at the family breakfast table . . . My father would read a selection from the Old Testament or the New and then ask what we thought the verses meant. If we were puzzled, he would briefly explain—in terms that were basically "believing" but allowed for questioning and thought and interpretation according to historical context or mythical meaning.

Aunt Becky was there—but never did she show any shock or disapproval. For a feisty person like her (and older than my parents)—not to protest and "interfere," as Fundamentalists so often feel called upon to do, says a great deal about the friendship and mutual respect between her and my parents . . . also her sense that children should not be drawn into theological contention any more than into making unnecessary sacrifices "out of sympathy."

Our first magazine subscription—just for Robert and me—was a gift from Aunt Becky. It was to *John Martin's Magazine* for children; and when it came each month, she enjoyed it with us (which made it much more fun for us)—exulting when we solved Peter Puzzlemaker's games and riddles—reading us the stories. And so it was Aunt Becky who introduced me to my first war-spy-mystery story . . . first and last for many years. It was entitled "The Secret of the Seven Stars"; it appeared in serial form in *John Martin's* and was a spellbinder, telling of how the curiosity and daring of some American children led to the discovery of German spies who were using an island off the East Coast as a place to send signals to saboteurs on the mainland.

It was Aunt Becky also who inadvertently gave us the chance to be in the Hangchow Armistice parade.

I can't say firsthand how the War had been affecting the consciousness and feelings of the general public in Hangchow, but the news of the armistice set off an official explosion of jubilation. The civic authorities immediately organized a great celebration, including an almost-impromptu parade. My father was invited to represent the United States of America; he would ride in the parade on a horse which would be provided for him. Someone suggested that his children—at least the two older (they didn't insist on fourteen-month-old DeWitt)—participate too; and this idea was presented and greeted with such enthusiasm that my father had to go along with it . . . especially since he knew we had an acceptable conveyance. We could ride in the custom-made sedan chair Aunt Becky had given us back at Ma Sze Gya when we had outgrown our market baskets. We had rarely used the sedan chair since moving to the Tartar City and I was much more excited over the prospect of riding in it again than about being in a parade. It was oval-shaped, with seats (one at each end) facing each other across a small table. Riding in it was like sailing through the air in a little wicker boat.

Sedan chair bearers were hastily hired, and Robert and I were bundled up in warm clothes against a bleak, chilly November day. At the last minute, Mother tied the laces of a blue serge bonnet under my chin, while I protested in vain; I wanted to wear my pretty white eyelet party bonnet, but she said it was for summer and wouldn't be warm enough. I was still feeling disgruntled when we climbed into the sedan chair and the bearers lifted it off the ground.

The parade began at the north end of the Great Street and pushed its way slowly southward. All I could see were the masses of people jostling and cheering—and behind us, separated by a dozen or more pedestrians (it was hard to tell which were part of the parade and who were spectators), was our father riding on a white horse. He was dressed in his Sunday best and wore a tiny American flag attached debonairly to the side of his derby hat.

The Great War was over. But it didn't leave our consciousness for some while; and for us children it seemed to become more real after its end than it had been while it was going on—probably because now we were old enough to understand the pictures we had seen in magazines of soldiers and sailors marching—of trenches and scarred battlefields—and of doctors and nurses ministering to the wounded and dying.

For a long time, the Kaiser was our arch-villain—a first-cousin to the Devil (he even looked like him, with his curling, pointed moustache and arrogant glare). We were still half afraid of him and used to feel quite daring when we and our small friends would choose the "It" for a game by chanting, "Eeny meeny miny mo. Catch the Kaiser by the toe. If he hollers make him say, 'I surrender, U.S.A!' "

(Where did we learn this? I suppose children of some family fresh back from furlough had brought it with them. American styles, popular songs, new sayings, games, and fads made their way to those of us in China in a capricious and sporadic trickle—some of them arriving months or many years after they had been in fashion back in the home country.)

Germans were *bad* people; they had started the war and had done many evil, cruel things to innocent people (I always connected "Germans" with "*germs*"; both were dangerous and indiscriminately bad). Imagine my incredulity the winter afternoon Robert and I were told to get ready to go call on a *German* family. I couldn't believe my ears and was too shocked to understand what we were told about them except that they were sad and lonesome and a friendly visit might cheer them up.

Years later I asked my parents about the family and learned that they had been missionaries up in north China and had come to Hangchow after the Japanese had displaced German control in Shantung Province. And now they had heard there would be no more funds to support them and their mission work and they would have to return to their defeated and impoverished homeland.

At the time, I was both surprised and puzzled—and I didn't know what to expect when we set out that cold January afternoon for their rented foreign-style house somewhere on a hillside outside the city.

Certainly I didn't expect the welcome—almost embarrassingly grateful—that we received on arrival . . . or the look of the parlor crowded with European furniture heavily upholstered and fringed in mustardy colors. Or the little Christmas tree—still standing on a small round table . . . still hung with ornaments that somehow seemed faded and forlorn. Christmas was long since over, and our tree had been taken down weeks ago.

We had tea—served to us, not at a table but where we sat. Were we served by a servant?—or our German hostess? . . . My recollection of this afternoon is, I'm sure, more subjective than accurate in detail, but the overwhelming remembered impression is one of melancholy and of a grownup couple who were bewildered and sad. And they were not bad; they were gentle people who somehow couldn't "put away" Christmastime. (Was it because it was their last one in a country where they'd come intending to live out their working years?)

So not all Germans were like the Kaiser and the fierce, scowling soldiers in their pointed helmets. The Kaiser himself came to lose his terror for us, and our arch-villain now became a Chinese—Yuan Shih-kai, traitor to the revolution and ambitious to become a new emperor of China. And, instead of the Germans, the enemies were the Japanese.

Aunt Becky is tied in with this development in my view of the world. But first I think I should "explain" her a little further.

She was—as I've said—a generation older than our parents and therefore seemed elderly to us. I could never imagine her as a child or even as a girl or young woman—nor in all the years I knew her did she seem to change or grow any older. In a way she seemed ageless—in that, like Dr. Main, she had never forgotten what was surprising, wonderful, or funny to a child. The communication between her and children was simple and direct without any of the barriers of abstraction, strained attentiveness, or kindly condescension often raised unconsciously by other adults.

Robert and I were usually at the gate to meet her when she came back from school in the late afternoon. When I close my eyes I can see her now, coming through the gateway, her step still springy, her eyes still bright behind her rimless glasses, even after a long day in the classroom struggling to impart the principles of the English language and of Christianity to Chinese boys who had had little previous knowledge of either. I see her always with her hair parted straight down the middle and puffed out slightly on either side of her face—a well-worn cardigan sweater (dark red) draped over her shoulders or on an arm—and, on her feet, sensible high-buttoned shoes, the tops concealed by her long skirt.

"Hey—hey!" she would call as soon as she caught sight of us running towards her; and when we reached her, she would stop where she was, to hear us report on the momentous events of the day. Every now and then, she would interject an exclamation of surprise or interest that never interrupted the flow of information but only indicated how eagerly she was following it.

"Goodness gracious!" she would exclaim. Or "Bless my soul!" or, most characteristic of all, "What-say? What-say?" with her voice lifting at the end as if she could hardly wait to hear more.

One day (Aunt Becky was not around at the time) I said, "Bless my soul" at what I thought was an appropriate juncture in a family conversation and was immediately reproved by my mother.

"What's *wrong* with it?" I asked in surprise.

"Well, you see, it really means 'God bless my soul'—and we shouldn't speak lightly of God. The Bible says not to take His name in vain."

"Aunt Becky says it," I argued—and was immediately sorry, because I didn't want to hear Aunt Becky criticized however obliquely. Besides, she probably had a pretty good right to call on the Lord's blessing, even in a light-hearted way.

In addition to being such a satisfactory audience, Aunt Becky was a lively talker herself and no matter how tiring her teaching chores had been, she was able to report of them with verve and optimism—and a sense of humor.

One of her classroom anecdotes comes back to me . . . My father had come home earlier than usual one mild, sunshiny afternoon and we were all out in the yard talking to him when Aunt Becky arrived. After we had greeted her, she told us that in one of her senior classes (she taught in a Middle School, which corresponds to our "high school"), she had asked the boys to tell what they hoped to be and do when they had finished school. One by one, the students stood up, each trying in halting and imperfect English to describe his particular goal or ambition. One of the brightest boys in the whole school was a member of this class, and Aunt Becky was hoping for something especially inspiring from him. When his turn came, he sprang to his feet, his eyes flashing fire.

"When I finish this school," he declared, "I not go university. I am going to be soldier and kill many Japanese!"

The whole class burst into applause.

"So much for all my attempts to teach Christian love," Aunt Becky concluded ruefully. "And," she added with a guilty twinkle, "the worst of it is that I had a hard time to keep from cheering too."

My parents laughed—even Mother, who usually reacted with shocked dismay at the mention of any kind of violence. My father, turning thoughtful, observed that this was an interesting example of the profound changes taking place in China—that only a few years before, no Chinese youth—particularly one fortunate enough to be a student—would have even considered becoming a common soldier. The soldier was traditionally the low man on the totem pole in Chinese society.

While the grownups talked, I was thinking admiringly of Aunt Becky's student and wishing I had been in the classroom to hear his stirring declaration. I would have clapped and clapped . . . If this sounds unnaturally bloodthirsty for a child of my background, I should explain that for as long as I could remember I had been hearing discussions of the humiliations that China, in recent decades of weakness and change, had been subjected to by certain power-hungry nations. My father and most of our American friends shook their heads over the "Unequal Treaties" and "Extraterritoriality" but spoke of Japan's "Twenty-One Demands" with open indignation, even outrage. Exactly what it all meant, I didn't know, but it was plain to see that, of all those who were treating my country so badly, the Japanese were the worst, and I felt that if I were able to, I would do almost anything to get rid of them and punish them—though perhaps *killing* them was going a little too far.

Through the classroom experiences and her interest in individual pupils that Aunt Becky shared with us all, Robert and I inadvertently learned a good deal about the temper and the dreams of the new student generation in China.

70

She also provided us with glimpses of what our other country (America) was like, in a way that most adults failed to do. I think it was because, when she referred to America, it was usually in specific terms and in a natural, un-nostalgic manner that gave it a solid reality, even though it was thousands of miles—weeks of travel—and years of absence away. It seems to me that most Americans living in China tended to speak of their homeland as though it were an idea and a sentiment rather than an actual place. For Aunt Becky, America had not ceased to exist and function fully just because she was not there. She never generalized about America or tried to describe it to us; but we got from her the feeling of its very substance from the seemingly ordinary but interesting living facts to which she would refer in casual, everyday conversation.

Besides, it was Aunt Becky who had subscribed to *John Martin's Magazine* for us—and when we had outgrown that, to *St. Nicholas*. These magazines gave us a real feeling of contact—almost of comradeship—with all the anonymous children back in America, who we knew must have anticipated every issue as we did (though they got them much earlier)—and read the same stories, did the same puzzles, laughed at the same jokes.

My father always had serious reservations about the wisdom of sending spinsters (an old-fashioned word now) to the mission field—or bachelors either, for that matter. He felt that normal family relationships were almost a requirement for healthy and effective adjustments. But he had no reservations as to Aunt Becky, who was brisk, tangy and wholesome as an ocean breeze.

Only once do I remember seeing her dauntless spirit threatened and even then it did not really falter. This was on a fine autumn holiday when she had sallied forth joyously for a long tramp in the hills. In the late afternoon, we heard one of the servants call out, "Wei-shaw-gee hwei-la-leh!" ("Miss Wilson has come back!") and we ran to meet her. Happily dishevelled from her wind-blown wanderings, she bore as triumphant trophy of the day an armful of brilliant autumn foliage.

"Oh, it was a wonderful day!" she exclaimed. "I wish you-all could have been with me . . . Bertha, here are some leaves for your vases. Aren't they simply splendid?"

Aunt Becky's enthusiasm for once had been misdirected. Only a little while later, we saw Mother hurrying along the balcony that led from our upstairs hall across the end of the concrete courtyard to the second-story rooms of the west wing. She was carrying bottles of lotion, towels, and a white enamel basin.

"Aunt Becky has been poisoned," she explained somewhat distractedly.

We followed along at her heels.

Aunt Becky was sitting in a chair on the balcony just outside her bedroom door, her face bright red and swollen beyond recognition. In fact, I wasn't even sure that it wasn't someone else till she raised her hand in greeting and spoke to us. Miserable as she was, she managed to turn her predicament into a joke on herself.

"Wouldn't you think I was old enough to know better," she said rather indistinctly—for by this time her face, besides being puffed out of shape, was well-caked with calamine lotion. "Those beautiful red leaves are exactly like the poison sumac back home. I should have paid attention, but I just couldn't resist them . . . Children," she warned us (and we couldn't really tell if she was joking or serious, but I have never forgotten), "remember that red is for danger—red flags for trains—red lights for street crossings—so watch out for red leaves, and never eat any red berries unless you know what they are . . . Thank you, Bertha," she said to my mother who was gathering up the first aid supplies; and we all half-tiptoed away, hoping that Aunt Becky wasn't hurting too much and that she would soon look like herself again.

Our New Boarders

After Aunt Becky left us to teach out at Hangchow College, we had two boarders instead of just one over in the west wing. Miss Margaret Mack and Miss Genevieve Lowry—newly-arrived YWCA (Young Women's Christian Association) secretaries—were more of my parents' generation than Aunt Becky. My parents called them "Peg" and "Gen"; they were "Miss Mack" and "Miss Lowry" to us children.

They participated wholeheartedly in special events and holidays like Christmas, but were never members of the family in the same way as Aunt Becky had been, since they spent most of their time at the temporary quarters of the YWCA they were organizing, and even arranged to have most of their meals (Chinese food) with the Chinese women who were their chief colleagues.

In later years, I gathered that my father had admired their zeal and their determination to identify themselves with their Chinese co-workers, but that, in a big-brotherly, exasperated way, he had found it hard to accept their "independence" and insistence on going it alone, when they might have saved time and trouble for themselves by following the lead of the YMCA in certain common problems of organization and establishment. My father felt they were being unduly feministic; but if there was pique on his part, it was purely professional and had nothing personal in it. Both Miss Mack and Miss Lowry were close and congenial friends to my parents—especially "Peg." (Miss Lowry's tour in China was brief and she never came back . . . but she used to send us marvelous Christmas packages!)

There were two memorable things about Miss Lowry. One was that she was "independently wealthy" and was paying her own way to work as a YWCA secretary in China. I don't know why that should have made such an impression on me; perhaps it was because the only "rich" Americans I had met (to my knowledge) were tourists, who seemed to have nothing to do but travel around enjoying perpetual leisure . . . The other memorable thing had to do with Miss Lowry's brother.

"Today is an important day," Miss Lowry announced to Robert and me. "It's my brother's birthday. His fifth birthday."

A birthday was always exciting—even of someone we didn't know, who was in a city (Philadelphia was Miss Lowry's home) that we had never been to. But what really surprised us was that a mature woman like Miss Lowry should have such a young brother.

"How old did you say he was?" we asked doubtfully.

"Today is his fifth birthday," she repeated. "Would you like to see his picture?"

She led us to her room in the west wing . . . You could see a faraway glimpse of hills—the Needle Pagoda and a tiny piece of the West Lake from the window, but we were too curious about her brother to look . . . She picked up a studio portrait from the tabletop where it had stood and held it for us to see. We were stunned into silence. The five-year-old in the picture looked exactly like a *grown man*! How could this be?

"How did your brother grow up so fast?" Robert finally asked in an awed tone.

"Well, I'll tell you," said Miss Lowry, as if about to explain everything. "My brother is really twenty years old, but today is only his fifth birthday."

We were as perplexed as ever.

"You see, he was born on February 29 and since that's Leap Year's Day and only comes around every four years, he can only have a birthday every four years."

I guess I am slow-witted, because it took me a long time to straighten all this out in my mind. For instance, could you call yourself nine years old when there was no birthday for it and when your last birthday, a year before, had been only your second? . . . I wasn't sure whether to envy Miss Lowry's brother for being so unusual or to pity him for all the birthday celebrations he must have missed. At any rate, this was something interesting to think about and to puzzle over for years to come.

Mr. Dzen

Finally—as a sort of ex-officio member of the household—there was Mr. Dzen, my father's Chinese teacher. He was one of the verities of my childhood.

Mr. Dzen did not live with us but came every day for a lengthy session of reading and translating with my father in his study at one end of the Flowery Pavilion reception hall (the east wing). If we were anywhere near by and stopped to listen, we could hear our father reading aloud, sometimes with a rhythmic fluency (there's always a singsong cadence to spoken Chinese)—sometimes haltingly—and often ending abruptly into silence which was gently broken by Mr. Dzen's voice explaining . . .

When my parents undertook to learn Chinese, there were no textbooks or manuals for teacher and pupils to use. I presume that my father's first solid reading—his first "textbook"—was the Bible in Chinese. By the time we were living in our new house, however, my father's reading ranged over a wide area of subject matter with a focus on religion, philosophy, and politics—which were his special interests. Of course, at my age, I didn't pay much attention, but in connection with what he was studying and reading with Mr. Dzen, I heard him refer to Buddhist teach-ings in the sutras—to K'ang Yu-wei and political activism—to contemporary writers and thinkers like Liang Ch'i-ch'ao.

In the beginning, Mr. Dzen was teacher only. Then, as my father's acquaintanceship in the Hangchow community grew and developed, Mr. Dzen came to serve as a sort of private secretary also, helping with the voluminous business and social correspondence which my father had to conduct in Chinese. Who knows what unconscious rudeness and gaucheries my father might have been guilty of if he had tried to compose letters in Chinese by himself or had had someone help him who was less well-grounded in literary practise and custom than Mr. Dzen? Mr. Dzen could always be counted on for correctness of style and expression, and he had an unerring knowledge (or sense) of the gracious and appropriate salutation, honorifics, and phraseology to use in every sort of letter to every sort of person.

He was one of a vanishing breed—the old style Confucian scholar. He had competed in the first round of the traditional scholastic examinations and had been one of the few (one percent) of the many competitors to pass and win the degree of Hsiu Ts'ai (Budding Talent). As hsiu ts'ai, he was qualified to teach—he was entitled to wear the badge of his scholarly rank, the black skullcap with a red braided button on top—and he could have competed in the second more difficult round of examinations given every three or four years in the provincial capital, which if he had passed would have made him eligible for certain important and desirable posts in the government. But in 1905, the ancient examination system was abolished by law—and Mr. Dzen had no chance to go any further . . . Was he disappointed? Did he feel frustrated? He didn't seem so. Maybe he had what he really wanted in life—not riches or fame or official position and prestige, but to spend his days in teaching and quiet study.

He must have been a superior scholar, a wonderful teacher and also a person of large wisdom and inner dignity to have elicited the kind of respect my father obviously felt for him. There was something of father-son in their relationship—and a great deal of the traditional respect of pupil for teacher in Chinese society. There was also a friendship.

"Mr. Dzen was one of my best friends," I've heard my father say—and once I chimed in with, "He was such a dear old man, wasn't he?" To which my father responded almost reprovingly, "He was a scholar and a true Confucian gentleman."

This took me aback at the time, because I had always pictured a "true Confucian gentleman" as someone who was stern, aloof, and chillingly proper—and that didn't fit Mr. Dzen at all. It wasn't till later when I really thought about the Confucian concept of *Jen* (poor translation *benevolence*) as the essential characteristic—the all-important virtue—of the "superior man" that I knew what my father meant.

I suppose that I had never noticed or recognized Mr. Dzen's correctness and propriety because they were not just a matter of form with him but were the natural expression of an inner benignity. His kindness and his courtesy were indistinguishable from each other, and they reached out and touched everyone he met with the gentle uncritical warmth of an autumn sun . . . It is not surprising that when I was of kindergarten age and drew pictures of the sun with a smiling face (a circle with two small circles for eyes, a dot for the nose, a wide upturned arc for a mouth and lines coming out from the edges for the rays of light) they always seemed to look like Mr. Dzen.

An encounter with him always made me feel better. If Robert and I were out in the garden playing when he arrived at the front gate, we would stop and wait decorously for him—watching while he bowed in courteous greeting to the gateman and then approached, head bent—lost in thought. The little round scholar's cap accentuated the roundness of his face and the curve of his shoulders, gently stooped from years of poring over books. He was dressed plainly in a cotton robe (well-padded in winter) with full sleeves, and he was shod with cloth shoes. He usually carried a paper-bound Chinese book rolled up in one hand—or, if it was cold, tucked with his hands into his sleeves. On rainy or threatening days he carried a large black umbrella; and when the weather was warm, he had a long, sturdy bamboo-and-paper folding fan dangling by a string from one of his fingers and every now and then would raise it and flip it open with an almost imperceptible flick of the wrist. He would wave it slowly back and forth for a time and then turn his hand in such a way that it would close again, the bamboo spokes coming together with a little glissando of clicks.

When he saw us, the meditative look on his face was replaced by one of pleasure and affection and his beaming smile seemed to light up the spot where we stood (I remember it now and the world is lit up).

If Aunt Becky was for us a surrogate elder aunt—wholly American-south, Mr. Dzen was a surrogate grandfather—wholly Chinese. Never would we have romped and teased with him as with our American grandfathers if they had been at hand, but he was a comforting, accepting, steadying grandfatherly presence filling a place that is important to every child.

It seems to me, as I recall our years in Hangchow, that I heard very little from my parents about which of their many, many Chinese friends and acquaintances were Christians. (Probably the majority were not.) And so it didn't occur to me to wonder about Mr. Dzen.

I've forgotten the context of the conversation, but not too many years ago, my father mentioned that at the end of a study session one day, Mr. Dzen said in the most natural way that he was "joining the church" on Sunday (I don't know which of the Hangchow churches he joined). This was a surprise to my father—and yet in a way no surprise. They had read the New Testament together, but had never discussed religion. My father had never tried to "convert" Mr. Dzen; it would have seemed inappropriate—even presumptuous. Mr. Dzen apparently had taken the step on his own—and in my view, he hadn't had to step far.

‖ Going to School

Kindergarten Days

Go out of our front gate and the little cul-de-sac and up the alley to the big street (Fa Yuanh Gya). Turn left—or away from the Lake; and down at the corner is the Wu Sanh Church ("our" church, where we attend Sunday School and morning worship—both in Chinese—every week). Go round the corner there and proceed southward a way on a street with a canal on the other side; then cross the canal on a bridge and you'll soon see the entrance, on the left, to the main campus of the Hangchow Union Girls' School and opposite this, the smaller entrance to its Primary School and Kindergarten.

These directions may not be one hundred percent accurate after all these years, and everything is different now; but this is how I remember going to kindergarten every school day after we had moved to the Tartar City. Unless it was too cold or wet, we walked to school and back with our amah. She left Robert and me at the kindergarten room and came back at noon to retrieve us.

This was not our first school. Before we moved, we attended a small mission kindergarten in the city. In a family album are a couple of faded, brown snapshots captioned "Fong-leh-gyao kindergarten Christmas 1916." Eleven small children—six boys and five girls—are standing in a double row against a vague background which appears to be a high compound wall. Nine of the children are Chinese—dressed in their padded winter clothes. At one end of the back row is my brother Robert, fair-haired and smiling sunnily; his younger sister is at the end of the front row, round of face and cheerful, a fringe of dark bangs showing from under a close-fitting knitted cap—and looking not very different from the little Chinese girls—except for her clothes (a heavy light-colored

78

sweater coming down nearly to my knees). Robert, of course, is obviously not a little Chinese boy . . . I don't remember this kindergarten at all, but judging from our expressions and demeanor, it must have been a happy enough experience for us.

We were the only foreign children also in our new kindergarten—which was a mission school too, but larger, better housed and equipped and more professionally managed.

The Hangchow Union Girls' School was popularly known as the Ong Dau, short for Ong Dau Niu Shwei Hsiau (its Chinese name in full). It had had its beginnings as a girls' school organized by the Southern Presbyterian Mission in 1868 and claimed to be the third oldest school for girls in all of China. It was now the cooperative enterprise of three missions, the Northern Presbyterians and Northern Baptists having joined the Southern Presbyterians in 1912 in the support and administration of the school.

In the same year, the school was able to purchase and begin to build on five acres of choice property at the inner edge of the Tartar City from which the defeated Manchus had recently been evicted. It grew and expanded until it consisted of six departments: Kindergarten and Primary (for both girls and boys), Higher Primary (I'm not sure if boys were pupils), High School, Kindergarten Normal, Primary Normal (these three for females only). Many of the girls were boarders. We used to see them every Sunday, dressed in the school uniform, filing into church and filling up about a quarter of the pews.

A beguiling and little-known fact about the Ong Dau and its premises is that there was a school for girls on the site before the Revolution of 1911. Exactly when it was in existence I don't know. A Manchu princess living in the Tartar City started it on her own—with no encouragement from anyone who counted and with the most reluctant and niggardly of support. According to the story, after begging and cajoling and badgering, she finally wangled classroom space for her school but no funds to hire a teacher ("that should stop her!" the powers-that-be probably thought). So she began to sell her jewelry and personal valuables to pay the salary of the teacher. Classes began. She insisted that little Chinese girls in the neighborhood be allowed to enter the Tartar City in the daytime to be taught along with the little Manchu girls . . . But finally she had nothing more of value to sell and no money for the teacher. She begged for funds to keep the little school going, but to no avail. So as a last recourse she let it be known that, without assurance of the necessary support for her school, there was nothing left for her to do but to commit suicide. She made all the preparations—in what must have been the most open and convincing way; and at the last minute the authorities in the Tartar City, in a panic of embarrassment over the possible scandal, gave in and the little school was saved . . . I heard this story from my father one day when I was recalling my Hangchow kindergarten days—and he was not one to fantasize. I've never seen the story in print. After all it was not a Christian Mission effort—or even a Chinese effort. But in my view, this unlikely but determined crusader for education and equal rights is surely worthy of remembrance . . . Through many centuries of Chinese history there had been educated women, including noted scholars and poets, but they had learned through private tutoring or kibitzing when their brothers and boycousins were being taught. *Schools were for boys only.* The early missionaries (usually the women) were breaking new ground when they began their first little schools for girls. The Manchu princess was a pioneer, too.

We never hurried to get to school on time. In fact, I don't remember hurrying to do anything "on time" in Hangchow—even though I know that none of us were late arrivals, whether at school, church, meetings or social occasions. Perhaps it was because we were all geared to the pace of a city where travel was mostly on foot and everything people did followed the tempo of its pedestrian traffic (the movement of the traffic on the canals was even slower). There was not the stimulation to keep up with anything faster.

Amah on her bound feet couldn't move briskly anyway; so, though we probably didn't dawdle, the walk to school was relaxed and pleasant— leisurely enough for us to observe the morning rituals along our alley (gateways opening for people going to work or market—or for housewife to hail a food vendor with his portable kitchen). As we neared the church corner on Fa Yuanh Gya, we were greeted by the several rickshaw men

80

who had parked their vehicles at the curb and were waiting for prospective fares. There was one who (if he was there) called out to tell us—in Chinese—that *he* knew how to speak *English*. We always stopped to listen admiringly while he recited a little sing song rhyme for us:

"*La* (a as in glad) *sze* come.
Chee sze go.
Ih kway yahng dienh—*one dah-loh*."
The translation (probably not necessary):
"*La* (in Chinese) means *come* (in English)
Chee means *go*.
Ih kway yahng dienh means *one dollar*"

From the church corner, we could see the canal that ran alongside the cross street. The canal just here edged the Chinese city and was very busy at this time of day. On the stone steps that led down to the water were women doing the family laundry, squatting easily on their heels and laughing and chattering to each other as they worked. They dipped the garments into the canal water, wrung them out, laid them on the flat stone surface of a step, and beat them energetically with their wooden staves—making a rhythmic, thudding accompaniment to the sounds of voices . . . Others, men as well as women, were washing vegetables or rice in the canal water. The fine-meshed sieves containing raw rice were lowered into the canal, swished gently to and fro and raised up to drain, the water straining off a cloudy white as the starch was washed off. The process was repeated until the water drained off clear—or as clear as canal water could be here, with its floating refuse of cabbage leaves, chewed sugar cane pulp (in season), and all manner of bits of this and that.

A little farther on, though, the canal was quieter and cleaner—and beautiful, with willow trees lining the grassy banks and looking at their reflections in the water below. And here we saw old gentlemen strolling alongside the canal, carefully dangling bird cages from their fingers as they took their songster pets for a morning airing.

Another thing I remember from the walk to kindergarten is catching a glimpse of a primary school class at their lessons . . . the children on benches in rows all rocking back and forth—though not in unison—keeping time to the words they were shouting at top voice. They were learning to read from the same little beginner's primer that had been used for generations: the Three-Character Classic, in which the rhyming lines of three characters each (drawing on the Confucian Classics and stories with moral and historic content) were learned and memorized by the pupils. Such total concentration and unrestrained vocalizing seemed like a lot of fun. Robert had a go at it when he was in the Primary School after we graduated from kindergarten; but I never had the chance.

The campus of the "big school," which we could see through its open gate was new and raw-looking, with no trees and few plantings to offset the grey brick of the recently-constructed western-style buildings. Across a large expanse of scraggly lawn was the main building—Administration and class-rooms. There was, I believe, a dormitory for the boarding students at one side and, closer to the campus entrance, to the right, was the Faculty House where the missionary teachers lived (and, I think, a few of the Chinese teachers)—all female. These are the buildings that I remember.

There was no campus as such for the one-story building where we had kindergarten. We entered a gate facing the big school, and then we were at the doorway to our kindergarten room. Beyond the building on the south was a small playground with a swing and a slide but not enough room for running around or for outdoor games.

On this south side of the kindergarten room were windows—almost a wall of windows—letting in lots of light. Child-sized desks and benches in straight rows faced the teacher's table and chair at one end of the room. On the wall behind the teacher's chair was a large blackboard. Almost a typical *American* classroom, except for the Chinese writing paraphernalia on each little desk, the posters and pictures on display around the room— and the flag, all of which were Chinese.

Our teacher, Miss Ganh, was a native of Hangchow and one of the three prettiest ladies I knew—the other two being my mother and "Aunt" Martha Wilson (no kin to "Aunt Becky") out at the College. There's an ancient Chinese saying to the effect that Hangchow and Soochow women are beautiful. Miss Ganh bore it out. She was slim and poised, with spar-kling dark eyes, pink cheeks, and a lovely smile (fifty-some years later, when I saw her last and she was well into her seventies, she was a beauti-ful woman—her hair black and glossy, her skin nearly flawless and her smile lovely and warm).

Miss Ganh had been a student at the Ong Dau from little girlhood and had recently graduated from its Kindergarten Normal Department. She was well-trained—but probably was also a born teacher of small children. The atmosphere in that kindergarten room was quiet but alive. What we did was interesting—sometimes fun—never stressful or anxious . . . nor, for that matter, out of control. Kindergarten was "school" to the Chinese and in school you obeyed and behaved, no matter how naughty or spoiled you might be at home. This was what was *expected*, of course; in practise it worked a lot better with a teacher like Miss Ganh.

Our lessons, stories, games, and songs were all in Chinese—which made not a particle of difference to Robert and me, since at this point of our lives we were quite naturally bi-lingual (as I've explained to people, that hasn't helped much in my adulthood. A kindergartener's vocabulary and comprehension of subject matter doesn't go far—and besides, the Hangchow dialect that we heard and spoke is not the accepted northern Mandarin).

The hardest work and the most fun (if that's the word) in our morning schedule was learning how to write our first Chinese characters—an effort requiring care and absorption, as each of us practised holding the writing brush correctly (the bamboo handle upright between thumb and the first and second fingers), wetting the brush end, dipping it on the ink tablet, and then forming the strokes (just *so*) of the character we were writing. Heads were bent in silence and Miss Ganh walked quietly here and there to help . . . I have no artistic skills and have never been able to create (by brush, pen, or pencil) a well-proportioned Chinese character, much less a beautiful one; but because of those kindergarten exercises, I've been able ever since to appreciate—to *feel* the aesthetics and expressiveness of Chinese calligraphy.

As in every good kindergarten, there was snack time. Ours was midmorning when we had "dienh-hsin." Our desks were cleared of books and writing materials. We folded our hands and sat straight and quiet—and eager—at our places. In came a servant bearing a large tray full of covered tea cups. He set one in front of each of us, then left and came back with the *dienh-hsin*, which he passed around the room. Often it was something like sesame buns, but if it was a specially cold day, it could be our favorite—*bao-tzus*—hot steamed dumpling-like buns, slightly sticky on the outside with a savory meat filling.

When everyone was served, we closed our eyes for grace (in Chinese) and then lifted the lids of our handleless cups. Steam billowed out. We picked up our cups with both hands (the warm cups felt comforting in winter) and sipped cautiously—put the cups down and nibbled (the tea was *green* tea—no milk or sugar, of course).

Miss Ganh was too good a teacher to expect children to sit still all morning. We had games that involved moving about and I remember doing some kind of setting up exercises beside our desks; but going outside to play was really a waste of time. Children were not supposed to "play"—not in public; and our fellow-kindergarteners simply stood about near the slide and the swing resisting Robert's encouragements to use them. So we stood about too; it wouldn't be fun without the others joining in.

Before school ended, there was always a small patriotic ritual with all of us standing up and singing to the flag at the front of the room at one side of the blackboard. It was the flag adopted by China after the 1911 Revolution to replace the Imperial Dragon Flag. It had five horizontal bars, the five different colors representing the principal peoples of the Chinese Republic. Our patriotic song, sung to the tune of "Bringing in the Sheaves," was as follows:

"*Ong—wong—lanh—beh—heh* (Red, yellow, blue, white, black)
(repeated twice)
Ngo-men do sze huanh-shee (We are all devoted to)
Ong—wong—lanh—beh—heh!"

The only unhappiness I recall from our kindergarten days was when, towards the end of a morning, we were marching around the room and Robert, looking behind him, ran into the corner of Miss Ganh's desk and—as we learned later when Dr. Main came to the house—broke his collar bone. Amah was already waiting to pick us up and we all three rode home in a rickshaw, Robert wailing aloud in his pain . . . After Dr. Main had set the bone and was about to leave, he spoke to me out in the front yard where I'd been worrying and wondering, and told me what a "brave little soldier" Robert was. Instantly my anxiety changed to sibling resentment and I felt like saying, "You should have heard him hollering all the way back from kindergarten!" But I didn't . . . When I saw Robert looking wan and heroic with his arm in a sling, I did feel sorry for him—and also envious. Mother obviously noticed that copycat little sister was feeling somehow left out and she took one of baby brother DeeDee's* diapers (no disposables then), folded it into a triangle, and put my left arm in a sling to match Robert's. I'm sure I tired of it pretty soon.

When we graduated from the Ong Dau Kindergarten, we received diplomas, and appropriate Chinese names had to be selected to be inscribed on the documents. Mine was easy: a girl's name was supposed to be pretty and decorative—no weighty significance necessary. For a foreigner, the characters chosen should sound as much as possible like the original name. By this time, my elegant name "Eugenia Mae" had, in good Southern U.S. fashion, changed for daily use to "Genie Mae." My Chinese name was (and is still, I suppose) *Chin Mei (Djin Mei)*. *Chin* can mean "gold" or "precious." *Mei* is "beauty" or "beautiful." I used to choose one or another of the meanings of *chin* for myself, depending on whether I wanted to feel gorgeous ("golden") or cherished ("precious"). The "beauty" or "beautiful" I didn't take as a serious attribute. It was mostly to match my American name, Mae.

The choosing of a boy's name was serious business—especially if it was for a first born son. It was made harder in Robert's case by the factor of having to match *sounds*, there being no initial "*r*" sounds in Hangchow mandarin; so how would the first syllable of his name be dealt with? . . . Several Chinese scholars were called upon to find a suitable name. They spent many hours separately studying their biographical dictionaries, historic records, and (for all I know) horoscopes and astrological data; and then met together to pool their findings and make a decision. Everyone was extremely pleased with the final choice, which met with all the requirements except for a compromise on the sound of the first part of the name. It was a name that reflected dignity and glory on my brother Robert—having connotations of nobility and brilliance and virtue. I believe it was derived from the name (or *a* name) of a first born son, back in the

---

* Younger brother DeWitt was called "DeeDee" ("Little Brother" in Chinese) until brother number three—Doak—came along four years later.

Sung (?) dynasty, who was brilliant and scholarly and a great credit to his princely family.

One day as I was thinking back to my kindergarten days and remembering them more and more clearly, it occurred to me with a shock that though I could *see* the room and my little desk and Miss Ganh and my brother Robert, I could not see the face of a single one of my other fellow-kindergarteners—not even those that sat on either side of me. I could not remember if my closest neighbors were boys or girls, tall or short, chubby or thin . . . When I'd begun years ago to be serious about writing my childhood recollections I had wondered if they would be too random and slight to be real or interesting; and my writer-aunt Lillian Smith (who was also something of an amateur psychologist) assured me that as I dwelt upon what I initially remembered, I would be astonished at how much more would come back to me. We never really forget anything, she contended; it's all stored away and retrievable. I've found this to be true to a surprising degree—except that I don't believe people remember what hasn't been significant to them or what they haven't focussed on or at least taken note of (whether as child or adult).

Memory is therefore selective according to one's nature or predilections (or prejudices?). I was shocked to find that my fellow pupils at Ong Dau were anonymous and faceless in my memory even though I'd been with them every day for months. Was this because of some hitherto unsuspected sense of superiority on my part? Had I failed to pay due attention to these other children because they were Chinese?

I was uneasy at the thought. It kept bothering me until after an occasion many years later at my parents' home in White Plains, NY, when I met and engaged in an animated conversation with a professor (a Chinese) who was married to the eldest daughter of close and dear Chinese friends of my parents. He was on the faculty of a large university in Texas. His field was physics, about which I never have much to say. But when I learned that he was a native of Hangchow, I was, as always, inordinately pleased and we began to compare notes. It turned out that he, like Robert and me, had gone to a mission school kindergarten in Hangchow—that it was the *Ong Dau*—that Miss Ganh had been his kindergarten teacher. And by reconstructing—each of us—personal factors such as age and the times and circumstances of our respective families, we came to the indisputable conclusion that we had been fellow-classmates in kindergarten.

It came as a welcome surprise that he had no more remembered Robert and me—the only foreign children in the class—than I had remembered him or any of the other Chinese children! So it wasn't a matter of prejudice at all.

Perhaps children have to play together to be real to each other. And playing together isn't always so easy for children out of different cultures. We American children had no problems of strangeness with our British friends because through our parents, we had a common cultural background. We knew that we were different, but we had our Christmas celebrations in common, our Easter Egg hunts, our games like Prisoner's Base and Cops and Robbers (which they called Bobbies and Thieves—to our secret amusement) . . . Playing with Chinese children was a puzzlement for us in those early days in Hangchow. It was simpler later on for children who via the movies could share cowboys and Mickey Mouse and Donald Duck—and who, still later, shared the ubiquitous daily costume of blue jeans!

The larger difficulty for us, however, was the matter of propriety—the proper behavior for children out in the school or social world. Decorum and dignity were required for most of the Chinese children Robert and I were acquainted with, and they raised a formidable barrier to our playing together and becoming easy with each other.

There was the time when Mother thought it would be nice to have a party at our house for her kindergarten-primary Sunday school class at the Wu Sanh Church, where (again) Robert and I were the only foreign children. The mothers were invited too and sat on the front porch having tea and being entertained in conversation with the hostess, while the children played games in the front yard. Robert was the "host" there and was in charge of organizing the games planned ahead of time. Nothing worked. The relay race, for instance, when we counted off by two's and lined up and Robert gave the starting signal . . . The two first runners set out at slow speed—glanced uneasily up at their mothers and then at each other—faltered and came to a full stop. That was the end of that. Robert and I looked at each other in frustration. Our guests couldn't bring themselves to be physically active in public or to compete (not to win would be humiliating; to win would be to make others lose face).

Our closest playmates, however, after the move from midcity, were Tsoo Ven Yau and Tsoo Ven Dzay—and the four of us always enjoyed each other's company.

Their parents, Mr. and Mrs. Tsoo Guang Hwa, were typical of certain leaders in the Hangchow community who were both thoroughly "Chinese" and "progressive."

Ven Yau was Robert's age; Ven Dzay was mine. A little later—about the time DeWitt was born—came two more boys: the twins Ven Bing and Ven Bay . . . which provided me with another rhyme:

Tsoo Ven Yau
Tsoo Ven Dzay
Tsoo Ven Bing
Tsoo Ven Bay (or leave out the surname *Tsoo* and it made an even bouncier rhyme).

Mr. Tsoo was a highly educated man. He worked (I am not sure in what capacity) for the Shanghai Hangchow Ningpo Railway and was an active member of the YMCA. He and Mrs. Tsoo were good friends of my parents.

They lived in one of the new residences in the Tartar City—a pleasant, but not overly pretentious home surrounded by moderately high white-washed walls. When we went over there to play and entered the front gate, we found ourselves in a sort of long, not-very-wide, stone-flagged courtyard with the house on one side and a steeply sloped garden space on the other. The garden, which was actually very small, cleverly simulated a natural hillside—with boulders and shrubs of various sizes, clumps of ornamental (but seemingly wild) grasses, a small tree or two, and a tall, fantastically shaped rock placed dramatically close to the courtyard. There was also one larger tree—near the base of the "hill"—which we could climb. The courtyard was where we four children did most of our playing, while our mothers visited in the house. And we played just as the spirit moved us—running, hopping, jumping, whatever . . . We probably played ball and threw beanbags; we probably kicked the shuttlecock. Whatever it was, there were no strictures on the Tsoo boys being naturally active, and we always had fun. And then we would be called into the house for refreshments.

There was an entrance directly from the courtyard into a bright, spacious, uncarpeted room with scrolls hanging on whitewashed walls, glossy, polished furniture of dark wood (chairs, end tables, and other pieces) set in their prescribed places. The square dining table and benches were at one side of the room at the end nearest the court—a corner that seemed more relaxed and informal than the rest of the room.

I remember the time we were invited to help celebrate a birthday, and were told that there would be *birthday noodles* for refreshments. Noodles (the long strands signifying long life) were the Chinese equivalent of our Western birthday cake. The Hangchow version was particularly delectable: freshly made noodles boiled, drained, sauteed in hot oil and dressed with a succulent mixture of vegetables, tiny shrimp, slivered pork or chicken—then brought steaming hot, mounded up on a huge oval platter to be served out in individual bowls to each person. There was vinegar and extra soy sauce available to brighten up your portion if desired and hot green tea to drink and freshen the palate—and as many "second helpings" as you could hold. And that was it . . . Even as a child with a sweet tooth, I would have chosen birthday noodles over ice cream and cake, except that cake was part of *our* celebration and there were candles to blow out.

On that birthday afternoon (whose birthday, I don't remember), the four of us children had been playing energetically outside and were hungry and expectant when Mrs. Tsoo called us in. As we were being seated, Mr. Tsoo appeared at the door to his study and came to join us, smiling and murmuring a greeting to each of the guests. He was thin, thoughtful, somewhat intense. She (Mrs. Tsoo) was large, cheerful, comfortable. Ven Yau looked like his father, Ven Dzay like his mother; and when the twins came along, they were not identical, but one was wiry and active; the other round-faced and placid. Such a well-balanced family, I used to think to myself.

When we were all in our places, Mrs. Tsoo announced (in Chinese), "Now we shall have the birthday noodles!"

Small bowls were brought in—one for each of us—chopsticks and porcelain spoons (why spoons?). Then the servant came in bearing in both hands a large, round, deep bowl and set it on the table along with a serv-ing-size porcelain spoon. Mrs. Tsoo beamed as she served out a new (to us) kind of birthday noodles—flat, oblong shapes of a chewy gray rice paste, floating in a sweetish slightly thickened soup . . . Mother looked sharply at Robert and me, hoping we wouldn't say anything to indicate our shock and disappointment (which I imagine she shared in a mild, adult way). We kept our tongues, and I hope that our friends didn't notice our lack of enthusiasm as we chewed on those birthday noodles. I hope they thought we were being extra polite and trying not to seem too eager.

How About School?

I wonder how much my 22-year-old, just-married parents-to-be had considered, before setting out for China, what having a family there would be like. 'Family' meant a great deal to both of them, and leaving home and parents and siblings in 1910 was hard and painful in spite of everyone's approval and pride in what they were doing and their own excitement at what lay ahead. There's no doubt that they expected and wanted chil-dren—a family of their own; but whether they talked much (or at all) about it during the courtship, I'm not sure. In 1910, *having babies* was a subject to be treated with delicacy before marriage (probably the phrase *become pregnant* was never spoken in the elder Barnett household). And in the whirlwind of activities after the wedding and before they left for China, there were so many more immediate matters to attend to—both those having to do with their service abroad and those relating to practi-cal necessities in the near future. There might have been some reference to family life during the days of conference and preparation at Silver Bay, but the YMCA workers there were going to many different parts of the world and were probably not told much about specific factors of family life in the various places . . . I believe that, like their missionary counter-parts (at least in China), the YMCA couples going abroad expected to bring up children there and counted on the children going on to college in America. Exactly what their education would be like before that— well, that might not have been clear, but they (the parents) would work it out.

The implications of having a family in China—particularly in respect to the children's education—struck suddenly, soon after my parents had

90

arrived in Shanghai. At a large social gathering of missionaries, they were introduced to a British couple who had just come up from Hangchow to take a ship back home: for furlough, the first in fifteen years. When they had come back to China at the end of the previous furlough, they had left their young children in England for their schooling. In a few weeks they would be seeing the "children"—now young adults—for the first time in fifteen years. Would they know each other? Would there be any real sense of connection? . . . Perhaps because the American couple about to go to Hangchow were so young themselves and were so sympathetic, the older missionaries completely forgot their customary British reticence and poured this all out in a sort of panic as if hoping for some kind of reassurance.

The fact that my parents re-told this episode so often in their later years is an indication of their surprise and dismay at the time—how sad and terrible it had seemed that parents should have to give up their children so soon and children be deprived of home and parents so early in their lives.

This is probably when my mother and father began to wonder about the education of their own children-to-be. And when they reached Hangchow and were living with the Stuarts, they were able to learn more about how Western parents in China had been dealing with the problem.

The early British missionaries (like the anxious parents in Shanghai) usually left their children "at home" in the British Isles or sometimes sent them there as soon as they were ready for school. The children usually boarded at school and spent holidays with relatives or friends—as was the custom of so many children of civil servants or army personnel posted in India and other parts of the far flung British Empire . . . The idea of sending young children to boarding school was not as strange as it would seem to American families. A common pattern in the home life of educated upper class Britishers was for the children first to have a nanny, then a governess and then to be sent off to a public school (that is, a *private* school with boarders) at the age of seven, eight or nine. But these facts and considerations didn't make it much easier, I'm sure, for the British missionaries in China, where separations, though perhaps no sooner than they would have been back 'home', were at such far distances and for so many long years (the only communication was by letter and the exchange of snapshots, which had to travel by "slow boat to China"—and then the other way—for weeks at a time).

American families, by instinct and tradition, stayed together as long as possible—the early missionary parents coping in various ways to educate their children without having to send them away too soon. The mother or father (or both)—using American text books—would teach the children at home. Sometimes there was a combination of home tutoring and attending a mission school, where many classes at the middle and upper levels were taught in English. And sometimes there was a variation of the British experience.

My parents heard from "Father and Mother Stuart" how they had gone on furlough—the first in fifteen years—taking with them four young sons, none of whom had ever seen America before . . . and how, at the furlough's end, they had gone back to Hangchow leaving the two older sons, Leighton and David, in Alabama to live with an aunt and uncle and cousins and to go to school. Before that, their mother had taught them at home, in Hangchow. I don't know when they saw their parents next, but Leighton continued his education in the States (as did his brother David, who became a doctor). Seventeen years later, after recovering from a long-lasting and violent aversion to being a "China-missionary-kid," he went back to China as a missionary himself (though never the orthodox kind) and to a distinguished career, which ended in his many years as president of Yenching University in Peking and finally in the aftermath of World War II, his serving as U.S. Ambassador to China in Nanking.

The third son in the Stuart family, Warren, had part of his schooling in the mission school in Hangchow. It was claimed in later years that Warren was the first president of the Ong Dau Girls' School YWCA (Young *Women's* Christian Association)—a story that always evoked smiles but that I find questionable or at least puzzling, in view of the fact that when the Ong Dau School came into being in 1912 the Rev. Warren Stuart (obviously no child!) was serving on the faculty of the (then all-male) Hangchow College . . . and when he was a boy going to the girls' school that later became part of the *Ong Dau*, there was no organized YWCA in the city of Hangchow—though there could have been one in the school (the YWCA first appeared in China in 1888 as units in schools). I suppose I am being historically picky . . .

As the number of Western families in China increased, schools for their children were organized in several parts of the county. One of the early boarding schools was in the Treaty Port city of Chefoo (Shantung province). It was run by British missionaries of the C.I.M. (China Inland Mission) and was rigidly strict and "moral." The American students who attended the Chefoo School apparently didn't mix much with the British, but kept to themselves and spent a lot of time discussing where they might be going to college in America. Thornton Wilder (later famous author and playwright) and his sister entered the school in 1910; his father served in Chefoo as U.S. consul-general. Another student at about the same time was an American missionary's son, Henry Luce, who was to be the founder of the *Time/Life* enterprises.

Down south in Shanghai, there were, by the early 1900s, the (British) Cathedral School for Boys and the Cathedral School for Girls which took both day students and boarders . . . I remember when Derek Strange was about to go up to Shanghai to enter the Cathedral School. The family (mother and children) came over to our house one afternoon on the brink of his departure. I think he was eight or perhaps just turned nine years old (I was about six). The Stranges were a British missionary family who were in Hangchow for several years. I was always somewhat bemused by them—partly, I know, because of the surname and the elder children's given names. Who wouldn't be intrigued by a family called *Strange* with a son (who was handsome as a prince) named *Derek* and a daughter (dark-haired and beautiful) named *Daphne*? There was also a *little* sister who was chubby and rosy-cheeked and cute—but I don't remember her name . . . I was impressed—almost overcome by admiration of Derek as he and Daphne and Robert and I shared each other's company that afternoon, so close to the time he was to leave the safety of home for faraway, alien Shanghai. I marveled secretly at his bravery—his *casualness*—that typically English air of studied though courteous masculine nonchalance—almost indifference, covering up who-knew-*what* intense emotions! (an air which in later years and in older English males used to pique and challenge my feminine interest).

At this time the older children of American Hangchow families were going up to Shanghai to be boarding students at the Shanghai American School, which had opened in 1912—two years after my parents' arrival in China.

There had been a predecessor—*Miss Jewyll's School*, which has always sounded so much like something out of Dickens to me that I thought it was British—and I still don't know much about it (or about *Miss Jewyll* herself) except that it was attended by first-generation American China-borns like the Fitches and Parkers. (Pearl *Sydenstricker* Buck and her sister were pupils in Miss Jewyll's School).

The Shanghai American School was the cooperative undertaking of the missionary and business communities. It was to be fully accredited to prepare its students for college in America and was to serve the children who lived in Shanghai and those whose parents were stationed elsewhere in China, mostly south of the Yangtse River. It offered twelve years of school: first through eighth grade (later kindergarten also) and four years of high school. Boarding students were accepted from fifth grade on up.

The Shanghai American School became a reality for me when, after studying at home with their mothers, the "big girls"—Elizabeth ("Nono") Blain and Janet Fitch who were nice enough to play with Robert and me now and then even though we were several years younger—went up to Shanghai to be boarders at S.A.S. From then on, going away to school was both exciting and fearsome to think about as part of *our* future.

A few years after we moved to Shanghai (thus depriving us of the initial terrors but also the superior status of being boarders at S.A.S. rather than mere day students), the number of Western families in Hangchow had grown, and the American parents established an elementary school so that the children could study together and wouldn't have to go away until after eighth grade. There was a small building and playground in a walled-off area of the Northern Presbyterian compound (Tsoo Jia Gyao). The faculty was comprised of one salaried full time principal-cum-teacher and several mothers taking turns teaching part time. From all accounts the Hangchow American School was a good little school with plenty of esprit among its lively and unusually bright students. I've often regretted that I wasn't one of them.

My parents may have been using Warren Stuart as an example when they enrolled Robert in the Ong Dau Primary School after our graduation from kindergarten. And of course it was so conveniently near.

I wasn't old enough to be in primary school. I stayed home—and I don't recall that this caused me any undue emotions, either of relief or of being 'left out'.

Small children don't have much conception of the passage of time, especially when it is being spent routinely; and I don't know how long Robert was in the *Ong Dau* School. Apparently everyone was happy enough about it until one day when Mother asked Robert a question involving simple arithmetic. His face went blank; he didn't seem to know what she was talking about. Somewhat alarmed, she asked more questions like: "What is three and three?," "What is two times three?" He didn't have a clue. He had been doing sums successfully on an abacus at school, but *plus* and *minus*, the multiplication tables, and division were out of his ken.

Our mother, who had always been a whiz at arithmetic and math in school, was dismayed. Something different had to be done about Robert's education.

In the meantime she had already taught Robert to read—in English, that is. Again, I don't remember when or how. I vaguely recall her pointing out words to Robert in a little book called a "primer."

I was never taught to read; like my young Chinese "sisters" of centuries past, I hovered and kibitzed and learned—only in my case, it wasn't that because I was a girl I wouldn't be given the same schooling as my brothers; I was simply thought to be too little to be interested.

One thing I do remember—and that is hearing Mother in her sessions with Robert explaining the printed word in terms of the sound of each syllable (*Phonics*). And I remember figuring out words (phonetically) for myself before I could really read. For instance, I could recognize scattered words in a book—or on a page of the *China Press*, the daily English-language paper that came from Shanghai (we took the *China Press* rather than the *North China Daily News*, because it was an *American* newspaper; the latter was British). I would find some familiar words on a page of the paper and then try to make out the sounds and meanings of words in between so that they would all come together to make some sense. I wasn't curious about the story or what was being said . . . what my father read aloud from the daily paper was obviously interesting to him but less than enthralling to me; I wanted to know what any string of words meant when put together. I wanted to know how to *read*. And so I did—and I don't remember exactly when it happened. It must have been as desirable and natural as learning to walk or talk or sing.

Nothing could happen in a hurry in Hangchow. Things went on as usual while alternatives to Ong Dau Primary School were being discussed. The "*Calvert Course*" began to crop up more and more often in family conversations; and finally it was known that Robert and I would be "taking" the Calvert Course with Mother as our teacher. It would be a *real* school with regular classes every morning. Our classroom would be one end of the east wing ("Flowery Pavilion" reception hall). We knew that all the materials would come from Baltimore (in America, a city whose name was familiar to us); we knew when they were ordered—and also that it would be months before everything arrived. I think we knew in addition that because there would be only the two pupils and I already was reading and learning how to write (that is, print), it made sense for us both to be studying at the same level rather than to have two "grades." So the order was for one set of teacher's plans for a year and double of the same set of materials for the pupils . . . And this is how my brother Robert came to be doomed to having a younger sister in the same class with him for the rest of his school days.

The months passed. Word came from the shipping company's authorities in Shanghai that the Calvert Course order had arrived and would soon be sent to Hangchow. We were about to open our own little Hangchow Barnett School.

City Streets

After we moved to the Tartar City, we delighted in its comparative openness and were constantly aware of how near we were to West Lake and how accessible to us were the hills and all its natural surroundings. But we were by no means cut off from the city itself, our home being on the "other" side (the *Chinese* side) of the former Tartar City wall. And we continued to travel the city streets for errands and shopping for visiting friends in the mission compounds and individual residences which were scattered throughout the large and crowded city. We accompanied visitors on tours in the city—chiefly in the south to see the great silk shops and other famous stores, the historic Mosque, and City Hill with its legendary and ceremonial sites and buildings (somewhat recovered from the destruction of the T'ai P'ing years). We went to afternoon church service held once a month for us "foreigners" in the tiny chapel of the CMS compound right in the middle of Hangchow. And we crossed over the east boundary of the city whenever we went to the railway station to meet someone or to take the train ourselves.

The Hangchow streets took on a different look according to the time of day. The morning scene was the busiest and liveliest, the afternoon more leisurely—and nightfall brought its inevitable transformation into darkness and quiet and mystery.

The look of the Hangchow street altered also with the seasons—midsummer and midwinter being quite different from each other and from the more clement spring and fall. It varied with the weather—sunshine or rain—and the rare snowfall. Or with the *horoscope*—some days being particularly auspicious for weddings or funerals. Then there would be the added crowding and color and noise of wedding or funeral processions though because of the narrowness of Hangchow streets, these never had the pomp and theatricality that I used to see later on the vast streets of Peking.

97

A Rickshaw Ride

Our most frequent and interesting journeys on Hangchow streets were when we (Robert and I) were sent off alone by rickshaw to spend the day at T'ienh Sway Gyao with our good friends, Carrie Lena and John McMullen. This was something that we did often, though not according to any fixed schedule—which made it more of a treat. A part of the treat also was going by ourselves without any grownup overseeing us.

We had no home telephones—and I wonder how Mother and "Aunt Emma" made the arrangements for "getting the children together" (there was probably an exchange of "chits" hand-carried by a servant). Mother usually told us about it the evening before—sometimes at bedtime just before or after hearing us say our prayers.

"Do you know what you children are going to do tomorrow? . . . Aunt Emma has invited you over to spend the day with Carrie Lena and John."

"Oh boy!" (Robert)

"Goody!" (me)

And the next morning, shortly after breakfast, Mother would go out with us through the double gate where a rickshaw was waiting in the *cul de sac* and would see that we were properly on our way, admonishing us to remember our manners—and "Be sure to give my love to Aunt Emma!" Off we would go, perched alertly side by side on the white cotton-covered cushion of the rickshaw seat.

It was about two miles from our house to T'ienh Sway Gyao—that is, I believe, as the crow flies. Actually, the travel distance must have been longer because of all the twists and turns, and would have varied according to the twists and turns chosen by the individual deciding on which route to take . . . for instance our rickshaw puller of the day. Once we were on the Great Street, the distance was easier to measure.

The Hangchow streets that we knew were probably at their most typical on a certain day in May when Robert and I made one of our journeys to T'ienh Sway Gyao (if what I recall turns out to be something of a composite, including scenes and episodes of other days, it shouldn't really matter).

I don't know exactly how old we were on this particular morning—Robert was about seven years old, or eight at the most. It was a fine morning.

Spring was near to turning into summer; it was the kind of day when the weather is not too hot, not too cold, but (like the little bear's porridge) "just right," so that you can forget about it and simply enjoy whatever is at hand to enjoy.

We were in such a mood as we gaily waved goodbye to Mother till our rickshaw rounded the corner out of our cul-de-sac and she was out of sight.

The alley leading to the street looked much as usual. Several of the neighbors' children had gathered in a group, watching while one of them was busily scratching some sort of pattern in the dirt with a stick—presumably for a game they were about to play. An older girl—ten or eleven—stood by with her baby brother strapped to her back. An old man—somebody's grandfather—sat on the lower step of an entranceway, half dozing in the sunshine. A doorway in the opposite wall opened; the housewife, dressed in her everyday trousers and jacket, stepped out to hail a peddler who was approaching from the street crying out his wares at full voice. He broke off his call and hurried up the alley, and he and the woman were beginning to dicker by the time we reached the street.

We had been moving at a slow and careful pace. Now as we emerged from the alley into the wide open spaces of *Fa Yuanh Gya*, we saw a lone rickshaw man sauntering down the middle of the otherwise empty street—his vehicle (unoccupied) tilted way back and the shafts, held loosely under his arms at their base, very nearly perpendicular. Catching sight of us, he gave a start of recognition and shouted out a greeting to our puller.

"Too bad your health is not good today," he added in a loud voice. "Only two small children to carry—and yet you go so slowly!"

Our rickshaw man snorted in reply and, as soon as we were properly on the street and pointed in the right direction, took a firmer grasp of his shafts, lowered his head, and away he flew. His friend gave a shout of defiance and followed after us and soon was galloping alongside, his empty rickshaw swaying wildly behind him. Robert and I gasped with excitement as we felt ourselves rushing through the air at what seemed to us a fearful and wonderful speed. We had never traveled so fast before—except on a train, and this *felt* much faster—as if we were being flown swiftly on a magic carpet.

Side by side, down the broad street, the two rickshaws sped till we had nearly reached the end of the long block, when both the men slowed down rather abruptly—and the race was over. Still exchanging cheerful insults, the rickshaw pullers went their separate ways—our erstwhile competitor stopping at the church corner to wait for possible fares, while we prepared to cross the canal which at this point marked the eastern boundary of the Tartar City.

Slowly up the stone arched bridge we went—over the canal—down the other side; and the city closed about us.

We had descended into a narrow street bustling with pedestrians, none of whom paid us any attention—so that our rickshaw man had to make his way cautiously, turning this way and that to avoid running into anyone. The crowd thinned out quite soon, however, and he was able to break into a half-jog, keeping a wary eye out for slippery cobblestones where a housewife or shopholder might recently have tossed out a bucketful of slops.

Presently we came to another busy corner. Several little streets and alleys came together here, with a space in the center almost like a constricted city square. It was half-filled with people walking to and fro across it between the small shops that surrounded it. Everyone seemed preoccupied with personal affairs of the moment, and we expected to pass over to the other side without any ado. But suddenly one of the pedestrians glancing at us, looked again, stopped short, pointed and exclaimed in apparent astonishment: "*Yang gway-dzz!* (Foreign devils!)" Others near by turned to look. They took up the cry; and before we knew it, we were surrounded. People had emerged with amazing rapidity from the little shops, the side streets—it seemed from out of the very cobblestones at our feet—all of them staring at us and yelling "*Yang gway-dzz! Yang gway-dzz!*" Our rickshaw man, uttering gruff commands, tried to push on, but he was ignored. He couldn't move in any direction, so thick was the crowd about us.

When this sort of thing happened and our parents were with us, Robert and I knew that we were all to keep quiet and patient and smiling, and after a while the crowd would have its fill of staring and shouting and would drift away. But the situation always seemed a little different when we were alone—and if necessary, we had our ways of dealing with it.

City Wall and Moat

A City Gate

A City Canal

A Street Vendor and his Traveling Kitchen

Peddler of Straw Sandals

Troupe of Strolling Musicians

Man Enjoying a Meal (Note the chopsticks, rice bowl, and typical square table)

Travel Before the Rickshaw: Eugenia and Robert in Market Baskets

At Ma Zse Gya Home: the Family with Eugene Turner (left) and Lawrence Mead (right)

Bride and Groom in Traditional Costume with addition of Western Bridal Veil

West Lake with Emperor's Island in Foreground

The Su Causeway (named for the poet Su Tung-p'o)

Fisherman on West Lake

The Needle Pagoda

Bridge on Causeway with Canopied Sampan (pleasure boat) Nearby

Sampan (without canopy) on West Lake Near the City

We waited for what seemed to me quite a while, but the crowd still jostled about us and the din of voices grew louder and shriller . . . I was beginning to be exasperated—we didn't want to be stuck here all day! Then came the last straw. A boy not much older than ourselves wriggled his way through the mass of bodies till he was almost against our rickshaw. He pointed at us in the most insulting manner, looked straight at us, and shouted in a loud, jeering tone over and over, "*Yang gway-dzz! Yang gway-dzz!*" . . . This was too much for me. How dare he look at me and talk at me as if I were really a—a *devil*, not a proper person like himself!

Robert's patience must have snapped just when mine did, because without any consultation, both of us were raising ourselves part way up from the rickshaw seat and almost simultaneously cried out in voices high enough to be heard above all the others.

"Ngo-men sze '*yang* gway-dzz' - *nee*-men sze *Chung-guo* gway-dzz!"

Having delivered ourselves, we sat back, pleased with ourselves and confident of the forthcoming reaction.

For an instant there was silence—not a sound . . . and then a burst of appreciative laughter. "Ha-ha-ha. *Hao! Hao!* (Good! Good!)" and our witty comeback was repeated and passed around through the assembled throng: "The small children say that if *they* are *foreign* devils, then we are *Chinese* devils!"

In the midst of all this, someone spoke out in a surprised tone, "They speak Chinese. The foreign children speak Chinese!" This remark too was repeated, along with nods of approval. People waved and smiled at us; we waved and smiled back—and the crowd began to disperse, melting away almost as rapidly as it had formed. Our rickshaw man, grumbling to himself over the delay—and probably to cover up his discomfiture at having been unable to do anything about it himself—began to move ahead and we were on our way again.

We were now traveling a poor-looking little street, partially unpaved. The buildings on either side were rickety, and their roofs nearly touched over our heads. Very little sunlight could ever reach down to clear away the shadows or to dry off the dankness. The random paving stones were broken and uneven, and our rickshaw bumped and lurched along unpleasantly. Pedestrians—who were few, fortunately—had to press themselves against the walls at the side or step back into doorways to let us by.

We caught sight of an even darker, narrower side street, which humped itself up almost immediately into an extravagantly curved bridge spanning a small canal invisible to us. An old man was climbing the steep stone steps of the bridge holding on at one side to the stone balustrade. I wished briefly that we might turn here and cross the old bridge . . . it would be fun to climb it—look down at the mysterious canal and to see what was on the other side. But we could never do it in a rickshaw.

Obviously we'd have been going in the wrong direction anyway, because now we swerved off to the other side into a quiet alley lined with blank walls. We made another turn—and then another; and for a while our rickshaw puller kept ducking this way and dodging that as if trying to escape an unknown pursuer . . . This part of our journey was always bewildering to me—my chief worry being not so much that we might be really "lost" as that we might end up back where we had started from instead of at T'ienh Sway Gyao.

"Where are we now? . . . Aren't we going the wrong way!" I asked anxiously.

Robert kept reassuring me in true big-brother fashion, but he was beginning to look serious and had just leaned forward to say something to our rickshaw puller when we were brought around a corner and found ourselves on a street that we both recognized immediately. It was quiet and full of sunshine—and fairly wide at this point, though it grew narrower further ahead. I could smell incense on the air and to our left we saw the warm vermilion glow of the outer wall of a temple. We knew where we were now, because we always passed this little temple on our way to T'ienh Sway Gyao—though I don't remember ever hearing its name. Though small, it was obviously well-used and cared-for. The double gate in the center of the vermilion wall was open, and looking through it as we went by, we could see the stone-flagged courtyard swept spotlessly clean. We could see the large bronze incense urn, nicely polished, standing squarely in front of the main temple building that faced us from across the rear of the court. Several long sticks of incense, recently lit, were standing upright in the soft ash that filled the urn—the grey ribbons of smoke floating off into delicate patterns with a puff of breeze. We caught a glimpse of gilded idols in the shadowy interior of the temple—and of red candles flickering on the altar table; and we saw a lone worshiper: a woman, neither rich nor poor by her clothes, who was probably the person who had lit the incense in the urn outside. She was moving about quietly making a series of quick, devout obeisances—the palms of her hands pressed together, fingers pointing upward, under her chin . . . She didn't seem to be praying *for* anything special, but simply worshipping—as we often did, at family prayers or Sunday school or church.

I took a long blissful sniff of the fragrant air . . . How I loved the smell of incense!

"Quick! Hold your nose!" Robert warned. Half-choking on a gasp and a giggle, I obeyed—and just in time. Not far ahead of us—as I should have remembered—was one of a few public latrines that had been installed at random in the city as a mark of modernity and progress. It was simply a space alongside a wall that had been partitioned off from the street . . . only semi-private, with an opening at one end, but no door. One person at a time (male) could use the latrine—a drain hole at the end of the cubicle toward which the paving stone conveniently sloped. The outer wall of the lathe-and-plaster partition was tinted a pale pink, on which the letters W C stood out in bold black paint. "W C"—as I had been told when I asked—stood for "Water Closet" . . . *Water Closet?* This seemed a *funny* sort of name for it; and it also seemed odd that English letters had been used, since who of all the passersby on that street could read English? . . . I don't suppose it mattered. Certainly the latrine was used—and the stench from it was almost strangling in intensity.

Robert and I had pinched our noses tightly and held our breaths as long as possible. But not long enough—and as we gasped for air, the odor from the latrine struck us full force.

"Pee-*yu-u*!" exclaimed Robert loudly and fervently.

"Pee-*yu-u*," I chimed in right after him, remembering there were no grownups about to hear us.

Taking advantage of our freedom from adult disapproval, we repeated the inelegant but eloquent expression a number of times, trying out different ways of saying it for better effect and continuing even after we were well out of range of the "bad smell."

Our dramatic reactions were partly involuntary and partly a joke at the expense of our elders. We didn't like this particular "bad smell" (it was pretty awful), but it wasn't all that bad to us—so part of the joke in our histrionic exaggeration was knowing how much better we could stand this and other strong odors than could any of the older-generation foreigners, our parents included. (Just to look at their faces—even the old-timers'—and to see the struggle going on between dismay and lofty unawareness at the encountering of certain disagreeable odors in the city or countryside gave us children a rare sense of ascendancy over those usually infallible beings, the Grownups.)

We had barely fallen silent again when a quick little wind blowing our way brought a whiff of another characteristic smell, which might have seemed unpleasant to some but which I liked and always found oddly exciting. We were approaching one of the larger of the city's canals and soon would be crossing over it on one of the stone bridges that were probably the oldest visible relics of Hangchow's long past. This bridge was wider and more gently arched than many. Instead of steps, there was smooth though well-worn stone paving underfoot. As our rickshaw moved slowly up the incline, a full current of cool dank air rushed up to meet us, smelling of water—of damp stone, mildewy and mossy—of floating refuse—of wet bamboo and the water-splashed varnished wood of the canal craft.

On either side of the bridge was a stone railing with balustrades that had once been richly carved but through the erosion of centuries now bore only the simplest shaping suggesting the original sculpting. The railing would have been only waist-high for a pedestrian and from our rickshaw perch we could easily see over it.

It was like looking down the length of an interesting little canyon. Continuous rows of small wooden frame buildings with dark grey tiled roofs faced each other across the canal. Some of the buildings extended several feet beyond the edge of the stone embankment from which they all rose and seemed to teeter precariously over the water. Almost all of them had little wooden balconies hanging above the canal. Here and there a doorway opened onto a flight of stone steps down to the water so that the householder could transact business with the passing craft and his wife could do the laundry, wash her vegetables, rinse out the rice, and scoop up water for the family's need . . . After dusk—perhaps sometimes in the deepest chill of winter—the little buildings lining the canal would be closed and shuttered tight and seem as still and lifeless as if abandoned or caught in a spell; but today the latticed windows were open wide. The little balconies were full of sunshine and brightened by the foliage and flower of potted plants; and freshly-laundered garments, white and faded shades of blue, were hung out to flutter and flap in the breeze.

But it was the lively scene on the canal itself that interested us most, and when we had reached the crest of the bridge, we called to our rickshaw puller, "Man-man-ti! . . . Dung-ee-dung . . . dung-ee-dung!"—begging him to slow down and wait a bit so that we could watch what was going on. He came to a halt, but held the shafts at the level so that we couldn't climb out and go to stand at the railing and look over—as we would have liked to do. He wasn't going to be responsible for one of us falling over into the canal.

We could see perfectly well from where we were . . . the canal choc-a-bloc with craft of all kinds and shapes, jostling each other in constant though barely perceptible movement. This was a major canal for transportation and traffic was at a peak. There were barges and rafts and many, many "houseboats"—which is what I always called the sampans that served as permanent floating homes for families of the "boat people." Some of them looked more like *houses* than others—the family living quarters being sheltered by a square wooden walled-about, roofed-over enclosure rising above-deck in the center of the boat. Others were smaller and simpler, with only a shallow arc of bamboo matting as a roof over the family living quarters below.

One of these had just moved into view from under the bridge, and I stared at it almost wistfully. On the tiny after-deck, the mother squatted on her heels stirring something that was cooking over a small earthen brazier. Close by her, the baby was crawling happily, trailing a long rope of twisted cotton cloth, one end of which was tied about his waist—and every now and then his mother darted a quick glance at the free end of the rope, making sure she could make a grab for it if the child ever seemed in danger of falling overboard. A scruffy dog lay on its side sleeping in the full sun; and several children scampered about him, vanishing down into the "cabin" and leaping out again, as agile and surefooted and playful as kittens. At a call from his father, the largest of the children—a boy of about Robert's size—clambered lightly to join him

113

at the prow and lend a hand with guiding the boat through the congested traffic . . . The children of the "boat people" always seemed to me so much freer, more active, and less inhibited than city children. It must be a wonderful life, I thought—always on the move with new scenes and adventures to enjoy without ever having to leave their own cozy, delightful little home.

I was interrupted in my thoughts by a shout from Robert.

"Hey—look! They're stuck! . . . they can't move!"

I turned to look at the other side of the bridge where he was pointing. At first glance it didn't look any different from normal, but then I could see that though there was a certain amount of shifting and rocking, none of the traffic was going anywhere. The sampans and other small craft, a heavy square-prowed barge loaded with sacks of something (probably rice), a narrow raft of large bamboo poles had all jammed together at impossible angles to form an almost solid mass for some distance back along the canal. Boatmen were leaping here and there with their long bamboo poles, trying to push their craft free. They worked swiftly and silently at first, but as their frustration grew, they began to yell at each other and then to curse loudly and eloquently. People appeared on the little balconies overlooking the scene and shouted down advice, adding their voices to the hullabaloo . . .

Our rickshaw man decided we had watched long enough. We started to protest as we felt ourselves borne away from the excitement and suspense of unresolved crisis, but subsided when we realized that we still had a way to go—we hadn't even come to the Great Street yet. So we fell silent and listened intently till we heard a low familiar hum from somewhere up ahead. It grew louder—separated into distinguishable sounds . . . And there it was—the Great Street—across the end of the smaller street we were on.

"Here we are—on the Great Street!" announced Robert, and I nodded with a sigh of cheerful satisfaction.

Great Street North

"The Great Street" was a name that had a good, satisfying sound. I liked to hear it and I enjoyed saying it myself. Yet the thoroughfare we were now traveling—bumping along in our rickshaw—didn't really fit my idea of something "great," like the Pyramids of Egypt, for instance, or the Great Wall of China. "Great" to me usually meant out-sized, grand, awesomely or dramatically impressive—and the Great Street was none of these.

To be sure, it was the longest street in Hangchow and the straightest and widest in the city proper. But a width of six to eight feet isn't impressive and when thronged with pedestrians seemed even smaller. What with all the people to weave through, our rickshaw had trouble squeezing by another coming from the opposite direction—the only other wheeled vehicle we would see from now on . . . The Great Street had no beautiful parks alongside—no imposing buildings—no historic monuments, even though it had been here from way back—hundreds and hundreds of years before—when Hangchow was just beginning to grow into a city.

But the Great Street *was* important, and I think I must have always sensed something of what it represented. The Great Street was "*Hangchow*"—not when it was dreamy or contemplative or romantic, but its down-to-earth practical self. This was the workaday, here-and-now city—prudent, productive, competent, and self-assured. Here in the shops and markets that lined the way, where goods and produce had been brought for sale, where craftsmen (and women) worked in full view fashioning with their hands their own products to sell, where people gathered daily to buy what they needed and wanted—here is where you could see how Hangchow made its living and how it lived.

A leisurely stroll would have been best in order to absorb all the sights and sounds and smells of the Great Street. As it was, we were kept busy looking from side to side at whatever particularly caught our attention, which was every now and then distracted by a sudden jounce or sway of the rickshaw . . . The Great Street here was paved with cobblestones at either side and a double row of long stone slabs laid end to end down the center. The stone slabs were fitted together rather loosely to allow water to flow through the cracks into the drainage canal underneath—the same sewer system that had impressed Marco Polo centuries earlier. The stone and cobbled paving was new since then, but was old enough to have been subjected to a lot of wear and tear. Some of the slabs were eroded; others had chunks broken out of them; and many rocked back and forth like seesaws under weight of foot or wheel. When this happened, we would give an appropriate squeal and each of us clutch at the arm rest nearest by. It was like being in a small boat on an uncertain sea, alternately smooth and choppy.

A ringing clang-clang-clang had us looking over to the left side of the street, where we saw a brassware shop. Two or three youths sat tailor-fashion on the floor near the open front of the one-story building, hammering out a staccato rhythm on the pieces of metal they were shaping. There were gleams from the finished products in the dimmer recesses of the room; and closer to the front an older man stood behind a wooden counter holding up a brass water kettle for a prospective buyer to examine.

As the sound of clanging and pounding diminished, I could hear a dry click-clacking from the other side of the street and saw a silk-weaving establishment—a small drab room, where a pair of looms reaching from floor to ceiling were placed side by side against a wall. Two women sat on benches in front of them, completely absorbed in what they were doing. Their hands seemed to move of themselves towards the loom and away from it to twist, loop, snap off or tie together silken threads. Oblivious of the noise and bustle of the street so near them, the women were as intent and serious as instrumentalists performing for some solemn occasion. But the only music was the clickety-clack as their feet pressed down on the treadles of the looms.

Across the way was a basket-weaving shop. Stacks of stout fiber baskets—the kind used by farmers to bring their produce to market—stood in rows along the rear wall of a rather large and high-ceilinged room. At one end a young man sat on the floor with his back against the wall very near the open store front, looking out at the passing scene as his fingers busily plaited strips of pliant reed onto a bamboo frame. He tossed a remark—probably an insulting description of someone in the street—over his shoulder to his co-workers behind him, and there was a burst of appreciative laughter from within.

A curious twanging sound came to us from farther on. As we approached, it grew louder . . . Twang-ng-ng. It quivered and faded, but before it was completely silent—Twang-ng-ng—there it was again . . . and again. We drew alongside the place where the sound was coming from just in time to see a white cloud descending and settling on a snowy drift heaped on the floor at one side of a small room. I heard the twang again—and a long flail-like implement with a thong attached swooped

116

down into the fluffy mound and sent up another cloud of white particles which went spinning up towards the ceiling before slowly floating down. The single man working the implement seemed to be rocking and bending tensely in a sort of rhythmic stationary dance. I don't remember the implement or the process exactly. Perhaps I was too mesmerized by the rising and falling of the snowy cloud to notice. I did know that this was the way silk fibers were converted into *ssu-mien*, the silk floss, light as thistledown and miraculously warm, used by those who could afford it for padding their winter garments and bedding. (The poor made do with cotton padding.) . . . On the other side of the room, a woman had just finished tying up a bundle of the floss and was lifting it lightly in her hands to put it with other identical bundles piled in neat rows on the floor and ready to sell.

Now we were passing a coffin shop—like most coffin shops, tidy and respectable. The coffins were on display on either side of the long rather narrow room. They were arranged neatly and exactly, end to end and several coffins high. Some were bright and sticky with fresh varnish or paint; others had been left plain so that the customer could buy at a cheaper price or order the personally preferred finish or decoration . . . Through the open door at the rear of the room I could see into a sunny courtyard and caught a glimpse of piles of lumber and of two men sawing a piece of it into boards. The two-handled saw made a pleasantly grating sound as it went up and down—back and forth. The smell of fresh saw dust and resinous wood drifted out and mingled with that of fresh varnish and paint . . . Coffin shops in Hangchow were almost invariably clean, dignified, and cheerful. I didn't know it then, but a common saying of the Chinese was "See Hangchow and die" . . . not (as could be assumed) because you'd finally had the privilege of seeing its beauty and now could die happy, but because you could buy a good coffin here at a bargain price—and what good Chinese would not live out his or her last days more happily and serenely in the knowledge of having a fine coffin to be buried in—moreover one that hadn't cost too much?

All this time we had been proceeding due north and coming closer to the most exciting—at any rate, the most frenetic—part of the Great Street: the Market section where every day, probably since the first beginnings of the city, farmers and fishermen had brought their vegetables and fruit and meat and fowl and seafood to sell. For a period back in the Sung dynasty, the markets had been open at night and the Hangchow *Night* Market had been famous for its wares, its crowds and its festive excitement; but now most of the buying and selling was done in the morning. I think we must have gotten there when it was at its height.

The street was jammed with people hurrying and pushing, their faces drawn into preoccupied frowns or lit with an almost holy zeal. Buying food was a serious business . . . A child toddled out into the street almost in front of us. His mother squalled wildly and snatched him up before he could get lost in the crowd. A chicken—escaped somehow from a farmer's basket—fluttered hysterically among dozens of cloth-shod feet. Vendors cried out their wares at full strength so as to be heard above the hubbub of all the other voices crying out "How much?"—the answers shouted back—the protests, arguments, and agreements.

Near by a man drew in a bubbly breath, hawked loudly, and spat—and there was a great blob of sputum on the paving stone in the middle of the street—another hazard for the busy and perhaps unwary feet.

The great market sheds were so full of produce—laid out on long boards set on trestles and standing in heaps on the floor—that buyers moved about with difficulty and there was an overflow out into the street beyond the overhang of the slanted roofs. Half carcasses of hogs and an occasional sheep, pale and smooth and clean and all wearing identical expressions of foolish and ineffable bliss, were suspended head downwards from rafter and roof beams—as were strings of dried sausages and clusters of pressed dried duck as richly glossy as polished mahogany . . . On the tables were smaller chunks of meat to be sliced or chopped as the customer desired—and pyramids of all sorts of strange-looking inner parts (tripe, brains, liver, kidneys). On other tables were taller pyramids of pale blue duck eggs, mounds of "hundred-year-old" eggs, and, filling shallow containers or brimming deep baskets—hundreds and hundreds of fresh chicken eggs. Live chickens, crowded into wicker containers set down on the floor or street, squawked loudly as they tried to free themselves—and every now and then a rooster or hen somehow scrambled out with feathers flying . . . White geese honked with authority, and ducks kept up a steady disheartened complaint out of similar cages.

Here were the vegetable markets with round cabbages and long ones, leafy "greens" of every shade, bright green scallions tipped with alabaster, white turnips, red radishes, mounds of translucent bean sprouts, knobbled ginger root, garlic, water chestnuts brown and shiny—kept fresh in tubs of water. And there were squares of dried beancurd, brown and rough on the surface, arranged in rows on wooden trays—and down below, fresh beancurd floated like large chunks of white junket in tubs of brine.

We were now passing by a row of temporary "kitchens" in the forefront of one of the market sheds. A customer had just been handed a blue china bowl full of savory hot noodles and a pair of bamboo chopsticks to eat them with. Next to the "noodle kitchen," large white *bao tzu* (dumplings stuffed with meat) were being steamed in a round bamboo container; and next to that was a cauldron of bubbling oil for frying the twisted golden-brown crullers which were skewered onto bamboo sticks and vended among the crowd. The tempting smells of hot oil and cooking foods mingled with the smells of fresh fruit and vegetables, of odd herbs and spices, and of greens and cabbage leaves fallen and bruised underfoot.

But all these interesting odors were overpowered and lost when we came to the fish markets. It was here that the combination of smell and sound suddenly crescendoed into *double fortissimo*—and where, when we had out-of-town guests along, we judged them for their stamina. Some of them, after an involuntary exclamation of dismay, buried their faces in their handkerchiefs. Some winced and grimaced. Others turned a little pale but kept on smiling bravely. My father always took this opportunity to explain in shouting tones to the guests near enough to hear that his Chinese surname *Bao* (chosen for its sound—the full name *Bao Nai-deh* being as close to *Barnett* as could be managed) was a character meaning "stinkfish" and referred to a certain kind of dried fish,* noted for its potent flavor and smell.

The Hangchow Fish Market on the Great Street offered every imaginable kind of seafood. There were the fresh fish still alive and swimming about in shallow wooden containers. There were tiny smelts crowded into wooden buckets and other buckets filled with sea slugs. There were clams and mussels . . . live crab and prawns. And there were the fish and other sea creatures that had been dried—salted—pickled—fermented. These gave off their own powerful odors, which encountered together with the

* Actually abalone—a mollusk

fresh seafood smells, suddenly and in volume, were like a surprise assault. And it seemed as if sounds had to compete with smells—the loud chatter and shouts of the other markets rising to a cacophony of shrieks and yells. It was overwhelming and exciting—and soon left behind.

And now it was relatively quiet on the Great Street. The shops were smaller, drabber. This section of the Street and all the city in its vicinity had been almost totally destroyed during the T'ai P'ing troubles. It had never fully recovered from the blows it had suffered then, and the hush of austerity and near-poverty lay upon it. In addition—though I didn't know any of this history at the time of the journey I am describing—it had lost the bustle and business once brought to it periodically by the thousands of scholars coming from all over the province to prepare for and compete in the civil service examinations which were held in an area not far from here east of the Great Street. These had probably enlivened the neighborhood somewhat even after the T'ai P'ing hostilities were over, but with the ending of the old examination system (in 1905), the stalls had stood silent and unused—then were razed to the ground and now were gone forever.

Though subdued, the Great Street here was not dispirited but relaxed and friendly. The sporadic trickle of pedestrians moved along at a slower, calmer pace; neighbors, bound for home with market baskets full, were no longer in a hurry and stopped to chat with each other on the street. It was the time of day when many families ate their morning meal—and, in more than one small shop that we passed, I could see the family at the back of the room seated at the square table enjoying their food in silent companionship under the approving eye of their Kitchen God, whose picture was pasted on the wall behind them.

In this little shop or that, there was a single customer making a leisurely purchase and passing the time of day with the proprietor. Going by a small rice shop, I saw a housewife standing in front of the wooden counter. The shopkeeper had scooped up a handful of dry rice and was letting it fall slowly for her to judge its quality. It was as if the white grains were precious as jewels and the feel of them pouring through his fingers beautiful and almost holy . . . In another shop, a stout round-faced merchant (he couldn't have been too poor) sat perched on a high stool behind his counter, smoking a long bamboo pipe and looking out at the street, taking placid note of whoever might be passing by.

We were nearing the end of our journey. I knew it by certain familiar, unmistakable signs. The sour and acrid (not unpleasant) smell of liquid dye came strongly from somewhere among the huddle of low-lying tiled roofs to the right. I couldn't tell which of the small buildings housed the dyeworks, but I saw the tall posts rising high above the roofs from some invisible courtyard and the newly-dyed cotton fabric hanging out to dry on what might have been the enormous clothesline made for a giant. The lengths of cloth hung in great loops—a harsh and brilliant blue against the paler blue sky. I wondered, as I often had before, what that bright blue stuff was used for—not realizing that I saw it every day in the clothes of almost everybody about me—but faded to softer and then duller shades through washing and wearing and exposure to sunlight, till finally in the garments of the very poor, the blue which had been so vivid it almost hurt to look at it, had become a sad, apologetic gray.

At the next corner, the Great Street widened to the right of us into an open space that looked like a poorly-defined village square. Over there across the space was a blacksmith's shop—a large, long building with a high-pitched roof and single airy room completely open along the front. The blacksmith was hammering at his anvil over the glowing coals of his furnace. He was stripped to the waist; his back and shoulders glistened with sweat, and his face and arms were black with soot. Sparks showered out from under his hammer as it struck the white-hot metal, and some flew up almost to the blackened smoky roof beams. A small boy stood near by holding a hand bellows, and at a word from the blacksmith stepped closer and pumped it vigorously—the coals brightening visibly with every puff . . . The blacksmith's shop was a fascinating place; maybe we could come here later with Carrie Lena and John to stand and watch at our leisure.

"The Catholic Place"

Close by us on the left roughly opposite the blacksmith's were the lofty walls of what we children always referred to—with a certain amount of awe—as "the Catholic place." (Founded in the early 1600s by the Jesuit missionaries—closed when all foreign missionaries were expelled from China about a century later, it now belonged to the French Lazarist or-

121

der.) Maybe what we felt wasn't so much awe as mystification and wonderment about something we didn't know too much about.

The walls were very, very high; they were plastered over and covered with a wash of smoky-blue color, which had been splattered with mud and was peeling off in white patches down close to the street.

There was something very strong and secret about those walls—and something almost forbidding about the huge, heavy dark gateway* set in the center. But more disturbing was the deep niche in the wall just beyond the great, closed doorway. Across the back of the niche was a dark wooden panel . . . "See that ledge there? (I'd heard it explained many times to out-of-town visitors) That's where unwanted babies are left for the nuns to take care of." And often—maybe in answer to a question—"Once they are left there, the families never see them again."

The words "unwanted babies" always struck a pang at my heart. I didn't really believe the word "*unwanted*." I'd always seen Chinese babies being loved and petted and enjoyed. But it hurt just as much to think of parents having to give up their *wanted* babies because they were too poor to feed them and loved them too much to see them starve.

I could never pass by that niche in the wall without imagining what must have happened many times—and might happen again tonight . . . A mother waiting in the shadows of a side street, holding in her arms a small bundle wrapped about in rags . . . slipping across the deserted square . . . hesitating and then laying the bundle quickly on the ledge and hurrying away before she could change her mind—but not going home to her sad little hovel—not yet. Not before she knew her baby was going to be all right. And so she would wait in the hidden recess of a doorway or the shadow of a wall, stifling the sound of her weeping and wiping away her tears so that she could see. A wail from the baby . . . the mother starts forward, but the panel has slid open and a pair of white hands appears from within to take hold of the small bundle and draw it forever out of sight . . .

I wondered intensely about the children who lived behind the blue wall. How did they feel living there cut off from the world? Did they ever

---

* The impressive entrance to the Roman Catholic Mission was built in 1661 with funds donated by one of the later Jesuit missionary priests—Father Martin Martini, author of a geography of China, *Atlas Sinensis*.

laugh and play and have fun like other children? Did they know that outside they had parents and maybe brothers and sisters? I never heard a sound from over those walls, and I never saw the heavy dark door open for anyone to go in or come out. For all I knew, no one ever did.

Yet a French Lazarist priest from "the Catholic place" was a member of my father's Bible study group at the YMCA—until the Bishop at headquarters in Shanghai heard of this dangerous fraternization with a Protestant and put a stop to it. And my mother had actually gone through the stately doorway herself. She sometimes took lady house guests to shop for table linens, handkerchiefs, and lingerie, exquisitely embroidered by the "orphans" (most of the babies left there were girls) under the tutelage of the French nuns.

For some reason, I didn't know about these visits—or about my father's friend, the Lazarist priest. If I had, some of the mystery would have been dispelled. The secrets of life behind the blue wall remained inviolate for me as long as we were to live in Hangchow. They continued to haunt my imagination and to hold a fascination that had nothing to do with the history of the place and its significance as one of the most important missions of the early Jesuits in China—which I must have heard my father talk about. (Maybe its "history" wasn't old enough to seem important or romantic.) Jesuits and Catholic missions did not capture my attention; it was the children who had been left as babies on that ledge who interested me.

I forgot all about them when we came to the street corner just beyond the Catholic Mission. We had almost *arrived!* Our rickshaw bumped over some flat stones laid side by side over a shallow ditch at the entrance to this smaller street. There was little or no water in the ditch—and the stones were certainly not "heavenly" in any discernible way, but I was literal-minded enough for all my flights of fancy to assume that this was the *T'ienh Sway Gyao*, the Heavenly Water Bridge, for which the Southern Presbyterian compound—*and* this whole area—had been named . . . Later I realized that this was ridiculous, but I still don't know whether I ever saw the *real* T'ienh Sway Gyao—not to recognize it as such, anyway.

The "smaller street" we were on was actually a *lane*. It had a quiet, almost rural look as it wandered (after it had passed the Catholic Mission grounds on the one side) between walls not so high as most city walls, with branches of leafy trees spread out above them, and garden bamboos leaning over their tops. At the very end, in the far, far distance was the Needle Pagoda, standing straight and slender and remote on its blue peak and pricking the paler blue sky with its pointed spire.

On our right now was "our" Compound wall—unpretentious and friendly-looking. It was quite low—not more than eight or nine feet high—and its surface was rough-textured and brown, for there was no plaster over it, and the mud and rubble of which it was built was frankly exposed. But it was a good sturdy wall and was neatly topped with the usual dressing of tiles.

The sound of children's voices floated out to us from the mission Primary School. We saw the upper branches of the great pecan trees that a young bride from Mobile, Alabama—Mrs. John Stuart—had started growing from the seeds (nuts?) she had brought with her from home. Now we were at the compound gates—always open wide during the day. We jumped out of our rickshaw and skipped up the low flight of steps, where the gateman welcomed us, smiling broadly and calling us each by name. Aunt Emma must have guessed to the moment how long our journey would take, because as we ran through the gate, there she was walking towards us and smiling, with Carrie Lena and John close by.

Mission Compound

I don't suppose there's a child in the world, however fortunate, who hasn't experienced moments of envy. (It's part of our common human nature—though as adults we should outgrow it.)

Robert and I were on the whole contented enough with our lot, but there were times when it seemed that other fields were greener than our own. Our most frequent moments of envy were of our young friends who lived such a gloriously free life "out at the College." But there were times also when we felt sorry for ourselves for not being privileged to live in a *compound*—which meant to me at this period the headquarters compound of a Christian mission (or when I thought of it, of a Western business like the B.A.T.—British American Tobacco Company—or Standard Oil, which had their compounds outside the city walls near the Ch'ien-t'ang River).

A compound seemed to me far more interesting than a single-family establishment like our home. It was populous—and *important*, with all sorts of people busy at a great variety of things!

The headquarters compound of a Christian Mission in a city like Hangchow was indeed an important, busy, purposeful place. It was the center of all the work and activities of the Mission—reaching out into various sections of the city, into the neighboring hinterland, sometimes far out into the province. There on its own grounds, it included usually a chapel, a mission school, a clinic or hospital, besides several residences for the foreign missionaries.

Each compound was a well-defined little community with an identity of its own; and as such it had its own hierarchy, ranging all the way down from its Chief Executives (the senior missionaries) to the compound gardeners, gateman, and messenger coolie.

But the real Aristocracy (and this must have been the source of much of our envy) were the *missionaries' children*: they were the favored ones—the "leisure class," free to wander about surveying—entirely without responsibility—all that was going on in the small domain and sure of being known and greeted wherever they went, often with deference—always with affection—respectful, interested, absent-minded, or exasperated, as the case might be.

Although Robert and I never had the satisfaction of being fully of the youthful elite in a mission compound, we were to some extent honorary members at T'ienh Sway Gyao. We were there so often either with our parents or "to spend the day" that we shared some of the glory of being recognized and accepted by practically everyone—the missionaries, of course, but also the servants, the Chinese teachers in the little primary school at one end of the compound, the earnest and ubiquitous Bible women, the visiting Chinese pastors . . . Besides, we knew that the middle house (now the Blains') of the three mission residences had been our parents' first home in Hangchow—and this knowledge somehow made us feel that we were not simply familiar guests but that we partly "belonged" to the compound and it partly belonged to us.

The two Hangchow mission compounds I was most familiar with were the Southern Presbyterian and the Northern Presbyterian; and I remember both of them as being good, cheerful, normal little communities. If there were serious personal problems or unhappy and abrasive stresses and strains among the adult missionaries, I was not aware of them—and I don't think our friends the compound children were either. We did catch inklings that certain unmarried lady missionaries who went out alone to evangelize in the countryside were becoming "odd" (heads were shaken sadly). But otherwise everybody seemed happy and normal. This may partly have been because our parents did not consider it kind or proper to burden small children with adult anxieties. But I believe also that there was an openness and vigor in the Hangchow atmosphere that affected the outlook of the Western missionaries there and kept compound life from being claustrophobic.

Carrie Lena (my age) and John (a year younger), who with their mother welcomed us at the T'ienh Sway Gyao compound gate that May morning, were our "best friends." They were the two older children of "Uncle Mac" and "Aunt Emma" McMullen, a Southern Presbyterian missionary couple who had arrived in Hangchow a few months after my parents and had succeeded them as boarders in the Stuarts' home.

At about the time the McMullens were allotted a house of their own on the compound, another young couple, the J. M. Wilsons ("Uncle Morrie" and "Aunt Martha" to us children later) came to join the Southern Presbyterian Mission in Hangchow—and they in turn began their language study and were initiated to life in China in the home of "Father and Mother Stuart."

The three youthful couples—Barnetts, McMullens, and Wilsons—all quick of intelligence, spirited, whole-heartedly dedicated, but full of laughter (and sometimes irrepressible merriment on occasions such as large mission meetings, which were often portentously solemn), found each other extraordinarily congenial from the very first. And as the children came along, *they* were 'congenial' too. The Barnett and McMullen kids in the city and the Wilson kids out at the College always enjoyed being together.

Aunt Emma greeted us, exclaimed (as if she really meant it—and we knew she did) "How *nice* you could come today!" She asked how our mother was—and little DeeDee, our younger brother, and the affectionate formalities being over, she told the four of us, "I have a meeting with some Chinese ladies in a few minutes, so I'll be going back to the house. You children have a good time. Just remember to be back home in time for tiffin. I'll see you all later."

She gave Robert and me each a fond little pat on the shoulder, smiled the nice smile that always made such pleasant crinkles at the corners of her eyes, and walked away leaving the four of us children standing together on the pathway between the front gate and the Blains' house. The Blains'—which had been the Stuarts'—stood in the center of the three mission residences. On the west of it was the McMullens' and on the east the "Ladies' House."

The compound grounds (which, as I've learned since, seemed diminutive and closed-in to children who came for visits from the wide-open spaces of the College) stretched out (for me) large and inviting. The gardens here in front were in full leaf and flower. A weigela bush near by bore a shower of pink blossom; there was a scent of mock orange on the air. The sun filtered through the leaves of the wide-spreading mimosa and the great pecan trees and dappled the grass with light and shadow. Down at the McMullens' end of the compound, a dense row of ornamental bamboo growing in the neighboring garden rose up feathery and graceful above the top of the intervening wall, a few of them leaning over in a way that was both inquisitive and protective.

I looked about me happily. Everything was as it should be.

And now—what were we going to do? None of us had any idea at the moment. No one had made any plans for us nor offered any suggestions. The hours ahead were ours completely. We were free to use them just as we liked. It was a beautiful day and there were four of us to enjoy it together.

A shrill chorus of voices came to us from the end of the compound beyond the Ladies' House.

"The Primary School is having recess," Carrie Lena explained.

"Let's go see," said Robert.

He ran on ahead along the walkway and the rest of us trailed after him—Carrie Lena and I practising our skipping while John tried to see how far he could hop on one foot before losing his balance. We passed the Ladies' house and joined Robert at the entrance in the low wall that separated the mission residences and their grounds from the school and other working buildings of the compound.

The sunny little play yard swarmed with children, all of them about the same age as we were. A Chinese teacher was trying to round up a group for relay races and after some delay had her children divided into two rather straggly rows. Some children playing closer to the entrance where we were standing caught sight of us and nudged each other and giggled. They stared at us; we stared back at them—all very amiably and mildly interested. It was fun for us to watch other children having their recess— and if any of them wondered how it happened we were wandering about instead of being in school ourselves, they probably accepted it as only natural, because we were foreign children and foreigners never seemed bound by the usual rules and ways of doing things.

A teacher hurried out of the building to the left and began to clang a large brass hand bell. Recess was over. The children were lined up and they marched back to their classrooms—a few looking back over their shoulders at us until they disappeared into the building. The playground seemed very quiet and empty.

We turned to leave but were halted by the wheezy sound of an organ. Glancing at each other, we turned back, passed through the entrance and hurried silently over to the open door of the mission chapel. Here we paused briefly and then tiptoed in. It was a plain, bare-looking room. Sunshine poured through the clear glass windows and shone on the white plastered walls, the single modest pulpit, the rows of plain wooden benches.

The music was coming from the farther side of the chapel just in front of the first row, where there was a small portable organ—the kind that has to be pumped by foot pedals. The organist, a soberly dressed Chinese lady, jounced slightly as her feet worked at the pedals while she leaned forward to peer at the hymn book on the rack and fingered out the notes of the song. Sitting on the front pew nearest the organ, four other women ("Bible Women," whispered Carrie Lena) were leafing through their hymnals. When they had all found the right number, they stood up and, at a signal from the organist, began to sing. Whether they were practicing the hymn for Sunday or holding a little private worship service of their own, I don't know—but they sang with great seriousness and sincerity of feeling. It was a hymn with many verses; they were still singing as we slipped out of the chapel. The wheeze of the little organ and the voices of the singers—not quite on key, not quite in unison—blended into a pleasantly ragged and dissonant sound that followed us back into the residential part of the compound.

(Throughout my growing-up years in China, I never really knew what the "Bible women" were. They were such a familiar and unobtrusive sight on a mission compound—going to and fro on their bound feet and in and out of the gates, always with their black cloth-covered Bibles held firmly and reverently in their hands—that I simply accepted them as a natural element in the compound scene. If anything, I assumed them to be devout converts who were extraordinarily devoted to their Bible study. Actually, the Bible women have been said to be among the "most effective evangelists" of the Protestant faith. They took their Bibles and the story of the Christian gospel into dozens and dozens of homes. They were non-professionals—volunteers receiving no pay. I don't believe that even the most cynical critic of foreign mission work in China could have called them "rice Christians." It would be fairer to say that in their humble, grateful, unassuming way, they were in the vanguard of *liberated women* in the China of that time.)

There had been no one in sight at the Ladies' House when we had passed it a few minutes before, but now we saw little Miss Boardman (born and bred in Virginia) tripping daintily across the porch and down the front steps. She greeted us kindly but vaguely; it was clear that she had something or someone else on her mind.

"It's the Ladies' leper," John informed us, as she hurried over to a poorly dressed Chinese man who was standing near by on the garden path. The two instantly fell into a friendly conversation that seemed as though it would go on indefinitely.

"He comes here all the time," said John.

"Not *all* the time," corrected his older sister. "Just every few weeks."

"The ladies give him money and clothes and stuff and talk to him," John went on calmly.

"Why doesn't he go to Dr. Main's leper place?" I wondered. "Maybe he could get well." I kept my eyes politely away from the man's puffy face but stared fascinated at his hands, which had been eaten away by the disease so that there were only spongey-looking stumps where some of his fingers should have been.

"You can't get well from leprosy!" my brother reminded me loftily.

I knew this, of course, but kept hoping it wasn't true. Besides, I had such faith in Dr. Main that I wouldn't have been surprised to learn that *he* had found a way to cure lepers, even though nobody else could . . . But apparently he couldn't do it yet—and suddenly I had an inkling of why the "Ladies' leper" hadn't chosen to take refuge in Dr. Main's Leper Asylum. I remembered how lonely and remote it looked down there in a valley behind the Needle Pagoda—cut off from all the busy life and different kinds of people in the city . . . even from a view of the Lake by the hill that stood between. I guess *I* wouldn't want to go there and live forever and forever.

Miss Boardman and her protégé were still engaged in the easy, interested conversation of old acquaintances as we went on. The leper seemed surprisingly cheerful and self-respecting; and in spite of his soft distorted face and slowly dissolving hands, I didn't have that sense of horror that I usually felt at the sight of a disfigured beggar beside the street or on the way to Ling Yin Monastery. Not surprising really. The spinster missionaries of T'ienh Sway Gyao were friends as well as benefactors; his illness was accepted by them without disgust; with them he knew that he wasn't just "a leper" but a person, a fellow human being.

As we walked on, the subject of our conversation was (rather naturally) *leprosy* . . . how you "got it"—how could you tell when you first had it (i.e., early symptoms)—what it *did* to you as it got worse . . . Our facts and opinions were varied and aroused some argument, but we all agreed on one thing—we never wanted to "get leprosy" ourselves. If it had been a different sort of day, the discussion might have developed into questions such as "Which would you *rather* have—leprosy or elephantiasis?"; but this was a day for activity, not for such difficult and serious considerations.

We were back in front of the Blains' house now, and Robert asked, "Do the Blains still have the rocking horse?"

The McMullen children nodded, and with one accord we started for the front porch.

There was a reason for Robert's question. The Blains had no children at home, now that "NoNo" (Elizabeth) the youngest had gone off to join her older sister Margaret at boarding school in Shanghai—therefore making her one of the "big kids," presumably too grownup for the rocking horse even when she was home for vacations. (Dan, the big brother, was *really* grown up—he was at college in America.) It would have been natural, we thought, for the rocking horse to have gone to a family with children our age.

We hurried up the porch steps of the Blains' house, knocked and waited till the houseboy came to the front door. He told us that Mrs. Blain was across the lane working in the garden. Off we dashed—out the compound gate. There was a narrow wooden door in the wall facing it. We pushed the door open and found ourselves in the mission vegetable garden—a rectangular lot enclosed by walls and closely laid out in long straight rows, where beans and peas and tomato vines, corn, okra, spinach and cabbage flourished in almost frightening luxuriance. You could almost see and hear them growing. The air was thick and warm and steamy and ripe with the smell of damp earth and growing things. The Chinese gardener was on his knees near by, working around the roots of a tomato plant. Further on, almost hidden between rows of pole beans was Mrs. Blain in a gingham dress. She wore a floppy cloth tennis hat as protection against the sun.

Mrs. Blain was famous for her green thumb and was the obvious choice to be in charge of the vegetable garden as well as the compound grounds. Her greatest pride, however, was in her wild flowers—rare and delicate plants that she had found out in the hills and coaxed into feeling at home in the flower beds at the foot of her own front porch.

We could see that she was busy now and quickly asked her could we ride the rocking horse.

"Yes—yes, of course," she told us. And back we went, up the sidewalk to the Blains' house—into the front hall and halfway up the stairs. There, in a small room off the landing, stood the rocking horse—all alone, but splendidly self-sufficient.

As usual, I was struck speechless. I'd never seen anything to compare with this magnificent creature—not even in the Montgomery Ward catalog—not even when we had been taken to view the wonders of the toy department of Whiteaway Laidlaws' in Shanghai. We walked about it, admiring the lustrous brown glass eyes, feeling the strong wooden teeth in its partially open mouth, stroking the "real" tail and the mane which had become somewhat sparse and ragged over the years.

We took turns at rides—Robert first because he was oldest, Carrie Lena next—either because she was the oldest McMullen or because she was bigger than I (though a month younger). John and I were about the same size, but I was the older—so my turn came after Carrie Lena. ("Taking turns" had to be fair, by following some kind of logic, however complicated.)

I clambered up onto the saddle, put my feet in the leather-and-metal stirrups, patted the horse on its hard cold flank—then on its neck, touched one of the leather ears, grasped the bridle firmly, and away I went . . . It may have seemed I was simply rocking back and forth—but I was far, far away on a wide and lonely plain and my horse was galloping, galloping as he carried me swooping and bounding through the air.

"It's my turn now," John announced; and I climbed down reluctantly.

We didn't pay much attention while John was having his ride. We had had ours—and began to chatter about horses and other animals and farms.

"Grandpa Smith has a farm in America," I said . . . I suppose it was the farms that made us think about the dairy.

"Come on, John," we said impatiently. "You've been riding long enough. We're going to the dairy."

Our Dairy

Leaving the Blains' house, the three of us—with John trailing behind—went out through the compound gate for the second time, and turned up the lane towards the Great Street.

The dairy (a perhaps euphemistic label) patronized by the few American families and households in this part of Hangchow was around the corner on the Great Street not very far away. We could smell it before we came to it.

We stepped through the entrance into the dirt courtyard. At one side were the stalls—a half dozen or so—and in each one stood a large gray water buffalo. Dried mud was caked in patches on their legs, sides—even their backs. No doubt they had been swimming in a muddy canal or rolling in a water hole during a recent foraging expedition outside the city walls. They looked patient and gentle standing there in their narrow stalls—until one of them shook its head fretfully and we could see from close up the sharp points of the long curving horns. They looked pretty dangerous and personally threatening.

The owner of the dairy had seen us enter and recognized us as children of some of his foreign customers. He seemed delighted at the visit—welcomed us and called out to his wife and other members of the family to join in the welcome. They appeared from out of the family rooms that opened onto the other two sides of the courtyard, smiling their greetings and obviously amused to see us backing nervously away from the vicinity of the fretful buffalo.

How to offer an expression of hospitality? . . . The dairy owner had a sudden inspiration.

"You children stay right here," he commanded in Chinese.

He hurried over to one of the stalls and led out a great, gray water buffalo, talking to it in soothing, unintelligible sounds.

"Don't be afraid. Don't be afraid," he told us reassuringly as they drew near and then stood still.

"Come a little closer," he said—and gestured for us to stand in a line.

Then he hunkered down on his heels and reaching for the animal's udders, pointed his chin at Carrie Lena who was standing at one end of the row. He didn't have to explain; as if by instinct she leaned forward and opened her mouth wide—and he aimed a thin spouting stream of milk towards it . . . The rest of us leaned forward and opened our mouths. Down the line he went. Some of the milk splattered on our faces, but each of us got enough in our mouths to roll about on our tongues before swallowing it down. ("It's *warm!*" I thought to myself, amazed at the discovery.)

We stood up straight again, wiping our faces and hooting with pleasure. Our host beamed proudly and indicated he was ready to give us another round of drinks. We looked at each other questioningly.

"It's not boiled," Carrie Lena remarked somewhat doubtfully.

"It came straight into our mouths," protested Robert. "*How* could it have any germs?" (This in some scorn.)

"It *couldn't* have any germs," we all agreed with vigorous nods—completely overlooking the fact that the milker hadn't washed the udders or his own hands.

Nevertheless, we decided not to presume further on the dairyman's generosity. We thanked him and skipped out gaily. Our day had been made! We had had milk straight out of a water buffalo! . . . Certain as we were that there was nothing out of the way (or unsanitary) about the treat we had accepted and enjoyed, I don't remember that either the Barnett or McMullen children ever mentioned it to their respective parents. We weren't deliberately secretive; it was just something we—all of us—neglected to report.

Tiffin Time

Our appetites had been whetted; it must be almost tiffin time . . . I never heard anyone in Hangchow—Chinese or foreigner—use the "pidgin English" that was so common in the port cities like Shanghai—except, that is, for single words like "chit" (used for a handcarried message) and "tiffin." For some reason, all the Americans in our part of China had adopted "tiffin" as the name for the noonday meal. One of the difficult, if unimportant, things a child about to visit America had to learn was to say "lunch" instead.

The sun was high overhead as we made our way back down the lane to the compound and through the compound gates. We went directly to the "Macs' " house and trooped noisily into the "front" door, which (a bit of a joke, I thought) was at the *side* of the house, next to the Blains'. (Along the whole *front* of the house was a porch.)

Aunt Emma met us in the hallway.

"*There* you are!" she said. "I *thought* you'd be coming back along about now. Wash your hands—we'll be having tiffin in just a little while."

The McMullens' house, like the other two mission residences, was large and, from the outside, had a homely, ungainly look that was somehow appealing. Inside, it showed the touch of its amateur designers of forty years back—those pioneer missionaries from the deep South. The rooms were high-ceilinged, ample in space, and airy. I liked especially coming through the front vestibule into a spacious, sunny hallway—almost like a room—with its large low window that opened onto the compound grounds behind the house. This back yard was deeper than the front; it was a flat, grassy expanse with the servants' quarters at one side. I liked the wide, easy stairway that began just beyond the window, climbed to a broad landing kept bright by another window, turned and continued on up to the second floor. The stairway had a fine, sturdy, well-polished banister—the best in the world for sliding.

We had washed our hands in the little room off the corridor down towards the pantry and kitchen and were gathered in the sunny hallway, when Uncle Mac and the Chinese pastor of one of the mission churches came out the door to his study where they had been in conference. Uncle Mac was still talking vigorously—wagging his head for emphasis—as he walked his visitor to the front door; and the Chinese pastor nodded earnestly, like a football player receiving final instructions from the coach before getting back into the game.

The goodbyes were said. Uncle Mac, still frowning in thought, turned around. His brow cleared and he boomed out his greetings.

"How's my best girl?" he said to me.

And to Robert—"Hey there! Have you been behavin' yourself lately?"

Uncle Mac was shorter and stockier than our father. His eyes were bright, alert, and quizzical under rather shaggy eyebrows, and his lower lip had a half-pugnacious, half-humorous thrust rather like that of a small boy ready to take a dare for the pure joy of it . . . When Will Rogers' face became familiar to all Americans (even to those of us out in China) people used to comment on the resemblance between him and "Mac." Uncle Mac had a drawl too—Kentucky, not Texas or Oklahoma (or whatever Will Rogers' was). It was slow, but not lazy—laziness not being in his nature. And his drawled remarks, often humorous, were always outspoken. Uncle Mac didn't believe in beating around the bush—and his forthrightness bothered people at times if they didn't know him well enough to be used to it or to recognize his essential good will and lack of malice.

(A typical episode: The Hangchow missionaries have gathered for a special meeting. All have arrived except for Mr. and Mrs. X who are always late for every such occasion. The others chat together for a while, then begin stealing looks at their watches. The minutes pass. Their patience is wearing thin. Finally Mr. and Mrs. X arrive, smiling and breathing their apologies. "Are we very late? . . . Have we kept you waiting?" . . . Through the soft chorus of "no-no's" and "It's all right," "Mac's" voice booms out, "Yes, you've kept us waiting—" pulling his watch from his watch pocket and holding it up ostentatiously, "for exactly forty five and one half minutes. But everybody's here now, so let's get started with our business." There is a flutter of laughter—partly to show the X's that this should be taken as a joke, but also because everyone is secretly pleased to have their feelings of annoyance expressed so neatly and bluntly. The air is cleared for action. What's more, "Mac" and the X's are still friends. In fact, if they are ever in trouble, he's the one they will turn to first for help.)

Aunt Emma's voice sang out from down the hallway. "Is anyone interested in food?"

"The Old Lady is calling. Come on. Let's go!" Off he marched, down the hall, leading a small parade of giggling children.

In the dining room, Aunt Emma was putting little Emma in her high chair. Uncle Mac took his place at the other end of the table, and the rest of us found our places at the sides. Before we sat down, we all linked hands and sang the blessing—"Be present at our table, Lord . . . " This was an old McMullen custom.

Tiffin was a merry meal. We ate with relish, talked between mouthfuls, and laughed at Uncle Mac's clowning. Aunt Emma, fair and sweet-faced, sat at her end of the table, quietly seeing to it that everyone was taken care of and smiling her enjoyment of our chatter and Uncle Mac's teasing and foolery. The McMullens' houseboy, who was very much a member of the family, stood by after he had served us, taking it all in. He didn't understand a word of what was being said, but his mouth kept twitching with the effort to conceal laughter and to preserve a suitable dignity.

Aunt Emma, seeing my plate was empty, asked the houseboy to offer me "seconds." He went from me to Robert and then in turn to the others of us, but inadvertently forgot Uncle Mac, who let out a bellow of dismay and indignation that so convulsed the "boy" that he had to make a precipitate exit into the pantry to recover his gravity before passing the tray to the master.

Uncle Mac pretended that it was all Aunt Emma's doing . . .

"You see how the Old Lady treats me," he remarked plaintively to Robert and me. "She wouldn't care if I starved to death."

We giggled at the ridiculous complaint—and I glanced down at Aunt Emma . . . Several times I had overheard little groups of missionary ladies (not my mother; she never gossiped) talking about how "Mac" was always teasing Emma—how awful it was the way he referred to her as "the Old Lady" or "the Madam." "Emma's a saint! I don't see how she puts up with it! . . . " I'd felt a bit puzzled at this feminine commiseration and headshaking over "poor" Emma's wifely tribulations; *I* thought Uncle Mac's teasing of Aunt Emma was pretty funny—and that it was a way of showing affection; and looking down at Aunt Emma, I was reassured that this was how it seemed to her, for her eyes were twinkling as she responded with mock sympathy to Uncle Mac's pitiful accusation, murmuring that it was "just too bad how he is mistreated" and asking us to notice how thin and pale he was—"simply wasting away!"

Uncle Mac had his second helpings, and the table was cleared for our dessert of fresh fruit. When we had finished and were sloshing our fingers in the brass finger bowls and wiping them on our napkins, and preparing to excuse ourselves from the table, Aunt Emma called for our attention.

"There's a surprise for you if you'll just wait a minute," she announced.

She leaned over to whisper something to the houseboy, who nodded and disappeared and came back holding aloft what was unmistakably a box of candy.

"*Chocolate* candy," Carrie Lena told us proudly, her eyes shining as she recognized the box.

"I've been saving them for a special occasion," said Aunt Emma, and explained that a house guest from Shanghai had given it to them and they had opened it at the time and had some of the contents. "But I counted the pieces before tiffin and there are just enough to go around."

"I bet there's not enough for *me*," Uncle Mac grumbled.

"There's one for you too," she assured him.

In Hangchow, any kind of candy was a treat—but especially chocolates. Occasionally someone sent us a box from America, but by the time they had traveled for six weeks or so exposed to all kinds of heat and punishment they were usually partly squashed and had acquired a stale grayish cast with a taste to match. These chocolates—probably from the recently opened Chocolate Shop in Shanghai—were a rich, glossy brown—and huge, each one large enough for two big bites.

"Maybe you children would like to go out on the porch to eat them," Aunt Emma suggested, as the box was being offered around the table. It seemed a good idea; so when everyone had been served, we pushed our chairs back and holding our precious chocolates carefully went out through the French doors and settled ourselves in the sunshine, dangling our feet over the edge of the low porch. I raised my chocolate slowly to my mouth and took my first bite. My teeth sank through the firm dark chocolate covering into a soft creamy filling, smooth as satin and meltingly good. I ate it just as deliberately as I could and then put the rest of the piece in my mouth, letting it dissolve on my tongue to make it last longer . . . But all good things come to an end, and though it seemed to me I could have eaten a whole *box* of these delectable morsels, I knew there weren't any more of them. I licked the last traces of chocolate from around my mouth and saw that my companions were doing the same.

Our noonday meal had been plentiful and satisfying. The noonday sun was warm and soothing. We were too comfortable and contented to want to do anything but stay quietly on the porch for a while talking together.

We talked about that vague and wonderful time in the future when we would be "grown up" . . . There was never any question as to where we might be when that seemingly impossible time came around—we expected to be right here in Hangchow; I don't think any of us ever supposed for an instant that this wouldn't be our home. (We would have to go to college in America, of course, but then we would come right back.) There wasn't any discussion either of *what* we were going to be. Little girls of that generation didn't think in terms of careers; you got married—or if romance passed you by, you were a teacher or a nurse. As for Robert and John, if they had lived in America they probably would have had burning ambitions to be a fireman—a garbage collector—a baseball player. But since these and other such heroes of their contemporaries back in America were not a part of their experience here in Hangchow, both of them simply took it for granted that when they grew up they would be doing whatever it was their respective fathers did every day to keep themselves occupied. For John this had something to do with Chinese churches and schools and mission meetings; for Robert—with going to the Hangchow YMCA every day and having "conferences" and conducting special study classes. Actually, the only urgent question to be considered was that of our matrimonial prospects. Marriage seemed to us to be the proper state for adults (and after all, if *our* parents hadn't gotten *married*, where would we be?) The problem was whom was each of us to marry?

"I know what we can do," John decided. "Robert can marry Carrie Lena." We all nodded in agreement.

"Little Emma and DeeDee (DeWitt) are just the same age—so they can be married," Robert contributed—and this further linking of the McMullens and Barnetts seemed a splendid idea to all of us.

"And John can marry Genie Mae!" Carrie Lena finished off triumphantly.

"But she's older," John objected.

"I'm older," I protested just as emphatically. The idea of having a husband younger than myself didn't appeal to me at all. Besides, I had never quite forgiven John for something he had said about me that I hadn't thought was very funny, though our respective parents had been highly amused. This joke of John's, basically a pun, had to do with Robert's name. The Hangchow Chinese, mispronouncing Ro-bert, called him "*Lo-Boh*," which sounds very much like their name for *turnip*. "We should call Robert "*Hung* Loh-boh" (*red* turnip or *carrot*), because he has such red cheeks," John had said. And after receiving an appreciative response for this sally, he had looked over at me and added, "Genie Mae is always kind of pale—

so I guess we should call her *beh ts'a* (white cabbage)."

Remembering this, I was not at all enthusiastic about having John as my future spouse.

"But you've got to, to make it come out right," insisted Carrie Lena; and, there being no immediate answer to her logic, John and I grudgingly gave in and agreed.

Hide-and-Seek

"Let's play Hide-and-Seek—not It!" Robert cried out suddenly all in one breath so that no one else could say "not it" before he did.

T'ienh Sway Gyao with its ornamental bushes, the healthy shrubbery against the walls, and the old trees with trunks thick enough for small bodies to hide behind, was an ideal place for games like Hide-And-Seek. (There was a sort of opposite version of it called "Ain't no Boogers out Tonight" that we used to play after dark. It was really scary and exciting!) We skulked and crouched and crept and raced and shouted until we were hot and panting and paused in the shade of the largest pecan tree to rest and catch our breaths.

I don't know when it was that Carrie Lena, Robert, and I really focused our attention on what John was doing. I had seen him put his hand down into a trouser pocket and calmly—there was nothing surreptitious about it—draw something out. It was something small and was wrapped in a piece of brown fluted paper, which he began to tear away gently and me-thodically. Suddenly I realized what the "something" was—and, apparently at the same instant, so had Carrie Lena and Robert. With simultaneous cries of outrage, we moved towards John. "Look what he's got!"—"John, you weren't supposed to . . . !"—"You can't have that!"—"Where did you? . . ."

Good mothers have a magic way of materializing at such threatening moments—and somehow or other, here was Aunt Emma murmuring, "Ju-ust a minute. Ju-ust a minute. Can anyone tell me what this is all about?"

We tried to tell her—all talking at the same time, spluttering in our excitement and pointing accusingly at John.

" . . . Chocolate! . . . " "He took another piece!" . . . "It's not fair! . . . "

Aunt Emma looked over at John who—quite unruffled—was crumpling the paper wrapper in one hand, while the other moved slowly towards his mouth and then paused in midair.

"Don't you remember? There were just enough chocolates to go around . . ."

"But we *saw* him eat his!"

"Well now—take a good look. There's just a half piece of chocolate . . . I guess John decided to eat part of his and save the rest for later."

"*Save-cat!*" said his sister in a passion of loathing.

"*Save-cat! . . .* he's nothing but an ole save-cat!" All three of us flung the scathing epithet at John. He was quite unmoved—and his mother ignored the name-calling, realizing that there are times when emotions are best vented in words.

"If John wants to save something of his, he has a perfect right to, don't you think?" she added—with the slightest glint of amusement in her voice and eyes, knowing that none of us would have had the foresight—or, if we had thought of it, the strength of character.

"*I* know why John saved it—so that he could have some when the rest of us didn't and could make us feel bad," said Carrie Lena bitterly. "Do we have to *watch* him eat it?" she cried out in an agonized appeal, as John began to lick at the surface of his half a chocolate. "Make him go away, Mother!"

"Turn around, John, so they won't have to see you," she told him firmly. Reluctantly he did so—and the three of us walked away far enough so that we couldn't hear him smacking his lips and making his quite unnecessary exclamations of pleasure. No one in the world seemed more hateful than John at this moment.

We came to a halt in the lee of a giant clump of pampas grass that towered over our heads. Something very small was hopping on the short-cropped lawn near its base. It wasn't a grasshopper . . . bending over to look, I saw that it was a tiny toad. And there was another—and another.

"Look at them," I cried to Carrie Lena and Robert—and immediately we were all three on our knees trying to catch one of the little creatures.

"I got one," Robert shouted in triumph and held out his cupped hands for us to peer into. The toad was unbelievably small and perfect. It gave a jump and Robert let go with a yell. "Ouch—it tickled!"

John joined us. We ignored the fact that he was wiping his mouth with the back of his hand.

"John," commanded his sister, "go get something we can put them in— a box or something."

He trotted obediently back to the house and returned presently with an empty Mason jar.

There in the early summer sunshine—all grievances forgotten—the four of us collected tiny toads, depositing each one tenderly in the jar.

When Aunt Emma came to tell Robert and me that she had to send us home now because she had promised our mother—and our rickshaw was waiting—we were dismayed. It seemed much too early to be leaving. But we didn't argue.

She let us go through a rather protracted ceremony of releasing our little prisoners—tilting the jar on the grass so that one tiny toad leapt out to its freedom—then a second and a third—until they were all free and the jar was empty again.

Sighing with satisfaction, we got to our feet, brushing some of the grass from our clothes and knees. And then we all walked to the compound gate. Aunt Emma, John, and Carrie Lena stood in its entrance waving until our rickshaw turned out of the lane into the Great Street and headed us for home.

Great Street South

Just off the southern end of the Great Street and almost in the shadow of the city wall was *Tsoo Jia Gyao* (Tsoo Family Bridge), the Northern Presbyterian Mission compound.

The War Between the States back in America had split certain of the church denominations, so that (in this case) what had begun as the *American* Presbyterian Mission before the Civil War in the U.S. was now two separate missions. The compounds were at opposite ends of the Great Street—the Southern Presbyterians at the north and the Northern Presbyterians at the south. The latter was quite a bit newer; the buildings were constructed and the compound moved into after my parents came to live in Hangchow.

The two missions had their own mission boards back home and their own programs in Hangchow. However, relations between the missionaries were relaxed and friendly and included cooperative planning and involvement in various areas of mission work.

For us children a trip to Tsoo Jia Gyao was a different kind of treat from spending the day at T'ienh Sway Gyao: it was nearly always an Event—a special occasion such as the Christmas party for the small British and American children of Hangchow, the annual Easter Egg Hunt, the celebration (for some reason) of May Day with a little pageant and a May Queen (Janet Fitch with a crown on her flowing golden hair), and every now and then a social afternoon of tennis for the grownups and an informal get-together for their children.

The compound itself seemed more novel to us, since we saw it more rarely; and it had a different ambience than T'ienh Sway Gyao. It seemed not only newer and tidier, but brisker and more business-like. But to offset and more than compensate for the more orderly, no-nonsense atmosphere, there was its closeness to the city wall, which gave it a historic "feel." And there was its indisputable glory, "The Rockery," preserved from a garden or courtyard of the former family mansion. What kind of exotic and beautiful setting it might have had before, I don't know and can only imagine. It rose now from the middle of an expanse of Western-type lawn—a wild little "mountain" with boulders and growing things, miniature ravines, and tiny paths to climb. It was the basis of comparison for all other garden rockeries wherever encountered and none other came close to being as satisfactory and exciting.

Another novelty about going to Tsoo Jia Gyao was traveling south on the Great Street. The only other times I saw this part of Hangchow was when, very occasionally, I was taken along with out-of-town guests who wanted to see its historic sights and visit its famous shops.

The Great Street changed character as it proceeded southward from midcity. I don't remember it in detail all the way. My recollections come in little pieces like pictures out of a story book. They are vivid, but not too reliable either as to place or time.

I can't be sure, for instance, where the Great Street lost its bustle and noise and became sedate and quieter and cleaner, with white-plastered walls on either side which receded now and then for dignified entranceways (a short flight of stone steps perhaps and heavy wooden double doors). The walls were well-kept and fresh-looking and indicated affluence but were not so high as to seem pretentious or too private. Trees rose above the tile-edged tops. Within the walls were the Hangchow guildhalls, financial establishments (bankers and leading pawnbrokers) and *yamens* (residence-cum-offices) of city officials. (I'm not *sure* of all this. It's what I remember hearing; I don't think I could have made it up.)

Somewhere farther along the Great Street, we passed the silver shops— the silk stores . . . the Fan Shop. Somewhere we passed the famous Medicine Store . . . the turn-off for City Hill—the turn-off for the ancient Hangchow Mosque.

Some of the side streets now were so narrow that a pedestrian could touch the wall on either side. These walls were exceedingly high—no trees could be seen over them—and they went on and on, blank and mysterious. Occasionally there was a discreet doorway to break the blankness; and once in a while there was someone, servant or tradesman, coming out or about to enter. Behind these walls were the homes of the old and wealthy families of Hangchow, too secret and removed from every-day life and humanity ever to be known or even encountered except in the imagination. Later on, I used to imagine scenes and persons with little resemblance to everyday reality . . . romantic and archaic as though materialized out of a silk embroidered scroll. But from my very first rememberings, those narrow, empty streets between their lofty walls that I glimpsed from the Great Street were intriguing and exciting.

One of my most cherished recollections of the Great Street South is also one that I am least sure of. Perhaps it comes from the earliest days when we still traveled longer distances in the city by sedan chair and when the famed luxury shopping area was exactly as it had been for cen-turies—untouched by modernism or foreign influence. In my memory I see the Street here quite narrow but paved solidly from side to side with long, smoothly fitted slabs of stone, giving it a clean, elegant look. The shops that face each other across the way are rich-looking, with great gilded characters engraved on sign boards above the entrances, brilliant red banners hanging from in front. The street is thronged—but not crowded—with pedestrians moving quietly, unhurriedly on cloth shod feet. There are no vehicles whatsoever. The closeness of the shops to one another—the people walking slowly to and fro—give the scene a look of dignified intimacy; the banners almost meeting overhead, the flashes of gold calligraphy suggest festivity and opulence, colorful but restrained. There is none of the compulsive shouting and jostling of the food mar-kets at the other end of the Great Street. *There*, people are shopping for the daily necessities of life; *here* it is for the specialties, the luxuries, the beautiful things that Hangchow has been famous for since long ago dy-nasties. Shopping here had always been something to enjoy in a serious way—to savor at leisure: The "picture" I remember is purely *old-Hangchow* "Quality Street"—completely *old China*.

As we neared the end of the Great Street, I remember coming to a curious little convergence of tiny streets (very tiny, sunless and dark), splay-ing off from the larger street like ganglia at the end of a nerve. Almost lost in the gloom was a tiny dark canal crossed over by a tiny hump-backed stone bridge. (Could *this* have been the Tsoo Family Bridge?) There was always an instant when I wondered if we were going to dive into the gloom and if so, which of the dark little streets we would choose;

145

but our rickshaws—which were our usual means of conveyance—took a turn to the right, and we were in a small cul-de-sac with the gateway to the compound in the high wall at the western side.

Another Compound

The heavy wooden door was opened for us to enter, and we stepped into the residential section of the compound. The high walls cut it off from the city outside, so that it seemed more closed-in than T'ienh Sway Gyao but at the same time more spacious. A wide, straight path lined with mulberry trees led between lawns (of the wiry, dusty-green grass common to these parts), with the compound residences set at some distance from each other on either side. The rockery (if I remember correctly) was in the lawn at the southern side, with the tennis court lying across its farther (western) end.

The homes for the missionaries, having been planned by and constructed under the supervision of a Western architect, were well-built and solid, more compact and more "modern" than the older mission residences in Hangchow. They were grey brick—three-storied; the rooms were not large.

As in the typical mission compound, there was the "ladies' house" for the several single women attached to the Hangchow mission (at this time—Miss Ricketts and Miss Peterson are the only ones that come to mind) . . . I never heard of a "bachelors' house" on a mission compound, perhaps because there were fewer single men in the field than "spinsters"— perhaps because the men didn't stay single very long.

The compound families—those with children—were the Van Everas and the Lassells.

Louise Van Evera was a little younger than I; her brother Carl was DeWitt's age. The Lassell children were Eldredge (my age), redhaired and stocky, his dark-haired brother Sidney (a year or so younger), and their little sister Ethel whom I recall as usually being sick or not quite recovered from some indisposition at the times of our get-togethers. I used to wonder why the Lassell children should ever get sick . . . their father was a *doctor*. But perhaps he couldn't help bringing germs to them from the sick people he treated.

In addition to the Van Everas and Lassells, there were the Arthurs, who were Canadian. They were childless, but the children of his widowed brother in Shanghai spent many of their school vacations with their aunt and uncle here on the compound, and so were among the British children we knew.

One of the confusions of my childhood was the word British. "English" and "British" seemed easily interchangeable, but how could Dr. Main, who was from Scotland, be British—or our sometime YWCA visitor from Shanghai, Miss Ella McNeil, who was really from Australia? And how about the Arthurs who were Canadians?

Certainly the young Arthurs seemed "British"—and sounded it, as I am sure did all their fellow schoolmates in the British schools that they attended in Shanghai. Rosamund, the oldest, was the *most* "*British*" in speech and mannerisms. I remember a tea party at Tsoo Jia Gyao one holiday season—the grownups at the big table, the rest of us at a separate, lower-to-the-floor round table drinking our "cambric tea" (hot water with sugar and milk added) and eating cake and cookies—the younger of us children listening with amazement to Rosamund's sprightly schoolgirl chatter which she sprinkled liberally with the adverb "horribly," pronounced more like "hoddibly." Everything was "hoddibly cold" or "hoddibly exciting" or "hoddibly boring." We younger American children were fascinated and listened speechless, but long after the visitors had gone back to Shanghai, we would remember and mimic her, using the word "hoddibly" as often as we possibly could, while crooking our little fingers and pretending to drink tea in the "fancy" way we attributed to our English/British friends.

James was the second-oldest of the Arthur siblings. I secretly thought him very handsome but with a somewhat condescending, almost scornful manner—or so it seemed to me, a small child and probably beneath his notice. Then came Charlie; he wore glasses and was the most friendly and outgoing of them all. He had a kind heart; he helped me find eggs for my basket one Easter, when he saw me standing bewildered and uncertain while all the older and more aggressive children swarmed over the Rockery, finding the eggs hidden there and then rushing off to other hiding places. Charlie helped me find a couple of eggs tucked away in crevices on the Rockery—which is where I *wanted* to find Easter eggs— and at the end of the Hunt, my basket was at least partly full, thanks to him, though by that time he was nowhere near by to claim any credit . . . Finally there was Bunty—pretty—quiet—a little remote.

147

The young Arthurs were very much a part of the seasonal get-togethers at Tsoo Jia Gyao. They definitely were not outsiders, yet they added a touch of glamor to the occasions—not so much because they were British (we had other small British friends in Hangchow) but because they came to us from Shanghai. Shanghai left its mark on everyone—Americans too. Going away to school in Shanghai wrought a change; never was a girl or boy quite the same after a time at boarding school in Shanghai. Something of sophistication had been added, something of belonging to Hangchow diminished.

The annual Christmas party, in the Van Everas' parlor, must have been held before the older boys and girls had come back for the holidays. Only the younger children were there, wide-eyed and expectant. Perhaps the older ones would have made the room too crowded; perhaps their presence would have spoiled the mood. Those of us there were still (all of us) believers in magic.

The room was almost filled up—mothers in chairs at the rear, children on the floor in front of them, the littlest on the very front row. The Christmas tree filled the farther corner of the room, opposite the door to the hallway; it was decorated rather soberly with paper chains and small ornaments but was exciting because of the packages of varying size and shape piled around its base.

The party began with a modest little program of appropriate songs and readings presented (for the most part either haltingly or as rapidly as possible) by performers whose mothers had been asked to volunteer their children's talents for the occasion. One year, Lillian Oliver and I were on the program. We had been drilled to sing the verses of a carol, "Once unto the shepherds, seated on the ground . . ."—from memory. We managed the whole song—every verse—without missing a word, by filling in for each other's lapses of memory. I don't remember applause—just the welcome sense of relief when I resumed my place on the floor.

At the end of the program, everything suddenly stopped. Nothing seemed to be happening—but something important was about to happen. I don't know if we children were "sh-h-h-ed" or whether it was by instinct that we sat where we were, as still as little mice, waiting and listening.

And then we heard it—the jingle of bells outside the house. I don't remember thinking "sleigh bells!" (where was the snow?) . . . only later did I picture the sleigh resting on the stubbly winter lawn near the front door. But when we heard the door open and the sound of a hearty, gruff voice, we all knew it was Santa Claus. In he came, bearded—ample about the middle, greeting us "boys and gir-r-rls" and asking us individually by name if we had been good all year. He sounded a lot like Dr. Main, but that wasn't surprising, because Dr. Main looked a lot like Santa Claus. That didn't mean they were the same person.

We were breathless and speechless with the surprise and excitement. Santa Claus handed out the gifts with great flair. Admonishing us to be good and he would come to our homes on Christmas Eve, he backed out of the room, waved to us from the parlor door, boomed out a cheery "Goodbye" and disappeared. We heard the front door close—the jingle of bells—and then the chatter began. "Was that really Santa Claus?" "Of *course* it was!" "What's your present?" "What did *you* get?" . . . I'm sure there were refreshments, but I don't remember them. Santa Claus's appearance was the significant event; the rest was nice but forgettable.

The Christmas party was always held at the Van Everas'.

The hostess, "Mrs. Van," was the person responsible for the special occasions for children at Tsoo Jia Gyao. She was tall, straight-backed, pleasantly authoritative of presence and manner. She was a gifted organizer; she initiated programs and group activities and made sure they came off properly.

The May Day pageant was one of her projects. I doubt that any of the other mothers would have thought of it. The Rockery, of course, presented a perfect outdoor setting for a queen and her court; apparently a Maypole and dance could be dispensed with. I have a photograph of Janet Fitch seated halfway up the Rockery surrounded by her retinue. She is in a long dress, wears a crown topped by a (paper) star, and is holding a slender scepter (probably bamboo). The members of her court— the "little kids"—are spring flowers with crepe paper head dresses and petals or leaves attached to their waists. There are no Barnett children in this photograph; I assume it was taken on a May Day after we had moved to Shanghai.

The only May Day that I remember is the one I missed by coming down with the mumps. This was one of the grievous disappointments of my childhood. I wanted to be a flower in the May Court. I'd *counted* on it. And then my jaw had started to feel funny and hurt, and I must have had a fever. The doctor came—not Dr. Main, but the one who was the father of Neville and Adrian—and said I had mumps and I must stay in bed and be isolated, especially from other children.

The worst of it was that, when the time came for the May Day celebration, off everyone went quite happily—leaving me all alone with Tsong Mah who had no idea what the event was all about that I was missing. Even Aunt Becky said goodbye to me in a heartlessly cheerful fashion— the only time she ever let any of us down. I have never before or since felt so abandoned or so *expendable*. Nobody seemed to feel that it made any difference that the buttercup (I was to be the buttercup) wouldn't be in the show.

The next day, I was over the worst of the physical misery, but still feeling melancholy and cut off from the rest of the world. I heard a scurry of steps and some muted commotion out in the hallway. Mother and Robert and Yienh San the houseboy were at the doorway to my bedroom. Mother took something from Yienh San's hands—said to Robert, "No— you have to stay out here"—and came to where I was lying, my head (with its swollen jaws) propped up on pillows. The "something" was a shallow basket (or tray) with four or five live baby ducklings scrabbling about in it.

They were my playmates while I was bedfast. They skittered about on the counterpane—fluffed their yellow down—made little busy clucky noises. They grew almost visibly. About the time that my face had resumed its normal look, I was alarmed to notice one of the ducklings with its beak pulled down and a swelling of the neck on each side. I was afraid that it had caught the mumps from me. Mother reassured me that it hadn't, but I was never completely convinced and felt apologetic every time I saw the bulges.

No one else in the household succumbed.

The ducklings were kept outside in the back yard after I had recovered. We were afraid they wouldn't learn how to swim without water to practise in. Robert and I gave them lessons in one of the large k'angs of rain water at a corner of the house. We held them perched on the edge of the k'ang and pushed them over into the water, ready to rescue any that might be in danger of drowning. It was gratifying—maybe a trifle disappointing—that none of them needed any help from us; but in any case we had given them the chance to have a swim . . . I don't know what happened to them when they grew up to be ducks—if they ever did.

Tennis Afternoons

My memories of the tennis afternoons at Tsoo Jia Gyao are suffused with a sort of timeless glow. They didn't happen often: the weather had to be right—and the Hangchow missionaries were a busy lot—too busy to set aside regular times on their calendars for such activities. So when there *was* a tennis party at the compound, it came about almost spontaneously and seemed to provide a complete escape from everyday concerns. At the same time, combined with the relaxed and carefree mood was the ceremonialism and orderliness that are part of the nature of tennis. In retrospect, these rare afternoons—in late spring or in the fall—have an idyllic quality.

It is somewhat ironic that tennis, which was generally considered back home to be a game for the wealthy and sophisticated, should come to be probably the favorite pastime of the low-income, unworldly China missionary.

The earliest Protestant missionaries—in Hangchow anyway—didn't play games at all. It wasn't what they'd come all this dangerous way to do; it wasn't what they felt was expected of them nor what they expected of themselves. In time, however, they became less stern with themselves. Dr. D. Duncan Main, the not-so-dour Scotsman who arrived in 1880, was one of those who believed that a person (even a missionary!) could obey God and serve others and still be merry of heart and enjoy life.

About the time that he joined the others in Hangchow, the game of croquet made its appearance at the mission compounds and was enjoyed by the missionaries at the little get-togethers with the knowledge and approval of their respective bishops and higher-ups. Croquet was an innocent outdoors game which could be played by a relatively few persons in a relatively small space. (I wonder though if it was the most benign game to encourage; I've found it to be potentially ruthless and contentious and it must have often been a test of Christian tolerance and good will.)

Tennis, like croquet, can be played without a large number of participants—and in most mission outposts the number of Westerners was small.
Also tennis didn't require much more space. And it was not expensive for
the missionaries in China where labor costs were negligible. A corner of a
compound could, at minimal cost, be converted into a tennis court; with
a modest outlay for a roller, the court could be kept in good playing con-
dition by the compound gardener and any other household servant or
relative he needed to help him. The basic pieces of equipment—regula-
tion posts and a net—were ordered from back home or from a sports
store in the nearest large port city (like Squires & Bingham in Shanghai).

The net lasted for years—until it was hardly more than a rope stretched
from post to post. Tennis balls were used till they had lost most of their
bounce at which time they were passed on to the children along with
warped tennis racquets. (Was it because or in spite of learning on these
hand-me-downs that many missionary kids grew up to be rather excellent tennis players?)

I remember an afternoon when my parents were invited for tennis at
Tsoo Jia Gyao and the children were asked to come along "to play."

It must have been early June—before wives and children made their
escape to the hills from the sweltering heat, the dysentery, cholera and
other diseases in the city . . . The afternoons were lengthening; this one
was pleasantly warm. The pathway leading from the compound gate was
spattered with fallen ripe mulberries.

We children dashed off to join Louise and Carl and Eldredge and
Sidney and whatever other small friends were already here—maybe the
McMullens, maybe the Olivers.

The grownups, meanwhile, proceeded more sedately to the tennis court
where there were wicker chairs at the shady side for those who would be
watching the play as they waited their turns.

This was free-time, frolic-time for us children—no organization from
above. We gravitated first, as always, to the Rockery and immediately
began to climb it—all of us helter skelter, fast or slow, up its tiny paths
and down again after reaching the top and calling "Yoo-hoo! I'm *here!*"

Someone suggested hide-and-seek and we all agreed, even though it
wasn't quite as good here as at T'ienh Sway Gyao, in spite of the Rockery.
After that—since there were enough of us—we played an exciting game

of Prisoner's Base with its attendant running and shouting and jumping up and down. And then, tired and out of breath, we trooped over to the tennis court and flung ourselves on the grass at the side opposite to the grownup spectators in their wicker chairs. A couple of the boys perched themselves on the roller near the corner of the court.

We had chosen a strategic moment to arrive. There was a break in the tennis; time for refreshments.

The men always played in the early part of the afternoon when the court was in full sun. They played to win—with vigor and gusto and exchanges of banter . . . singles first, while the wives at the sidelines visited happily with each other and occasionally thought to take note and cheer after a good play.

After the singles, there were sets of doubles for the men, and it was at the end of one of these sets that one of the compound ladies was seen approaching the court, holding a large pitcher. She was followed by a servant carrying a tray full of glasses and another servant with a plate in each hand. (Sandwiches? Cookies? When he came closer, we could see it was cookies.)

Hearty shouts of approval came from the men on the court who were wiping their foreheads with large white handkerchiefs. We children jumped up from where we were and unobtrusively joined the grownups at the other side of the court. We watched while glasses were filled, first for the ladies and then for the gentlemen, with a fruit punch that was a specialty of the Tsoo Jia Gyao ladies.

It was made from a fruit which we always called "Chinese strawberries." "Chinese strawberries" grew on trees; they were deep red (almost black)—round—and about the size of small plums. The surface of the fruit was rough and nubbled and vaguely resembled the exterior of the genuine strawberry. They were too sour a fruit to eat raw, but poached in a sugar syrup they had a pleasing flavor and the juice was sweet and tart and a most beautiful color. This was what was used as a base for the famous Tsoo Jia Gyao punch (non-alcoholic, I shouldn't have to add).

When we children were served, I took a quick thirsty gulp and then held my glass up to the sunlight. It glowed and sparkled like a glass filled with melted rubies.

Still nibbling at cookies—our energies recharged—we skipped back to the lawn for a final, breathless game of tag and then returned to the court where play had been resumed. We rested and watched idly—jumping up occasionally in a race to retrieve a ball that had gone astray.

Now with the afternoon cooling was the time for the ladies to play, pairing off with the men for mixed doubles. It was tennis of a gentle, decorous nature. The men were gallant; the ladies in their long skirts tripped daintily to the balls that bounced near them and patted bravely at them. More often than not they seemed to be trying to *push* the ball over the net rather than *hitting* it as if afraid of causing it pain. The ladies served underhand and the men pretended not to notice if his partner or his opponent's happened to step over the line when serving. Occasionally the lady player on either side would stand aside and watch and admire the male partners carry on a spirited rally. Then the play would return to its leisurely, ceremonial pace. The non-participant adults at the sideline relaxed in their wicker chairs and called out in encouragement and praise— careful to show no favoritism.

A set was completed. Another foursome began to play.

The sun was now slanting golden rays across the compound wall at the farther end of the court and shadows deepened and lengthened. One by one the players discarded their cotton tennis hats—the men tossing theirs carelessly over onto the grass where they lay in shapeless white splotches.

Now the sun dropped out of sight behind the walls. Here in the compound the light suddenly dimmed; but it still glowed on a high spur of ground that rose up just beyond the compound walls—and on the city wall that crested it, climbing briefly into view and then descending out of sight. For a moment or two, the upsweep of hill and the massive crenellated wall were bathed in light—green-gold, grey-gold—against the clear evening sky. Then, unseen from where we were, the sun sank behind the western hills far across the Lake, and the radiance faded here. In that instant, a bugle sounded the hour of sunset—a sound that was lonely but steadfast . . . each note clear and strong at first—held long and thinning out and quavering into a final silence. These were ancient sounds in a minor key. The bugler was a soldier of today. But for how many centuries had there been a garrison there in the shadow of the city wall? Had the sun been bade farewell and the coming of night saluted by these same minor notes back in the Sung dynasty a thousand years ago—or even

154

long before? Perhaps not with bugle notes; yet the past was present in these sounds—vague intimations of old wars and past glories and the eternal loneliness of a soldier far from home.

Did I as a child know enough about the history of Hangchow or, for that matter, about the life of a soldier to be so affected by the melancholy sound of a bugle at sunset? Probably not—but somehow I *was* affected. Why else would the memory be so clear and still so rich with feeling and fancy?

In the growing dusk the tennis game went on—until the ball seemed no more than a will-o-the wisp darting erratically back and forth over the court. The players struck out wildly too soon—too late—and finally gave up, laughing.

Children were called and sorted out—racquets, balls, hats and other paraphernalia collected by their respective owners. We straggled down the mulberry-spattered walk to the front gate, accompanied by several of our Tsoo Jia Gyao hosts. The gateman opened the gate. Rickshaws were waiting outside—enough for all the guests. A pause at the threshold while *thank you*'s and *goodbye*'s were said. And then into our rickshaws and off for the journey home across the city.

By then it was deep dusk. Already the streets were silent with only an occasional pedestrian hurrying quietly homeward.

At nightfall Hangchow became a different city. All the humanity that had bustled and surged along its thoroughfares during the day vanished from sight. All the activity that had been exhibiting itself so busily and matter-of-factly in shop and market place ceased. Life disappeared and took refuge behind walls and bolted gates, closed doors and boarded-up shop fronts. The hum of voices, padding of feet, clanging of metal, clatter of loom—all had been hushed into a deep, breathing silence—a silence not of a dead city but of a city at rest.

Down at the other end of the Great Street where businesses were smaller and less pretentious, the boarded-up shop fronts would be outlined by ribbons of amber light shining out from candle or lamp through the slits between the panels. (Not too much later the lights would go out for the rest of the night.)

Here, though, the great shops of Hangchow were altogether dark. Instead of coziness there was mystery. Now suddenly the narrow side streets

155

seemed to go on and on, narrower than before; their high walls seemed even loftier and more secretive and strange.

It was almost fully night now. The rickshaw men had been prudently saving their kerosene; but now they called to each other—stopped—set down the shafts—and each lit a lantern that hung near the footrest. This done, the cavalcade proceeded. The lanterns swung to and fro with the swaying of the vehicles and threw glowing shafts of light about, revealing here a doorway, there the curve of a roof. The stone slabs of the street itself appeared in bold outline. Where the street widened temporarily into small squares or open courts in front of entranceways, these were lit dramatically like scenes from a play—stage sets empty of characters except for ourselves. Shadows in corners seemed darker and more velvety in contrast with the light. Tree tops plumed out black as smoke over the crests of low walls.

No one talked; even the rickshaw men were silent.

Leaning against my mother's knee in our rickshaw, I tilted my head back to see the river of stars above us. My heart seemed to stretch out wide—to fill up and spill over with a wonderful feeling, deeply peaceful and yet charged with excitement. In the silent, dark, deserted streets of Hangchow, I felt utterly at home with the whole quiet city—the stars above—the world . . . a sense of awareness and of belonging that I've never experienced since in quite the same way.

It followed me home that long ago evening, and I've never forgotten it. (It is probably one of the reasons I am writing this book about Hangchow.)

West Lake

My fairy godmother (if I had one) must have been feeling generous when she came to my crib side. "This child will have the good fortune to spend her early years in Hangchow—and for four of those years she will live near West Lake!"

Of course, at the time we were actually living near the Lake, I took it more or less for granted; though I remember being aware (even at four) that part of the anticipation of moving to our new house in the Tartar City was that we would be near West Lake—and the Needle Pagoda— and the hills.

What I didn't realize until I was grown (in fact when I was up north living in Peking and experiencing its splendors) was the unique appeal of West Lake and the natural surroundings of Hangchow for people in other parts of China. Scenes of Lake and hills and valleys and bamboo groves and the Ch'ien T'ang River, pagodas and temples and tombs and grottos were celebrated in poetry and prose, in painting and (in more modern times) photographs, and were familiar to people everywhere in China. Best known and most loved was West Lake itself. Everybody (I kept learn- ing) knew of West Lake and longed to see it in its reality, at least once.

And there in Hangchow, for four years, we had lived with the Lake close by—only a few minutes' walk away!

It would be stretching it to say that we had a view of West Lake from our house, though I believe a tiny piece under the Needle Pagoda was visible from a window upstairs in the west wing. There was also the view from the attic—which was hardly one that could be enjoyed in comfort- able contemplation, but was an exciting experience when rediscovered twice a year.

Our attic was large and had windows, small and high up, on every side, giving it a fair amount of natural light. It was where bedding and out-of-season or out-of-style clothes were kept stored in trunks or chests. But it was neither antique enough nor dark enough to be interesting, and most of the time I forgot we had an attic.

For a few days, however, in fall and spring it became a busy place—when, in autumn, winter clothes and blankets and quilts were being retrieved for use in the cold months ahead . . . and then (again) in the late spring when they were being laid away with moth balls (from Montgomery Ward) or (in the case of blankets) with layers of dried China-grown tobacco leaves.

These were dress-up times for us children—especially for me. We could rummage in the trunks and try on old clothes and hats and—every time (for me) a mosquito net for a bride's veil.

In the rummaging and going from trunk to trunk, we would remember our own special view of the Lake. The window to the south—like all the others—was too high to see out of from floor level. But underneath it was an outsize trunk, one of those that had carried household belongings all the way from north Florida across the continent of North America across the Pacific Ocean to China. It was sturdy and deep, with a flat top (not rounded like some of that era). It was a scramble to climb it, but from the top, we could peer out the window towards the west and "There's West Lake!" It seemed very far away and not quite real—a magic lake. It was wonderful to see it from our very own house.

It was different seeing the Lake close to—but then (as Chinese poets have pointed out) it was never twice the same no matter where you were—on the shore or from the heights or while on its waters. This was part of its charm—seeing the same components but always in different contexts, at different distances and in different lights and shadows.

We saw it most often from along the northeastern shore. I wonder how often we took that impromptu walk—with house guests or just the family. It could be any kind of day—any time of day—probably most often in the afternoon. Someone would say, "Let's take a walk to the Lake."

So we would set out—down the alley into Fa Yuanh Gya (Law Court Street), wide and quiet. Often there was no one else in sight and we had the whole spacious street to ourselves. There was no hurry. We children walked alongside Mother and the other grownups (if there were any) or dawdled behind or ran ahead, skipped, hopped, ran backwards, kicked pebbles . . .

Always we paused briefly and respectfully in passing an ancient stone well in a corner of the sidewalk where two white-plastered residence walls joined at a right angle. The stone rim of the well was rounded and worn smooth by age. A weeping willow tree leaned over it.

Mother—or any other Hangchow adult who was with us—would murmur, "Here is where the official's daughter drowned herself—" and we were all pensive and sad for an instant or two before moving on.

The story was that an official in the Southern Sung dynasty court (eight centuries ago) had been falsely accused of misdeeds by an envious fellow-official and was sentenced to death. His daughter protested but to no avail; and so, to prove her father's innocence, she leapt into this very well and was drowned. Her father was exonerated . . . and soon after, a willow tree grew up beside the well—to mourn the daughter's death and honor her loyalty and self-sacrifice. Or was the tree her spirit, transformed and living still?

We passed the block where the Manchu wards of the city lived. Another long block or so and we came in sight of the building that housed the Provincial Law Court for which our street was named. And soon after that we were at the lakeside, breathing in the freshness of the air blowing across the water and making sure everything was where it should be.

First we looked for the Needle Pagoda, slim and tapering, on its high bluff to the right of us—and then, facing it on a lower rising far across the Lake, the grand old russet-red hulk of the Thunder Peak Pagoda (we called it *Thunder Pagoda* for short). And then we checked on the nearest causeway—the one that led to Emperor's Island [now called *Gu Shan*], the largest of the islands . . . and the other causeway, with its willow trees and its bridges . . . and the other islands—particularly our very favorite, which we called *Three Lantern Island* and was a special place for picnics.

Down the lakeshore from where we were, little sampans, tied to posts sunk into the lake bed, bobbled at their moorings. The boatmen were near by, passing the time of day together as they waited for passengers.

"Can we go out on the Lake?"

"*May* we—not *can*," Mother would correct us almost automatically. "No—not today" and she would give a negative wave of her hand to the boatmen who had caught sight of us. If they kept coming towards us, we would wave our *no*'s too.

So we picked up flat pebbles and skipped them on the water or walked on the ledge of the stone embankment ("Be careful! Don't fall in!")—looked up at the Needle Pagoda and asked if we could go there—and Mother would say, "Another time." And then it was time for us to go home, turning our heads for last looks at the Lake before we left it.

Our other most familiar view of the Lake was from Needle Pagoda Hill—a place we also went to on numerous extemporaneous excursions. We even *lived* on Needle Pagoda Hill once for two whole weeks—one early, early spring when Dr. Main sent us up to stay in his Convalescent Home to recover from the after-effects of the flu . . . But those two weeks in that rather grim, very British house, with the pagoda on one side, the cave and the tumble of huge boulders on the other, and the steep little overgrown path down to the lakeshore (when we had picked up our strength enough to maneuver it) gave us—or, at any rate, gave *me* a lasting sense almost of ownership of that whole bluff.

From the top of Needle Pagoda Hill we could see all of West Lake except for the little hidden coves and mysterious inlets that made it seem to extend to unknown boundaries . . . We saw the causeways, the islands, the Thunder Pagoda across the way—and over and beyond the hills that bordered the Lake there in the south we could see the River, looking grand and majestic even from so far away in its sweep by the city on its way to the sea—or more specifically, Hangchow Bay . . . To the east was the city—to the west and northwest a whole panorama of hills and valleys—and below us, to the northeast were plains with squares of rice paddies and thin ribbons of canals.

We had many, many expeditions to the Pagoda and to other places in the nearby hills. Mother in her gentle way had an adventurous spirit, and she loved the outdoors. My father used to call her a Gipsy. Now that we were living where an enticing outdoors was so accessible, she didn't wait for the planned excursions and outings and picnics that were a part of the Hangchow way of life, but would simply pick up and go when the spirit moved her and she didn't have serious matters to attend to. And usually it was with Robert and me as her fellow-wanderers.

Sometimes we were looking for a particular place or site. Sometimes we had a special project—like collecting leaves to take home and iden-tify—or seeing how many different birds we could discover and (later) name and record in a notebook. The Hangchow region was in several ways an extended bird and wildlife sanctuary because of its temperate climate and its natural fruitfulness and its Buddhist traditions. Especially where there were monasteries and shrines with their shade trees, small creatures lived unharmed and birds nested and sang and flew unafraid.

Often we simply went roaming with no specific destination or pur-pose—simply adventuring—following tiny footpaths along steep, brushy hillsides or wider, stone-flagged walkways in the narrow valleys. When we grew tired, there was always an old and tree-shaded tombsite where we could rest a while, leaning against (or perched upon) a part of the low wall that encircled the grave mound and extended out at either side. Maybe we would have a sandwich—or a tangerine . . . Maybe our only refresh-ment would be the shade with sun flickering through—the breeze—the utter quietness except for leaves rustling and the twitter or song of birds. When I wonder if there is or ever was any real peace and serenity in this world, I have this to remember.

When there were more than the three of us on these impromptu outings, it was usually "Aunt Lucille" and Lillian and John Oliver who were with us.

Not too long after we moved from midcity, the J.C. Olivers had come to join the Hangchow YMCA staff. Like the Barnetts, they lived first in the city in whatever mission housing was available, and then moved to a newly-built bungalow in the Tartar City not far from the temporary quar-ters of the Y . . . The word "bungalow" fascinated me. It sounded both cozy and somehow free-and-easy, and I wished *we* could live in a bunga-low until I saw it for the first time after the Olivers moved in. Maybe for a bachelor it would have been cozy and free-and-easy; for a family it seemed crowded and constricted. (I suppose I was unconsciously com-paring it to our house with its high ceilings and cavernous rooms.)

Before the Olivers,* the American YMCA secretaries had been (for varying periods of time) Eugene Turner and Lawrence (Larry) Mead. Both were bachelors, until "Uncle Gene" was married to a sparkling-eyed

---

* When I refer to the Olivers joining the staff of the Y, I mean that Mrs. O was typical of the American wives who felt themselves full partners with their husbands. Even more than my mother, she became personally engaged in many of its activities.

missionary lady who naturally became our "Aunt Mary." (Robert was ring bearer at the wedding; I was flower girl.)

Mother used to tell me that when I was a chubby infant, my father and Uncle Gene would toss me back and forth between them like one of the YMCA gymnasium medicine balls. I must have loved it; Mother must have been terrified. And a favorite story is one my father told me in later years—about the summer Uncle Gene (still a newcomer and bachelor) stayed in a Buddhist monastery in the Hangchow hills to concentrate on his language study—and someone going there to deliver a message found him in a tree-shaded temple courtyard teaching the happily-bemused grey-robed priests how to play softball.

The Turners both were Southerners (Uncle Gene with the gentlest of slow, genial drawls). Larry Mead—a gifted amateur photographer, among other things—was from New Jersey. On one of our home furloughs his sisters arranged for our family to meet and visit with Thomas A. Edison in his home-cum-laboratory in West Orange, N.J.

The Olivers were mid-Westerners—outgoing, zestful, unaffected, unceremonious. They took to Hangchow immediately and unreservedly; and "Hangchow," though startled sometimes by their breezy directness and disregard of certain old-time conventions and proprieties, accepted them completely.

With their coming to live in the Tartar City, the Barnett children had other American children close by "to play with." Robert and I should have been overjoyed, but I have to say that in those early days our response to being told we were to play with Lillian and John, whether here at home or elsewhere, was "Do we *have* to?"

For one thing, they were younger—Lillian a year younger than I and John close to little brother DeWitt's age. And they were "different": they hadn't been born in China—and in all of us China-borns in Hangchow there was a sort of sense of territorial imperative that made us feel superior to non-China-borns. At the same time there was unease about our comparative status as Americans. Lillian and John—especially after the first family furlough—spoke of certain places back in America with an aplomb and a familiarity that the rest of us could never have even pretended to feel. This gave them an edge over us which we wouldn't admit but found annoying.

None of this mattered in later years when all of us were older. But even in that early time when Lillian and John seemed like little children to Robert and me (who weren't so big ourselves), they were enthusiastic playmates and sturdy little troupers on our hikes and expeditions.

"Aunt Lucille" (it occurs to me that most of our adopted aunts and uncles were from the American South—none from anywhere north of Pennsylvania or from the West or Midwest except for the Olivers. Should I take time to figure this out?) . . . To resume—Aunt Lucille, about the same size as Mother, had dark hair, snapping dark eyes, tender sensibilities, and a quick wit. Like Mother she was a Gipsy at heart. And so, on a fine day when the outdoors was calling, she would appear with Lillian and John in tow to ask if we would like to go along to wherever we all wanted to go. This was all the invitation needed.

As I recall, we almost always decided to go to the Needle Pagoda—partly because it was close enough for a spur-of-the-moment trek, but also because it had its own particular excitements to offer.

The Needle Pagoda

The fun began after we passed by an old temple, somewhat dusty and untidy, at the base of Needle Pagoda Hill and began to climb. The path wound its way up at an easy grade. It was wide and pebbled, with stone slabs down the center and every now and then a series of two or three shallow steps. We didn't *walk* this path; we ran up it a way so that we could fly back downhill to where our mothers had climbed more sedately. Then upward again faster and higher—and back down. Always someone fell and skinned a knee—which delayed the climb—or we stopped for breath and looked at the rice paddies below us north of the city. Then we were at the top, with the level grassy ridge before us—the Lake below us on one side, two widely separated western-style buildings on the other, the pagoda in the center, a small t'ing-tzu (pavilion) and a great tumble of boulders at the farther end.

The first of the square, two-storied buildings was Dr. Main's T.B. Sanatorium. We could see three or four patients, bundled up against the breezes, taking the sun on the open verandah, but we never got close . . . Germs! With scarcely a glance at the ancient pagoda or at Dr. Main's Convalescent Home, we made for the piled-up boulders ahead of us—and the cave. And first we had to go into the cave. As caves go, it wasn't impressive—just a shadowy room that had been formed by nature, as if some giant hand had carelessly dropped several enormous rocks on each other in such a way as to leave a hollow space at the lowest level. The exciting part of this cave was looking up at the ceiling of those carelessly tossed giant rocks and wondering if one of them might jar loose and smash us like little bugs. We talked about that, and we also tried to guess where the precious stone might be—the legend being that in one of those boulders was a jewel worth more than any other jewel in the world. Where was it hidden? Would anyone ever find it?

At the farther end of the cave, there was an opening barely wide enough for a person to go through. It led into a rocky passageway out onto the hillside beyond. On a longer expedition we might have left the cave by that exit to follow along the ridge on our way to the Purple Cloud Cave or the old Taoist Temple.

Now, however, we left our cave by its larger entrance and scampered up the sides of the great rocks outside. We were sure-footed as mountain goats—thanks to our American Keds (sneakers). When we reached the top, we were kings and queens of the mountain!—with the winds blowing soft and clean about us and the whole world spread out below. West Lake was more beautiful than ever. We could see the islands, the causeways—all of it except for the teasingly out-of-sight borders of coves and inlets. We saw randomly scattered sampans, like tiny toy boats that seemed not to be moving until we stared long enough to see the silken filament of a trail being spun out behind each one.

A call of "Do you kiddies want a surprise?" from Aunt Lucille brought us scrambling down the rocks. Aunt Lucille never went on an outing without a "surprise" for us all to picnic on. It could be simple—dried fruit or crackers and peanut butter (which could make us pretty thirsty and ready to start for home) but it always was a welcome surprise. Everything eaten out of doors *does* taste better.

(Robert and I wondered why Aunt Lucille called us "kiddies" and were told by our parents that it was another way of saying "little *kids*." "A kid is a baby *goat*!" one of us would protest. "Well, isn't that what you children are like when you're out climbing?"—which was mollifying until we remembered that we were being called "baby goats" whether we were climbing or not.)

While we nibbled, we gazed up at the pagoda. It was very old with only its core remaining. It didn't occur to me to try to picture it as it had been long ago with its tiers of encircling eaves and perhaps bells hanging from the upcurved roof corners to sway and chime in the wind. I wondered instead about whether there was hollow space inside; if someone could climb through one of those indentations on the grey brick-and-stone facade that looked like blocked-up openings, what would there be? Would there be space enough for steps or for anything or any person? Maybe for a child . . . But I liked the Needle Pagoda as it was—straight and slender, tapering upwards. Delicate vines and small plants that had rooted in crevices of its crumbling surface softened the grey exterior and somehow gave the ancient pagoda a young and living look. Way up, close to the narrowing top, floated the spokeless metal wheel (attached by prongs to the body of the pagoda) through which the iron spire rose and pierced the sky.

While we gazed, a quickening wind blew random clouds across the sky above us.

"It's *falling*! It's *falling*!" someone screamed—and indeed, seen against the scudding clouds, the pagoda was swaying and bending and seemed about to topple down upon us. Shrieking wildly in not-entirely-simulated terror, we children ran from this side to that to escape imminent doom.

This was a strategic time for our mothers to suggest our leaving the danger zone and starting for home.

There were two ways to take. One was by the same way we had come; the other was a narrow path that plunged down towards the lake by steep, uneven stone steps between walls of natural rock and overhanging shrubs and small trees. This was the path we chose.

Everything smelled bosky and damp—of moss and wet leaves and hidden flowers and other fragrant growing things. Somewhere on the way down, the stone stairway came up against a solid slab of rock and had to take a sharp turn to the right. Stopping to crane our necks to look at the flat upper surface of the rock, we could see indentations in the shape of a giant hand, thumb and four fingers splayed out realistically from the palm.

165

This was where the great Buddha had rested his hand when he came (flying) from India and arrived for his visit to Hangchow. And when we had turned the corner, we stopped again to see the enormous imprint of the Buddha's foot on the perpendicular surface of the rocky cliff to our right. Was this made too on his arrival? or was it left there when he took off to fly back to India after his visit?

The placement of the hand print seemed logical to me. But the foot-print?—firm against the perpendicular wall? Had the Buddha been in a horizontal position when he sailed in to land? or when he pushed off? It made a picture in my mind that I couldn't help giggling at—*secretly* (knowing it wasn't respectful, as we were supposed to be in regard to any religious stories and beliefs).

So many stories or fragments of stories were attached to Hangchow, West Lake, and the whole region. Some had their origins in fact—natural or historic. The Buddha's visit may have been myth born out of deep religious faith—or might have been a popular belief based on the true stories of the real-life priest who came from India and founded Ling Yin Monastery in the year 326 A.D.

Other stories seem to have been pure fantasy that somehow became "real"—like the legend of the White Snake supposedly entrapped and imprisoned in the foundations of the Thunder Pagoda.

The Thunder Pagoda

We didn't visit the Thunder Pagoda very often though we looked at it a lot from a distance and were always conscious of its presence. It wasn't graceful and soaring like the Needle Pagoda, but it had a kind of benevolent majesty that was affecting and compelling at whatever distance . . . and when it glowed rich red in the light of a setting sun and was reflected in the lake below, it was achingly beautiful.

The pagoda was built in 975 by Huang Fei, a woman of wealth. According to her wishes, it was to be 13 stories high, and probably taller than the Washington Monument. Her funds were insufficient, and when the pagoda was completed, it was about 170 feet high with five stories instead of 13. It was massive and dignified. The superstructure—like that of the Needle Pagoda—was long gone, burned away several centuries before our time by Japanese pirates who were invading and raiding the rich coastal cities of southeast China. They were never able to broach the city walls of Hangchow and loot and sack the city, because the pagoda was used as a watch tower and the pirates' approach up the river was always seen in time for the city garrison to be warned and on guard and all the city gates closed and barred. The frustrated pirates, so the story goes, were so furious that they took revenge on the pagoda by setting it afire. It burned for three days and three nights. When the flames died and the smoke cleared away, the people saw that the pagoda still stood, but with only its hulk remaining—and a strange thing had happened: the grey brick of its outer surface had been burned red by the intense heat. Maybe it was survival and this transformation that gave the Thunder Peak Pagoda its supernatural aura—something beyond the popular belief that it had been built to imprison the beautiful but mischief-making immortal who often took on the form of a White Snake.

Ancient and benign, the pagoda seemed to stand guard over the city and the lake. Pilgrims from far and near came to see it and feel its gentle power. The bricks of which it was constructed were believed to have miraculous healing properties; and many who came chipped away a tiny piece to take home and make into a powder to heal a loved one grievously ill. This had been going on for goodness-knows-how-long, so that the base of the pagoda as high up as people could reach had been deeply eroded—and had been "repaired" in recent times by filling in the surface with layers of plaster.

"Some day the whole thing is going to collapse," worried some observers.

Seen close to, the Thunder Pagoda was even more impressive—and poignant—than from a distance. Here we could look up and see great gaping holes in the sides—vines, shrubs growing out of its surface, and even small trees where birds had their nests and flew out and about . . .

A hollow pagoda was far and away more interesting than a solid one. Everyone knew that the Thunder Pagoda had a hollow interior which people in the past had entered; but now that it was in partial ruin and there was no easy entrance no one went into it any more. What would it be like inside? Here was a mystery.

One day we were there with out-of-town visitors. A Miss Margaret Mitchell (YWCA secretary, I believe, from Soochow). And from Shanghai, Mr. Arthur Q. Adamson, a handsome widower and gifted architect, who always stayed with us on his trips to inspect the building of the Hangchow YMCA (Later he was to be chief architect of the YMCA building in Jerusalem.) We were always delighted when—as now—he brought along his son George, who was Robert's age.

As we stood at the base of the pagoda looking up, Mr. Adamson—no doubt with an architect's curiosity—suddenly said, "I'd really like to see it from the inside . . . How about giving me a hand?" This to my father, who while we watched with dropped jaws and rounded eyes made a "step" with his linked hands for Mr. Adamson to climb on. We watched him clamber up the rest of the way and pull himself into the nearest crumbled opening above our heads and disappear. Soon he was at the opening again. His eyes were dancing. "There's a good, solid floor," he called down—and then, "Give them a hoist, Gene, and I'll haul them the rest of the way." And before Mother could protest effectively, my father was boosting us up, one by one, and George's father was catching hold and helping us in.

What I remember most is the hush and the sudden sense of being away from the ordinary world—completely away from the outside that we had just left. All the inner structure was gone, so that it was like being in an immense dungeon tower of a giant's castle—except that it wasn't fearful. If I had ever been in a gothic cathedral, I might have thought this felt somewhat the same—quiet, solemn . . . All around and all the way up were the crumbled openings with light filtering through vine tendrils and leafy branches that partially reached out across them. At one side of the very top was a ragged hole, through which I could see the faraway sky. For some reason this broken place made me feel sad.

We all spoke softly, as if not to disturb . . . what? We joked a little about the White Snake somewhere underneath where we were standing— whether she might be getting angry about it. Then someone caught sight of something on the floor way across from us—a small heap of what looked like the blue cotton clothing worn by most people. Someone else— some ordinary mortal human being like us—had been here sometime not *too* long before. Why? Was it to take refuge from the weather? Or from pursuers? Why were the garments left—if that's what they were? They looked somehow insignificant and pathetic in this awesome place. Indeed we ourselves seemed small and humbled.

When we were helped out of the pagoda and were safely on the ground again, I could see Mother's relief, still mixed with vexation. Something terrible could have happened. I don't know if she had been imagining that the pagoda might crash with the three children (and, of course, Mr. Adamson) inside . . .

From Robert F. Fitch's "Hangchow-Chekiang Itineraries": "At about half-past two o'clock on the still afternoon of 25th September, 1924, the Thunder Peak Pagoda sank into a shapeless mound of bricks. Among the ruins all sorts of treasures have been found."

This was only three or four years after our adventure. We had moved to Shanghai, but we heard there was great unease and commotion in Hangchow city for several days after the collapse. (Was the White Snake free now and ready to do mischief?) There was conjecture as to why this had happened so suddenly and completely. One theory was that cannonfire in the fighting between the armies of two contending warlords in the vicinity of Hangchow may have set up reverberations that jarred the already diminished and unsteady base—and so "the walls came a-tumblin' down." In fact, the whole thing! No wonder our realistic mother had been anxious . . . I've always been glad of seeing the pagoda from the inside. It was even more mysterious and beautiful after that. And after it fell, the memory—the idea—of it was still so strong that its presence could still be felt. (Decades later, the Chinese characters for Lei Feng T'a—Thunder Peak Pagoda—still may appear on maps of Hangchow and West Lake, and the pagoda is sometimes pointed out to tourists even though there's no pagoda there on the Peak.)

There is still so much to wonder about. The White Snake legend in all its ramifications (most of which I never knew as a child)—still known and relished all over China . . . when was the story first told? And where did the story come from? Was it purely fanciful or did it spring out of something that really happened?

And how and when did the Pagoda come to be more than a historic monument built to honor a tenth century Buddhist priest? When did it come to be a sort of guardian spirit—not personalized exactly (though compared in poetry to an "old monk")—but something more than inanimate matter? How does spirituality come to invest something made of brick and stone?

Our Favorite Island

Three Lantern Island—out in the Lake—had its stories too—many of them in bits and pieces and having to do with how the island was created (in the early Sung dynasty when the poet-essayist-landscape gardener Su Tung P'o was Governor of the province and living in Hangchow).

The charm of this island was two-fold. First there were the three stone lanterns rising out of the water at some distance from each other (like points of a triangle) at a fair distance from the western shore of the island. The bases were firmly fixed to the lake bed—and the story here was that the "lanterns" had been placed there to trap forever three evil spirits which heretofore had been (somehow) luring unwary fishermen to their vicinity and dragging them from their boats to drown . . . I heard it said about the lanterns that on a certain night each year when the moon was full, they seemed to be lit up from within and cast their three reflections on the water in a magical way . . . Some day, when I was old enough, I was going to stay up all night and see this magic!

The other aspect of the Island's charm, and its true delight (certainly for us on our sojourns there) is in its composition—a rim of land enclosing gardens mostly of water, so that essentially it is a lake-within-the-Lake.

In those days a visit to the Island was a long, leisurely outing, not frequently taken either by tourists or Hangchow residents, Chinese or foreign. The boat trip itself in one of the small pleasure boats (called *sampans*) was perhaps the more important part of the outing; and the time spent on the Island for a picnic or simply for strolling was a sort of an extra enjoyment . . . The Island was never crowded in those days.

Once in a long while, it was chosen as the site for a communal picnic—like the one celebrating the engagement of Miss Kitty McMullen (sister of our "Uncle Mac") to a fellow missionary, John Farrior. The whole American missionary (and "Y") community participated—which I should point out wasn't all that large a number, even including the children, who were also invited.

It was a gleeful occasion for us children, from the initial gathering of everyone on the eastern lakeshore where a small covey of sampans—all fresh and clean with white, scalloped-edged awnings overhead as shade from the sun—had been hired to carry us to the Island.

The landing place was on the farther (western) side of the Island. As soon as we children were helped out of our respective boats, we went on ahead, leaving the adults to unload the picnic gear—baskets, ice cream freezers, and all. Almost immediately we were crossing water on the Bridge of Nine Windings—a level, zig-zagging stone walkway set on stone posts over water where lily pads floated, crowned with pink or yellow blossoms. It was too early for lotus flowers, but the leaves were full-size and a sort of smoky green and held drops of water large and round and clear as crystal.

The rustic wooden rail at each side of the bridge was hardly enough to keep anyone from falling into the water below. "Be careful, children," called our mothers. "Don't run so fast!" "Don't lean on the rail!" "Don't get so close . . . !" "Remember Miss Ricketts!"

So we would repeat to each other one of our own little West Lake legends—about Miss Ricketts and her tennis hat and how it somehow dropped over the rail into one section of the pool and . . . here the story took off and developed its own variations. One version was that she couldn't reach the hat and a gentleman in the party gallantly jumped into the water to retrieve it. Another—more dramatic (and preferred by us)—was that Miss Ricketts herself, in reaching for her hat, fell into the water— and one of the gentlemen gallantly leaped in and rescued her (and the hat?). The story made the traversing of the zigzag bridge much more interesting—and I think it made us more careful.

The meeting place for the picnic was the so-called Swastika Pavilion, where the Buddhist swastika was the motif of the carving of the open woodwork of railing and other decoration. (The Buddhist swastika, we were usually reminded, went in the opposite direction of the swastika of Europe—a comfort to remember in later years when it was the Nazi symbol.)

It was late spring—sweet pea season. The ladies had brought sweet peas from their gardens and festooned the whole pavilion with bunches of them—tied to the posts, the under-eaves—everywhere.

A communal picnic like this used tablecloths and real dishes—and the food would be wonderful (ending with the homemade ice cream and cakes for dessert). But this time, after all was ready, we had to wait; and after a suspenseful period, we could see approaching on one of the paths, several of the men carrying the groom-to-be on their shoulders. The grownups laughed and cheered. I was somewhat shocked—or maybe disappointed is more like it. I thought it undignified—not to say, embarrassing (for the hero of the occasion)—and certainly not very romantic. The adult jocularity and merriment was hard for me to understand . . . There was no accounting sometimes for the childishness of grownups!

Leaving the island was always from the other side, where our sampans had gone and were at mooring to wait for us.

I remember one communal picnic when a violent storm blew up and everyone took refuge in a small enclosed garden at that side of the island and stood under the overhanging eaves of the memorial temple there honoring the poet Su Tung-p'o and other eminent scholars of the region. A modest but elegant building with wooden tablets engraved with characters—no images. The storm was so fierce that the Lake was whipped into waves that seemed too threatening for voyaging in our little sampans. A brave boatman ventured out into the wind and rain and waves to hail one of the large, beautifully decorated pleasure boats (like floating pavilions) that I had always thought would be so wonderful to ride in; and we all hurried through the wet and clambered in to make our way back to the city shore.

It was a clear, calm day all the way through, however, for Kitty McMullen's engagement party, and as the afternoon waned, we climbed into our respective sampans and started back across the lake. The sun was setting. The water sparkled and glittered, and then there was a path of gold and flame and rose that Janet Fitch told me was the reflection of the Queen of the Fairies and all her attendants dancing just above the water. (*They* were invisible, of course.)

When the moon came up and there was a silver path, *that* (she said) was reflecting the King of the Fairies and his retinue, who were all dressed in silver.

Thunder Peak Pagoda
(from booklet of Chinese paintings of West Lake scenes)

Pavilion of Calm Lake and Autumn Moon
(from booklet of Chinese paintings of West Lake scenes)

Rice Paddies

*Farmer and Water
Buffalo Working in
the Field*

*Measuring
the Rice*

Curing Tea leaves (the ovens are heated by charcoal)

Raising Silk Worms

*1913 Reception given by Hangchow officials for American residents
to celebrate the recognition of the Chinese Republic by the U.S.A.*

The Hangchow Fire Brigade

The Six Harmonies Pagoda overlooking the Ch'ien–T'ang River

Bamboo Grove in the Hangchow Hills

On the Grounds of the Ling Yin Monastery

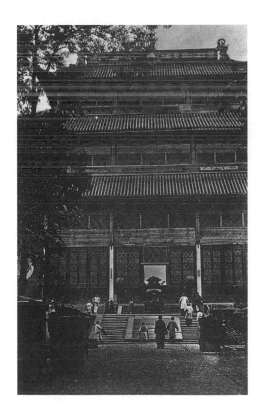

The Main (worship) Hall at Ling Yin Monastery (founded 326 A.D.)

Canal in the Countryside

*The Family at their
Home in the
Tartar City*

The big picnics were exciting and memorable, but the best times on the Lake were when there was just one sampan or two—sometimes the Oliver family in one, our family in the other . . . with whatever visitors or friends we might have asked to join us.

We children always liked to have a turn at rowing (Lillian and John called it "*oaring*")—which our respective boatmen smilingly or reluctantly allowed. On the island it was always quieter and more leisurely, with time to explore before having our picnic.

Going back, we always sang. Lively songs first . . . "Polly Wolly Doodle" and "Oh Susanna," "I've Been Workin' on the Railroad," "Daisy, Daisy, give me your answer true," "The Animal Fair," and "There's a bulldog on the bank (ladies and children)—There's a bullfrog in the pool (the men's voices going down   *down   down*) . . . " And then there was "Juanita"— "Love's Old Sweet Song"—"There's a Long, Long Trail A-Winding"— "Swanee River" . . . When the sun had set and there were soft colors behind the velvety hills and on the water, we sang "Day is Dying in the West" and "Now the Day is Over."

In fair weather, during the daylight hours the Lake was dotted with little sampans. On our way to the Island we could see them widely scattered—and occasionally one of them came close enough for us to hail the passengers and to see them taking tea from pots on the small table (like ours) in the center of the boat or leaning back, idly nibbling on watermelon seeds while savoring the scene all about them. Except in the summer, however (when people might seek respite from the heat by staying up all night), most of the little pleasure boats had carried their passengers to shore—to reach their homes before dark. There may also have been a residue of habit from the time not so long before when it was necessary to enter the city before the gates were closed at sundown.

Often in the gathering dusk we seemed to be alone on the lake, and in between songs, all we heard was the soft plashing of oars and the softer sounds of our boat moving through the water. But one time, as a song of ours was sung to its end, there was a continuing of sound which seemed to flow from our harmonizing into a single pure, winding melody . . . the sound of a bamboo flute floating, serene and haunting, through the clear air. We could dimly see the other sampan some distance away. My father called a greeting across the water; someone called back cheerily. There was a friendly and appreciative exchange of compliments for the music—ours for the flute playing, theirs for our singing; and we moved on into the darkness as did our fellow travelers. It's odd. It was only when falling silent that we could hear the other music—and I think it was the same for them. The two kinds of music did not disturb each other—and when heard separately, each was appropriate and beautiful in its own way.

As we came nearer to shore, we saw points of light flickering at the end of the shore where the large, several-storied resort hotels stood. The reflections lengthened and brightened the closer we came to land. They were like streamers of light, moving in parabolas, breaking apart with the rippling of the water and rejoining. I was mesmerized.

I can vaguely remember arriving at the shore and being helped out of the gently rocking boat onto damp, shallow stone steps, and then feeling firm ground underfoot. But I never can recall the rest of it . . . going back to our alley, through the gate, into the house—getting ready for bed. I guess I was too full of happiness.

Chinese poets have especially loved West Lake in the rain or in light drifting mist. Painters have loved it in winter after a snow, when all the shapes of stone bridges and curved roofs and branches of trees in the scene were delicately outlined in white.

At various periods of history, the scene has changed. In our day, the hills around the Lake were bare of trees, except where there was a monastery or temple or tomb; and I loved the contours of hill and valley and the way they changed texture as they caught light or were in shadow. In the spring the brush that covered the hillsides burst into glowing color—the "brush" being a profusion of azaleas growing wild. Now that the hills and valleys have been re-planted with trees, the wild azaleas have been shaded and crowded out. The shapes of the hills have softened and they are lush and green and are beautiful in a different way . . . perhaps not entirely a new way, because I have seen paintings of times past where the hills were wooded, not bare. But for me they are always the eternal hills—and whenever I hear the words of the psalm "I will lift up mine eyes to the hills—from whence cometh my help . . ." they are what I see in my mind's eye.

One time, I saw West Lake in a morning mist—not the usual light filmy mist trailing here and there, but one that was dense and mysterious. West Lake was a sombre yet alluring ocean with no visible shores or outer boundaries. The causeways and the islands appeared in glimpses and disappeared. Strangest of all was Three-Lantern Island, which seemed to be floating in a sea of cloud—far away and then looming up darker and closer than usual but always insubstantial—a faery, phantom island.

One winter, West Lake was frozen over—a rare, perhaps once-in-a-lifetime occurrence, and it didn't stay frozen for very long.

But we were there to see it. It was late afternoon—the sun low over the western hills. Everything was absolutely still—motionless—and clear cut in the cold transparent air . . . the hills, the Needle Pagoda, the islands, causeways and bridges sharply etched, three-dimensional, almost touchable, yet remote and dreamlike. The whole far-reaching surface of the lake, held taut by its thin skin of ice—pale and gleaming—took on faint colors as the sky brightened in the west and then turned opalescent, reflecting the rose and amber, turquoise, lilac and pale green brighter than they were in the sky and seeming to fill the very air with light and color, a soft unearthly radiance.

The colors dimmed and faded; the light drained away and the briefly shining world was now sober grey with only a sheen like polished pewter on the Lake—and that would darken and vanish soon in the growing dusk. It was cold. Time to go home.

But what a sight to have seen!

Of all the times I have gazed at the West Lake scene in childhood or later, this may have been the most extraordinary. All—with their obvious or subtle differences—refreshed the eyes and spirit . . .

Thank you, fairy godmother, for giving me West Lake to remember!

School in the Flowery Pavilion

*O*ne fine day, before our Calvert School shipment arrived, we heard a bustle at the front gate and saw a couple of workmen enter, each carrying a small desk attached to a bench with a back rest—our school furniture, which Mother had the men take into the Flowery Pavilion.

The "school furniture" had been custom-made for us by a Ningpo carpenter. (Most carpenters and furniture makers in Hangchow were from Ningpo.) It was child-sized—painted black. Across the top of each desk was a shallow indentation for pencil, pen, or brush; in one corner was a round indentation for an ink bottle. The top was hinged and lifted up over a storage space for writing paper and work books. It was empty now—just waiting.

Our desk sets were placed side by side facing the teacher's work table and chair at the end of the room nearest the main house. Robert and I decided who was to have which desk. I don't know how the choice was made since they were identical, but from then on each was to be sacrosanct to its owner.

At the opposite end of the room was our father's "study"—two chairs and the table at which he and Mr. Dzen read Chinese every afternoon; and in the middle section were our larger toys, like my doll house (also custom-made probably by the same Ningpo carpenter) neatly arranged against the wall. Latticed windows along the longer sides of the pavilion let in plenty of light—even on cloudy or rainy days.

Now we were ready for school except for books and supplies—and they were due to come down from Shanghai very soon.

It was a red letter day when the packing boxes were delivered to us and put down on the front lawn to be opened.

Everything needed for school was there—from the teacher's daily lesson plans and the pupils' text books and daily worksheets to all the materials such as writing paper, blank notebooks, pencils, pens, crayons, water colors, construction paper. And *books*—hard cover, honest-to-goodness books: collections of stories, poems, fairy tales, biographies of famous men (I still remember Alfred the Great, King Canute, Robert Bruce and the spider) and famous women (Jenny Lind's story I was to read and reread many times). There was a small volume of Lamb's *Tales From Shakespeare* and one of Early Greek myths and history—another with stories of Early Roman gods and heroes. All these were arranged in our schoolroom book shelf to be taken out to read at any time.

One small box that we opened that day was tightly packed with pictures—photographs of famous places, buildings, works of art. For some reason the prints were not black and white or sepia like most photographs of that day but were in blue and white like architectural blueprints. On that morning we became acquainted with—or at least introduced to—the Parthenon and the Colosseum, the Taj Mahal, the Pyramids, the Sphinx . . . the *Sistine Madonna* and *Last Supper*, Corot's landscapes, and Landseer's and Rosa Bonheur's beautiful animals . . . the Winged Victory and Venus de Milo. There was a lonely and awesome picture of the Great Wall of China too (named as one of the Seven Wonders of the World). While Mother was discovering and sorting out and deciding how to store the more mundane supplies, we looked at the treasure box of pictures and then carefully repacked them in their container. Like the books, they would be returned to often in the future.

Whether it had been openly discussed beforehand or somehow obliquely and tacitly agreed upon, we were determined to have a *real* school.

That meant, first of all, having a school bell. Actually it was a brass gong—from Ka-shing (where the best brass gongs came from). Yienh San took it out on the front porch, held it up by its string loop, and banged it at its center—a round circle painted black—with the wooden knocker. (It was a wonderfully resonant, politely authoritative sound—and I still regret the loss of that Chinese gong. Some years later Mother lent it for use in a play at the Shanghai American School and it was never returned.)

At the signal, Robert and I left the big house and walked to school in the east wing—either out through the front yard or (short cut) along the porches. We took our seats at our desks. Our teacher was at the table in

185

front of us.

"Good morning," she said.

"Good morning," we responded.

And then we sang: "Good morning to you . . . Good morning to you . . . We're all in our places with sunshiny faces . . . for this is the way to start a new day." (Our teacher believed in positive reinforcement . . . as she also did as Mother.)

The daily lesson plan for the teacher was clear and explicit, so that there was no need to fumble or be confused as to what the pupils should be doing as the morning progressed. There were the drills and disciplines of arithmetic and spelling and writing (printing at this stage)—which were laborious and tedious at times, but had to be done and could even afford a sense of accomplishment now and then . . . and there was reading—and some memorizing (which I liked), and there were projects.

However it had been put together, it seems to have been both exact enough and flexible enough to be stimulating and absorbing for the three of us. It turned out to be a *real school* with solid, conventional learning plus "extras" probably not common to grade schools back in America. It also allowed for the carrying out of ideas that bubbled forth out of our teacher's creativity and enthusiasm.

Real school and real teacher. From the beginning our mother was teacher during school hours. We did not presume on our relationship; we did not whine or complain or quarrel and take sibling grievances to her (as we certainly did at other times). In fact, we were too busy and interested in what we were doing even to compete with each other . . . And where had we acquired the notion that politeness and respect were due a teacher in a classroom even more than to older persons at other times? Had we inherited a family respect for the process and the purveyors of learning? or was it a part of our Chinese 'heritage'?

Sometime about mid-morning the gong sounded for a brief recess. Robert and I went outside or to the playshed to run about and stretch ourselves. Mother used the time to check on household matters.

The gong sounded again for a return to the classroom and then once again (Yienh San was kept busy) for the end of the school session, to wait for our father to bicycle back from the YMCA and for us all to have our midday meal together.

186

About once a week, Robert and I had a Chinese lesson with a Miss Nyi, daughter of a Chinese pastor. She was young and serious and earnest to the point of anxiety . . . I don't think we ever saw her smile; her sense of responsibility permitted no relaxation.

I vaguely recall using brush and Chinese ink to practise simple calligraphy as we had begun to do in kindergarten. I don't remember reading out of any Chinese primer. What I do remember is the set of stylized pictures on coarse, yellowish rice paper illustrating stories and fables that she told us—just as they were taught, I believe, to all young school children in China at that time. I remember best the pictures and stories having to do with resourceful—or naughty—children who grew up to be famous scholars.

One picture—very dramatic: frantic children near a large water *k'ang*. An adventuresome and foolish playmate, having climbed up to its rim, has fallen in and is about to drown! But see what one clever boy has done while the others are dancing about in helpless panic: he has taken a large, sharp rock and broken a hole in the base of the *k'ang* and the water is beginning to gush out. (The foolish playmate is saved. Some grownup person will come to haul him out—and no doubt give him a hearty scolding.)

Another picture and story also have to do with water. In this story a ball has fallen down a deep hole formed in the roots of a large tree and the resourceful child (to be a famous Sung dynasty scholar) is pouring water in the hole to float the ball up where it can be retrieved. The other children stand watching in hope and admiration.

The "naughty" child—as everyone will know who ever began language lessons at the College of Chinese Studies in Peking—turned out to be the most famous of all: the Confucian scholar and philosopher Mencius (B.C. 372-289).

When Mencius was a small boy, his father died, and his mother (a woman of character and learning) had to support her son and herself which she did as a silk weaver. Her young son instead of studying spent his time with idle playmates out in the streets . . . The picture showed Mencius who has just come home from his playing. He is shocked to see his mother seated at her loom slashing across a great length of fabric she has just woven. He protests—and she replies that wasting his time and gift for learning is far worse than destroying and wasting a piece of silk. And so he forthwith abandons his frivolous ways to pursue his studies and to become one of China's greatest scholars.

Not scheduled during morning school hours or at any special time that I can remember were our piano lessons. Our teacher in this case again was our mother, who after all was a trained music teacher. She probably worked in our piano sessions (held individually) whenever it was feasible. After a while she gave up on Robert. She concluded that Robert considered playing the piano was for girls (and grown ladies); but she had hopes of arousing his interest when she heard that a young American business man from Shanghai who would be staying with us was an amateur pianist—and what's more he was skilled in sleight of hand tricks. This should inspire her son to go back to trying to learn how to play the piano. She made sure that during our visitor's brief visit he gave both a musical and a magic performance. Robert may have been impressed, but the piano was not for him. (Later, in Shanghai, the cello became his instrument—after he had tried out the violin for a while.)

Music lessons and Chinese were "extracurricular" activities for us (though we didn't know the term). We had projects that grew out of our lessons or were somehow fitted back into them; but *real school* was the weekday morning session. These mornings passed quickly. We were never bored—not even when trying to learn the multiplication tables. (Hard work—but not *boring*.) We never felt threatened—or embarrassed, as would inevitably happen in the larger classrooms of our future.

But we knew that school children were supposed to be happiest when there was no school; and so (such is the consistency—or perhaps, in this case, the perversity of the childish nature) we were appropriately enthusiastic about our weekends, holidays, and vacations.

Every Friday at noon, Robert and I closed our desks with exclamations of joy. "Tomorrow is Saturday. No school!" And we marked off school holidays on our classroom calendar so that we could count the days until the Thanksgiving, Christmas, or Easter holidays. Our second Calvert School year, we made our own calendars to check on each day: a page for each month with an original seasonal illustration above and the spaces for the weeks and days beneath . . . Robert had an especially fine picture for December—of Santa Claus in front of a realistic brick fireplace (such as we never saw in China).

Learning from Visitors

The more I think about it, the less reason there seems to have been for us to pretend we were having too much school, for in addition to the weekends and the seasonal holidays—not to mention a long summer break—we had a great many unscheduled days off when house guests had to be attended to by both our parents or often, if our father was too busy at the "Y," by our mother—who was also our school teacher. No teacher—no school . . . though you might call our going along on sightseeing tours with our guests as field trips and therefore a part of school.

Every Western household had its quota of out-of-town visitors. Besides being an attractive site for regional mission meetings and conferences, Hangchow was becoming a popular holiday retreat for Westerners from Shanghai and other parts of China; and more and more it was included on the itineraries of tourists from abroad as an important city to visit.

But no Western-style hotel existed in Hangchow at this time and no one recommended that foreigners stay in a Chinese inn—not even one of those large, new buildings near the lake shore. They were new, but they were not "modern." Few Westerners would know how to cope with the lack of familiar facilities; few would be equipped with the bed roll and other necessary paraphernalia brought as a matter of course by Chinese tourists and travelers. (There was a story of a romantic young American who insisted—against all advice—on taking his bride, who was fresh from America, to a Hangchow inn for their honeymoon. It was a disaster; and the poor wife never fully recovered from the culture shock . . . or so it was said.)

So the Hangchow "foreigners" were accustomed to hosting not only their out-of town friends and colleagues but also friends of friends or friends-of-friends-of-friends.

We had all of these and more, as my father increasingly saw part of his YMCA role as being a sort of liaison person between Orient and Occident—particularly between China and America . . . an interpreter of each to the other and encourager of mutual understanding and respect. As such and with his friendships and working contacts in the Hangchow community, he helped to initiate and set up many official and semi-official events involving visitors from the West. And so we had diplomats, lecturers, evangelists, educators, government and church and business representatives among the succession of our house guests. My father joked about "Bertha running a hotel."

The longer we were in Hangchow the more guests we had, but somehow they didn't interfere too much with our sense of family life or with its basic routines. Most of these visitors were simply absorbed into the general atmosphere and were steered somehow into the activities they'd come for.

As individuals they added peripherally to our "education"—Robert's and mine. In the general conversation at the breakfast table—and sometimes at noon—we heard lively talk on whatever topics our current guests were interested in. The Student Movement—education—politics—religion—international affairs—usually relating them to immediate realities in China or more specifically Hangchow itself.

We heard about Health and Sanitation from Dr. W. W. Peter, the dynamic YMCA secretary who traveled to all the important cities in China lecturing on how to prevent disease and promote health. Crowds in the thousands came to hear him. After his visit posters were seen all over the place reading—in English—"SWAP THAT FLY."

Another YMCA secretary was sent out by the National Committee headquarters in Shanghai—in this case to introduce elements of modern science to people all over China. This was "Big Robbie" Robertson. Robert and I were taken to one of his appearances (presentations—lecture-cum-demonstrations or scientific "shows") when he visited Hangchow.

It was an exciting event to look forward to and we were not disappointed although I wasn't always quite sure what scientific principles the experiments we watched so intently were supposed to prove. "Big Robbie" was *big*—six feet four or more—with a majestic look about him. He was not flamboyant; he was dignified and serious; but as he talked and performed the accompanying illustrative experiments, he somehow induced a subdued sort of excitement and expectation that was irresistible—even to a small, unscientific person like myself. It was like watching a magician. He used simple props—bells and wires and batteries and light bulbs— and weights and ropes and pulleys and buckets of cold water or steaming hot water to dramatize the laws of physics and chemistry and physiology that he was offering to people in a society which for the most part was still in the Middle Ages. Of course, I wished that he could have made someone fly—or disappear (and re-appear, I would hope)—or produce a trayful of glittering jewels . . . fairytale magic, but it was exciting all the same.

World-famous evangelists and lecturers stayed with us. They drew great crowds too. Sherwood Eddy and E. Stanley Jones (author of "Christ of the Indian Road") were among our evangelist-guests.

Dr. John Dewey came to China as an Educator and was our house guest during his Hangchow visit. I am not sure whether he "drew crowds" or even lectured to large groups. He may have had meetings with individuals or selected groups of government officials, professors, school administrators and the like. Education in China was undergoing revolutionary change with the abandonment not too many years before of the old examination system based on the study of the Confucian classics . . . How to introduce new subjects of study and new ways to teach . . . how to educate the whole population . . . how to change the whole philosophy of education. I have no idea what the great American educational theorist John Dewey had to say to the Chinese on all the crucial questions of teaching and learning in the new republic. What I do know is that my father had the deepest respect for him and seemed almost in awe at the honor of having this Great Man of our times as a guest in our home. I accepted that and was ready to be impressed. I rarely saw him which wasn't unusual with important and busy visitors.

But I remember specifically not seeing him at our morning prayers (at the breakfast table on weekdays—in the parlor on Sundays). And I asked where he was. Surely, I thought, a great man like Dr. Dewey would want to share with us our Bible reading and what we said about it—and maybe would want to join in the discussion, which was followed by a prayer; and maybe he would like to say the prayer if my father asked him . . . If my father didn't answer the query the first morning that I missed our guest, I must have asked again. I can't recall exactly what my father said—but he was honest. He didn't make up excuses. What I understood him to say was that our honored guest was not sure about God and could not pretend to worship when he didn't believe. I could clearly see how that would be so. But it was something of a shock and continued as a puzzlement.

Considering that personal encounters of us children with Dr. Dewey were so few, perhaps it shouldn't have surprised me decades later when I learned from my mother that Mrs. Dewey had been with him on his trip to China and that they both were with us—for at least a couple of weeks . . . They must have stayed in the West Wing. It was extremely hot weather (very late spring or early fall) and Mother told me, (with an involuntary shudder of embarrassment) that Mrs. Dewey kept herself cool by dipping a bed sheet into a water k'ang, draping it over her otherwise unclad self and walking about so that the wetness would evaporate and cool her off. "I was so afraid the servants would see her!"

Among the houseguests were a number of repeat visitors who were especially welcomed by the family, children included. One of them was Charles R. Crane, U.S. Minister to China (China did not rate an ambassador then) who stayed with us on his official visits from the capital in Peking.

We could expect him on an evening soon after his arrival to come upstairs to see us about the time our supper was over. We were still sitting in our little wicker chairs and at our little bamboo and wicker table when he came in and spoke to us. While he talked of this and that, he put his hand in a pocket and drew out something which he held up for us to see. It was a small pair of scissors in the shape of a bird . . . a crane, of course. ("Just like my name!") Then we saw him move his hand towards his face. He opened his mouth and closed it quickly. The scissors were gone. He showed us his hand; it was empty. Our eyes got bigger and bigger as we watched him swallow and swallow until it seemed the scissors had gone all the way down his throat. How he did all this without ever losing his dignity, I don't know—but he did. Seemingly relieved to have finally gulped down the scissors, he began to chat with us again—and walking over to Robert in his little chair, casually reached down behind his ear and pulled something out—lifted up. Presto! it was the pair of scissors shaped like a crane! We loved the trick and its variations and were surprised every time he performed it for us. And we liked having him come up specially to see us.

We had other return-engagement entertainers among our house guests. Miss Tuttle, a missionary lady of indeterminate age from the Southern

Methodist Mission in Soochow, was one of our favorites. Her specialty was the Uncle Remus stories which she told verbatim in dialect with such exactly-right inflection, expression, and timing that Joel Chandler Harris would have been highly gratified. Brer Rabbit talking his way out of his predicaments with Brer Fox had me laughing so hard one time that I tumbled out of my little wicker chair onto the floor.

We were introduced to Kipling and the *Just So Stories* by Miss Ella McNeill, newly arrived from Australia to serve as a YWCA secretary in Shanghai. I remember how she looked on her first visit to Hangchow—dressed in middy blouse and skirt, her hair worn long with a large school-girlish ribbon bow at the back of her head. She must have been barely twenty and was fairly bursting with vitality and good spirits. She bubbled; she effervesced. Her enthusiasm never flagged. We children were charmed and delighted. (I think our mother found this typically Australian inexhaustible zest somewhat wearing.) Robert was duly impressed when someone told us that Ella McNeill was a champion swimmer and—what's more—had saved at least three people from drowning back home in Australia . . . Like Miss Tuttle, she knew her stories by heart and they flowed and bounced out, natural and true, with those wonderful phrases and rhythms—" . . . the great grey green greasy Limpopo River, all set about with fever-trees . . ." and "Still ran Dingo—Yellow-Dog Dingo—always hungry, grinning like a rat-trap, never getting nearer, never getting farther."

Hangchow being such an important craft and trade center, I am sure that my father must have received a number of letters like the following . . .

Dear Gene,

I have been talking to a Mr. X, who is here in China to study sericulture . . . He is most eager to visit Hangchow which he has heard is a center . . .

I wonder if Bertha out of the goodness of her heart could put him up for a couple of days—and perhaps you could help arrange for him to see what he is after . . .

A letter like this one probably is why Robert and I had the chance to see silkworms being raised (maybe missing a school day). I don't remember how we got there but it was far out of town on a quiet, open hillside with no one about and only the one low-lying single-story build-ing, simple and rustic. As soon as we entered the doorway, we realized we would have to be very quiet ourselves, for we were greeted in a cour-teous and cordial *whisper*. Silkworms do not like noise. So we fairly tiptoed from room to room and could hear the silence in the first room (where the tiny hatchlings were feeding) change into a faint rustling that developed into almost a chomping sound where the silkworms had attained their full growth and were devouring quantities of mulberry leaves at a voracious rate. In each of the rooms we could see the little creatures feeding on the fresh leaves spread generously on shallow bam-boo and woven reed trays. The final room was the most fascinating. This is where the full grown silkworms had been provided with small straw cones, tied at the top like toy tepees, on which to climb and attach themselves as they wove their cocoons. We watched them work away—and I hoped they didn't mind us watching and I wondered how did they know how to do it and what was it like to go to sleep in your own little perfect, dark house.

———

How many official "school days" did we actually have during the first year of our Calvert Course school—or the second year? How many *unin-terrupted* days?

Even when we had a full morning with the gong sounding at the proper times, there could be unexpected interruptions that our teacher had to deal with—and some that she didn't seem to mind at all like the day when Yienh San came bursting into our classroom breathless with ex-citement and urging us (in Chinese) to come and look! The three of us hurried outside and he pointed up at the single wire that carried electric-ity to the house. On it—as if waiting for us to come and admire—was perched the most spectacular bird we had ever seen, with the snowy plum-age of an extravagantly long tail hanging down like a waterfall. We just had time to stare and gasp, when the wonderful bird rose into the air and flew away. Yienh San, who seemed to know about all our projects whether we'd told him or not, wore a big smile of pleasure at having gotten us out in time. We returned to our school room to try to identify this new bird to add to our list of Hangchow birds we had seen. We identified it as a Paradise Flycatcher. We never sighted another one.

Anything having to do with a wonder of nature merited an interruption to classroom work . . . the discovery of a lunar moth—seeing snow begin to fall. At the sight of early snowflakes we were kept at our desks to finish whatever we were working at—and then school was let out for the rest of the day so that we (teacher included) could watch and marvel at the falling snow and the changing world.

When the winter sun no longer provided enough warmth for the Flowery Pavilion, the classroom moved to the main house and we worked at the long dining room table (part of the handsome teakwood set purchased from a departing British family) sitting at the side nearest the iron coal-burning stove where the room was coziest. Our books and writing materials were spread out in front of us. Since Mother was more accessible here, she was frequently called on by one or another of the servants with questions or messages. Every now and then Yienh San came in to open up the little door in the stove and poke up the fire, add fresh coals, take out the ashes from underneath. (It was exciting to see the rounded sides of the iron stove glow red hot.) It wasn't so much like real school in here and it wasn't as easy to concentrate. It was good to be back at our desks with some space around and our bookshelf of special books and the teacher's desk and chair facing us—and a blackboard . . .

By the second springtime of our school, we had so many little projects going or completed that our teacher decided we should put together an Annual as a record of the current school year—its activities and accomplishments. We created it all—from the covers (pasteboard colored a festive red) on in. The contents were samples of our best work—having to do with geography or history, our neatest writing (or printing), most artistic or interesting pictures. An original story by each of us was included and my first poem.

Graduation Day

Mother's next inspiration was for us to have graduation ceremonies after the last day of the school in June. Whatever surprised or facetious comments my father surely made, they did nothing to dampen her enthusiasm, and he cooperated, at least in his admiring interest in the plans and preparations and then in his actual participation when the Event took place.

It was a perfect June day. Our guests—a select few—assembled in the Flowery Pavilion. At the farther end, my father's "study" had temporarily vanished to be replaced by a platform, constructed of wooden packing boxes from the storeroom in the West Wing, which had been fitted together under Mother's direction by Yienh San and the gardener . . . the former happy and buoyant as usual, and the gardener willing but glum. It was a fine platform, with a matting rug to cover the cracks and potted plants and flowers for decoration. The American flag hung behind. Chairs for the audience had been arranged in front. Elsewhere in the room were displays showing what we had worked at and accomplished during the school year . . . our Annual, the calendars we had made, the booklet with dried leaves or trees we had identified, our record of bird-sightings, and so on.

The program was well-composed but not long. Our father was master of ceremonies. There was an introduction and a song. Robert and I each read or recited a piece of literature. There was a short speech—another song. And then one of the other grownups—I think it was "Uncle Jay" Oliver—called the graduates back up on the stage and handed out the diplomas, which were properly rolled up and tied with red ribbons. The audience applauded. Then everyone went outside for a party in the front yard—sandwiches and cookies and iced tea . . . with *ice*. Mother had heard how to make "safe" ice by putting boiled water in the ice cream freezer with plenty of local (*dirty*) ice around it and lots of rock salt—but not (of course) turning the freezer handle. Result: a large cylindrical chunk of clean, sanitary ice.

The chief reason for our Graduation event was to recognize what we had been doing and achieving in our little school during the year. But it also was a good excuse for a party; and the clincher for Mother was that she was going to surprise (she hoped) the gathered guests with *real iced tea*. It was a lovely little garden party with everyone happily shaking their tall glasses and exclaiming to hear the clink and tinkle of the ice! Meanwhile the honorees were more or less forgotten—which didn't bother them at all, as long as they could have their share of the refreshments.

Tours, Shops and City Hill

My parents introduced many guests of ours to Hangchow as China, recommending tours or actually conducting them—often with Robert and me going along.

All of our guests saw West Lake. All of them were taken to Ling Yin Monastery with a stop on the way at the Sacred Fish Pond ("Gem Spring of the Dancing Fish") and probably another at the tomb of Yo Fei, the great hero-general and patriot of the Southern Sung dynasty when Hangchow was imperial capital. Some were taken to what we called Emperor's Island—perhaps to sip tea and look at the Lake from a pavilion on a site dating back to the T'ang dynasty (618-907 A.D.) or to see where the great Imperial Library—or replicas thereof—had been housed by order of the Manchu Emperor Ch'ien Lung of the Ch'ing dynasty in the 1700s. And they might be taken to City Hill with its great historic significance . . . and, before that, to the Medicine Shop on the Great Street—simply because it was quaint and interesting—and perhaps to the Mohammedan (so-called in those days) Mosque, first built, it was claimed, in the early seventh century on that same site near the base of City Hill.

I never saw the inside of the Mosque, but the Medicine Shop was a favorite place to visit. It had been in the hands of a Ningpo family for a few generations—not terribly long by Chinese standards. It was a smallish, one-story typical shop building—not modernized. With one step over the threshold, there was a marvelous pungency in the air like nowhere else in the world—a blend of aromas and spicy smells and strange emanations from dried plants and herbs and gnarled roots (hanging in small bunches from the ceiling beams above the counter)—from nuts and seeds—from old animal bones and horns and antlers, crumbled or ground to powder and heaped in mounds or stored in jars. Some of the

197

horns and antlers were still whole and hung on the wall behind the counter.

Behind the counter, the shopkeeper-chemist was listening to a customer describing symptoms of pains or illness that had to be treated—most often it seemed for a family member. The shopkeeper listened—asked questions—reached for this or that and measured the ingredients out onto squares of coarse paper. Each of these was weighed using a scale made from a bamboo rod with a shallow tray suspended from a string at one end and the weights (metal discs) to be added or taken off the other end till the two sides balanced. If the remedy was to be taken as a single "medicine," the ingredients were carefully combined and poured onto a larger spill of paper, which was closed by folding and handed over to the customer with instructions on dosages. The buyer counted out coins for payment and hurried out of the shop . . . comforted and hopeful.

At the rear end of the shop was a door that opened into an inner courtyard as lush and green as a miniature jungle. What a fantastic surprise here in the crowded, congested city! There were grasses and shrubs and a small rockery with plants and mosses and small trees with overhanging, leafy branches. I think there was the sound of water falling on rocks. And as we stood there at the entrance and watched quietly, we would see something moving in the green foliage and a small deer would appear, serenely feeding on leaves and grasses. If we waited long enough, we might catch sight of another. Always we saw at least one small deer—raised there for the antlers which were trimmed (without *hurting*, I was happy to be told) and used for medicine.

Hell and City Hill

I don't remember going to City Hill very often. I vaguely recall that at its base were small portable tables and stalls for fortune tellers, professional letter writers (how sad, I thought, that grownups couldn't write their own letters), and astrologers who advised on such matters as when the geomantic influences were right for betrothals and weddings, funeral practices and burials.

City Hill itself, in the prestigious southwest corner of Hangchow and overlooking West Lake, was virtually a wasteland after the T'ai P'ing occupation, its memorial buildings, temples and official *yamens* having been largely destroyed by the rebels. I remember going up long, wide flights of stone steps with rubble and nothing much else at either side. (I have to remind myself that I was small and couldn't see very far.) A few historic temples remained. The one we children relished—and, I must admit, the only one I remember from those days—was the Temple of the Sacred Mountain of the East, dubbed the *Temple of Hell* by the Hangchow foreigners because of its graphic representation (Buddhist conception) of the tortures of the damned in the afterlife. This was (as I recall it) in a large enclosure in front of the temple hall . . . a panoramic view in highly colored plaster or terra cotta relief of the wicked drowning in seething waves or being engulfed by flames or attacked by devils with pitchforks— not too different from a Dante-esque depiction of Hell. The entire scene and all the figures and creatures in it were so grotesque and exaggerated as to be unbelievable. We children were horrified in the same deliciously shivery yet satisfying way as when listening to certain fairy tales and to the horrid things that happened to the wicked Giant or Witch or other evil characters in the story. In those more innocent days, before the daily disclosures of real violence and horror in the media, we saw in our fairy tales the confrontation between Good and Bad and the resulting rewards and punishments in a symbolic way, vivid and lively but not related to everyday life. Underneath the scariness, it was all quite clear-cut, unambiguous, and reassuring.

The Temple of Hell, therefore, did not give us nightmares, but something to mention now and then . . . at least in part because it gave us a chance to say (without fear or hesitation) the word "hell," which otherwise was not permitted. (There were a few hymns that were enjoyable because we could *sing* the word.)

There were certain strictures on language for all of us young American children in Hangchow—probably much the same as in similar households back in the States. "Darn—gee—gosh—golly" were taboo. You could get away with *telling* on somebody . . . "I heard So-and-so say 'darn!' "— dropping your voice discreetly on the "bad" word. Or you could somehow drag in the mention of *darn*ing a sock or stocking, accenting the first syllable and laughing loudly.

"Sex" was a word conspicuous for its absence in our vocabulary. I can't remember hearing it or reading it except when it was used in such gallantries as "the fairer sex." Having seen thousands of Chinese babies with their slit trousers and hundreds of older children stark naked in the sweltering summer, none of us had any need to be curious about the "difference" between little boys and little girls. We were familiar with the sight of mothers breast-feeding their infants; we (most of us) knew that babies grew inside their mothers—and how they came out into the world. All this was interesting and taken for granted . . . How did babies start in the first place? . . . Parents prayed; God decided when it should happen and made a little miracle.

Some expressions were peculiar to us or had their own connotations which I'm not sure that even our parents understood. "C.I.M. missionary," for instance. *C.I.M.* referred to the China Inland Mission, whose missionaries seemed to us to be dowdy, intense, humorless, out-of-touch with any of the normal, enjoyable things of life. They were odd and different—and the term always elicited spontaneous childish laughter . . . Don Quixote is on the surface a ridiculous character and so was "C.I.M. missionary" to us. (On the other hand, I took Don Quixote and his story with complete seriousness and sympathy.) Stereotypes can apparently come easily to children. It wouldn't be hard for me to explain how this one came to us, but it doesn't seem important—except that it wasn't very kind and it stayed with me. I was astonished when looking at old photographs with my parents in their retirement to see the picture of an early Hangchow friend of theirs whom I didn't recognize . . . an exceptionally handsome, attractive, intelligent-looking young man. "Who is that?" I asked. My father told me his name and that they had had many wonderful and stimulating conversations together before he left Hangchow. Was he a missionary? Oh yes . . . *C.I.M.* So much for my stereotype.

The antithesis in our lexicon of words and expressions was "stylish." This also was spoken with exaggerated emphasis and in an amused tone. It was not complimentary. It was usually applied to visitors of a certain type from Shanghai or the U.S.A. who seemed to us to be worldly and affected in manner. "Stylish" suggested phoniness and superficiality. We used it in a slightly derisive sense; but underneath there was a certain wary defensiveness . . . on behalf of our parents perhaps? who were not "stylish." Or was it possibly a reaction to what I imagine some of these strangers felt about us—precocious, prudish little creatures (not like *normal* American kids!)?

I came to dread the coming of guests who might be "stylish." They were usually American tourists—friends-of-friends-of-friends . . . seemingly affluent. The ones I remember were female—the kind who when introduced to the Barnett children took note of Robert's bright expression and Anglo-Saxon coloring and exclaimed, "What rosy cheeks!"—and cooed at roguish little DeeDee with his yellow ringlets—and then, turning to look at their sister, could only say, "Oh isn't it too bad that the little girl has the straight hair!" Upon which, her companion might hasten to add, "She certainly has thick hair! (Straight, thick, *fat* hair . . . that's how it sounded to me. And of course no mention of my cheeks. How could I help it if they weren't like Robert's?) One time when we were about to meet some new and obviously touristy guests, I hurried upstairs to Mother's dressing table and took her hair brush and whacked vigorously with the *bristle* side, first on one cheek and then the other. I felt them glowing as I trotted back downstairs. I don't know that anyone noticed, but *I* knew that I was rosy-cheeked and that helped.

Shopping

From the visits of some of these more worldly female guests, I learned the exquisite boredom of going shopping. Mother was the guide for the tours that focussed on shopping. She took pride in showing the beautiful crafts and handiwork of Hangchow to strangers in the land, and through all her life enjoyed looking for "just the right thing" or happening upon a meaningful treasure—most preferably at a bargain price. (Back in the States, she loved auctions and acquired some worthy Chinese pieces in Westchester County—bargains, needless to say, but to be appreciated by her as by no other possible bidder.)

And so I doubt that she ever understood my lack of enthusiasm when I was taken along on an official shopping tour of the important Hangchow shops—the most prestigious of which were towards the southern end of the Great Street.

"Shopping" didn't apply to what went on when peddlers came to show us their wares. I liked it when the gateman came to Mother to say that someone was out there with dried dates to sell—or walnuts from north China—or fresh persimmons in season . . . or silver trinkets—or embroideries (including mandarin coats and skirts so recently out of style) which when unfolded sent forth a characteristic smell of camphorwood and must. Best of all were the curio peddlers who spread out large squares of dark blue cotton cloth on the grass in the front lawn and set out a marvelous miscellany of small objects—tiny cloisonne vases and boxes, silver and enameled jewelry (including long, curved fingernail protectors), porcelain bowls or tea cups, wooden prayer beads (Buddhist), leather tinder pouches with a metal base and usually (in the pouch) a stone to strike against it to light the dried mossy-looking tinder . . . Some of these fascinating objects had become obsolete; a great deal of it had come from the households of Manchus, now out of power and favor and forced to sell their belongings for income until they could learn how to cope with their present reality.

I liked our family shopping expeditions into the city—usually Mother, Robert, and I—looking for something special. For instance, we might visit a store that sold nothing but paper, where we could buy what was needed for making Halloween decorations (black and orange) and for wrapping Christmas gifts (red and green, some of it figured or embossed like Hangchow silk fabrics).

I also liked going to the new Hangchow Bazaar near West Lake— its connecting two-story buildings enclosing a large, square, unpaved courtyard and offering in its small individual shops every sort of product (except fresh foods) for local use—everything from cookware and cotton bedding and clothing to Hangchow scissors, writing brushes and inks and beautiful (but porous) writing paper, and Hangchow parasols—and little brass pocket knives in cases shaped like squirrels or fishes . . . This is where we came in mid-fall to shop for Christmas gifts to wrap and pack and send to grandparents, aunts and uncles and cousins in America . . . allowing at least six weeks for the parcels to get there.

But to *go along* on a shopping tour with visitors was painful. I was just *there*—uninvolved, invisible, forgotten; and time went on—and on—and on. Would it be forever?

And yet—I must be honest. I was not subjected to the numbing torture of these shopping tours very often, and without them I would have missed some important glimpses into Hangchow life and character.

The Silk Store

There was more of Chinese tradition and significance in the Silk Store than any of the others. (It was also where the ladies spent the longest time looking and deciding and where it seemed to me there would never be an end to the waiting.) It was a serious, almost solemn place. Coming off the Great Street through a heavy double wooden gateway, we stepped over a high threshold into a small stone-paved courtyard enclosed by high walls. To one side was a large, dark building with tiled roof—all very traditional. Inside there was dark wood paneling and a vaulted ceiling with dark exposed wooden beams—the long counter—and the bolts of silks and satins on shelves against the wall.

The look and atmosphere of the Silk Store, I know now, came out of the thousands of years during which the production of silk, from the raising of the silkworm to the spinning and designing and weaving, was held in respect mixed with reverence such as no other craft in China evoked. One of the most precious of Chinese legends is that of the "discovery" of silk (the silkworm and the cocoon) by the Empress Su Ling, wife of the legendary Huang Ti (Yellow Emperor), and from early times, in the spring when the Emperor plowed the first symbolic furrow in behalf of good crops for his people, the Empress blessed the silkworms and later offered sacrifices to the goddess of silkworms.

For Hangchow to have been known for centuries as a major silk-producing center and to have been famous for its own distinctive kinds of silks and brocades was not simply a matter of economic and commercial importance: it added another dimension, deeper and more emotional, to how it was regarded and admired all over China.

It was quiet and dignified in the Silk Store. When a bolt of fabric was taken down to be shown, every motion was practised, measured, and sure—almost ceremonial. Flip—flip—flip on the counter top and the fabric flowed out across its length smooth and wide and shining—colors brilliant or subtle . . . lustrous satins—rich brocades—softer silks with delicate floral or geometric "figures" woven in . . .

I liked it when a decision had been arrived at (partly because I could hope for an end to the waiting) and the fabric was measured out. Then came the cut with an outsize pair of scissors that went *sz–z–z* across the silk—swift, straight and clean. A wonderful sound. The material was folded *just so* and wrapped *just so* in paper with ends folded into corners that were tucked under larger folds to make a neat and elegant package. No string was used or needed.

A visit to the Fan Shop on the Great Street was a more light-hearted experience. Although it was also in the crowded southern area of the city, I always thought of the Fan Shop as being near West Lake, catching reflections from the water as well as light from the sky. The courtyard was sunny; the building was airy and full of light, and the walls of the show-room were plastered white (not paneled in dark wood). On them were hung unmounted fan paintings. In showcases below were fans already on their frames; and there was one showcase with the mountings (handles and spokes) to be chosen by the customer as desired. These were in sandalwood, bone, ivory, tortoise shell, fine dark woods, polished bamboo.

At one side of the room were straight-backed chairs with small square tables in between. Visitors, after being welcomed into the room were invited to "Ch'ing tso"—"Please have a seat," and lidded cups of hot green tea were brought in and served. It was a gracious social occasion—and I was offered a seat (my feet dangling far from the floor) and was served a cup of tea as politely and cordially as anyone.

Hangchow fans—especially the folding fans—were prized all over China. The paintings and calligraphy of many were by famous artists. Some were on gold leaf, others flecked with gold. They pictured birds—flowers—bamboo branches—West Lake scenes. I could look at the fans, handle them, open and close them, sniff at the sandalwood (my favorite)—and the time passed. I couldn't complain of being bored there.

Our Silk Venture

Some of our visitors I remember partly because of their names. One was Mr. Viloudake (pronounced Vill-uh-dock-ie), a middle-aged Greek-American business man from Shanghai with a round face and gentle dark eyes. He stayed with us for a few days in April, and when he said goodbye to us children out in the dewy springtime garden, he presented us with our first candy Easter egg (probably from the Chocolate Shop in Shanghai). It was covered with chocolate and beautifully decorated—and it was *solid* . . . all *candy*. And what's more, when Mother sliced it across the middle and the two halves fell apart, we saw that the inside was just like a real egg (hard-boiled). The yellow center (we discovered when she cut it into smaller slices) was of course the "yolk"; it was orange-flavored. The white may have had a touch of vanilla or almond; it was satisfactorily sweet and candy-like. We had several "treats" from this wonderful egg. How could one ever forget Mr. Viloudake?

Or Mr. Nightingale, whom I remember as the young man who played the piano. Or do I only remember it so, because someone named "Nightingale" surely must be a musician?

There was Miss Olive (sometimes in later years referred to not too kindly as Colossal or Supercolossal), a teacher of singing and choral music in a Shanghai or Soochow middle school. She was an enormous person, though light on her feet—somewhat mannish. She had a trained solo voice; and when she sang for us in our parlor, it was not in the big dark deep voice I had expected but in a heavenly high soprano like an angel's.

I don't remember the name or look of the guest who made a casual remark about our mulberry tree. Perhaps it was someone interested in reforestation in China—something that the YMCAs were interested in promoting. "*We* have a *mulberry* tree?" It was a surprise to us. He pointed at the medium-sized tree standing inconspicuously against the farther wall beyond the front gate. The mulberry trees that we saw out in the country, alongside canals and irrigation ditches were pruned heavily in the off-season so that in winter the shortened branches were gnarled and twisted in a distinctive and recognizable way; and they were well-shaped and full when leafed out. This tree of ours was somewhat formless and unimpressive. But it was healthy enough and was full of leaves—our own mulberry leaves.

Now all we needed was some baby silkworms. They were procured from somewhere or other; and we raised them in our schoolroom in the Flowery Pavilion, feeding them daily on fresh leaves from our mulberry tree. Mother had had Yieneh San and the gardener rig up a sort of trestle table near the entrance to the room where there would be sunlight. The flat basket tray was placed on that. We tried to do everything the way we'd seen it done out in the Hangchow hills, though I'm afraid we forgot to keep as quiet as we should; but the silkworms thrived and grew until it seemed they might be ready to make their cocoons. The gardener constructed the little straw tepees for us to set up on the tray. We wondered if *our* silkworms would climb on them and spin their cocoons about themselves. They *did*.

The final step in our silk producing project was when boiling water was poured over the cocoons in a pail and we watched while Yienh San stirred the water with a long pair of chopsticks and lifted up strands as fine as cobwebs. *Silk*. It was *silk*—and we had helped it come to be. We were all outside in a sunny spot near Mother's flower garden. She had supplied us with empty spools and we tried to wind some of the strands on them but gave it up. We suggested to Amah that *she* do it; she shook her head and explained that the single strands were too fine; they had to be twisted together before they were thread that could be put on a spool and she didn't have time to do that.

Somewhat to our surprise, Yienh San asked Mother if he and the other servants could have the remaining silkworms, now divested of their coverings and thoroughly cooked, for a special snack . . . They didn't look too bad—round and brown and nutlike; but though we children had begged such things from the servants' table as sea snails (to be sucked noisily out of the shell), somehow I didn't care about sampling our little worms that we had raised on leaves from our own mulberry tree.

The River Beyond the City

*O*ur Hangchow world reached out to include the Ch'ien-t'ang River and the College to the south of the city—and Ling Yin Monastery in its secluded valley beyond the Lake.

The Ch'ien-t'ang River itself—even though it was outside the city walls and even though it was not always in sight (as it was for our little friends out at the College) seemed closer to our everyday life—a continuing part of our sense of 'place' . . . of mine, anyway. I was conscious of its being *there*, just as I was aware of West Lake being 'there' when it was beyond actual view.

People have said that Hangchow without West Lake is "unthinkable"; but so is Hangchow without the Ch'ien-t'ang—especially for anyone who knows how much the river has had to do with the shaping of the character of the city, with its history—and at times its very existence.

I didn't know much of this in my childhood. I didn't even know that the name of our province was taken from the early name of the river—the Chê Chiang, which we had anglicized into *Chekiang*. I knew about the famous Hangchow Tidal Bore; and I knew that the *Liu Ho T'a* (Six Harmonies Pagoda) on its bluff above the River on the way to the College, was one of Hangchow's three most famous pagodas; but I *didn't* know about the great local hero, Prince Ch'ien, who in the tenth century had ordered the building of the pagoda in order to control the geomantic influences and protect against the destructive forces of the tides.

I don't remember hearing how the river acquired its 'new' name (in 25 A.D., according to one story)—the *Ch'ien-T'ang* (or *Dzien-Dong* in Hangchow dialect) but always, rather improbably, I thought of the River when we had a certain kind of locally produced malt syrup at breakfast, to use on pancakes or French toast. (For *waffles*, it was Log Cabin syrup ordered from America—a rare treat, poured from the little tin chimney of the little tin house.) The malt syrup was pale amber, not too sweet and very thick. We children could dribble it from a spoon held high and 'write' our initials on the surface of pancake or toast. Did the hot cakes get cold during this exercise? Did the others waiting for the syrup get impatient? I don't know. I was just as interested when my brother was writing his initials as when it was my turn. And all the while I was thinking of the name, dzien-*dong-lo* (syrup) and wondering what connection it had with the Dzien-dong River.

Mostly, however, the name brought to mind the view from the steeply pitched hillsides of the Hangchow College campus . . . with the River, wide and majestic, lying below . . . and, moving slowly and at random, the stately junks with their brown or patched sails—the smaller craft—the rafts of logs floating down from the forests to the southwest . . . all these spaced far apart and never hurrying. From any high place, the River far to the west could be seen to have made an extravagant swing from the south-west—almost like part of the letter Z—before straightening out on its flow eastward to the sea. In later years I heard about the narrow and fantastically wild and beautiful gorges in the mountains of the southwest through which the River made its tumultuous way—and I know now that even stretched out wide on the level plain, it had its storms and turbulence; but I never saw it stormy or turbulent. Even the knowledge of the awesome Bore somehow failed to intrude upon my image of the River in its amplitude and serenity.

The Bore

You'll find the famous Hangchow Bore listed and described in encyclopedias along with other well-known tidal bores. I heard it discussed fairly often in our home—particularly when there were visitors who may have come to Hangchow primarily for a viewing. The first pun I ever invented was a riddle: "When is a bore not a bore?"—which I thought clever and funny, because a great tidal wave rushing inland up a river was certainly not boring!

To my best recollection, I have 'viewed' the Bore three times—and one of those was by accident and not in my early childhood.

There have been explanations and accounts of the Ch'ien-tang River

Bore from ancient legend, through history and in more contemporary records—some of them kept by Western observers of the nineteenth and twentieth centuries.

Put in my own words briefly and I hope, accurately, Hangchow Bay, into which the river empties, is funnel-shaped with the narrow end of the funnel at the mouth of the river. When the Ch'ien-t'ang flows out into the bay through the narrowing opening and meets with an incoming ocean tide, the waters build up into a wave that is forced back inland against the current.

When the tides are especially strong—as on a few days during the spring or autumn equinox—the tidal wave or Bore will reach its greatest height. A storm at sea or a typhoon (not uncommon in September) can raise it even higher. It was at these times that visitors came to Hangchow specifically to see its famous Bore. Eastward along the sea wall between the city and the Bay were stations where onlookers could view the tidal wave as it moved inland. The choicest station was at Hainan some twenty-five miles east of Hangchow. Here is where the Bore could be seen at its highest and most spectacular.

The two expeditions that I remember were not to Hainan—which would have been a long journey in those days, especially for children—but to a nearer station.

The first time, we traveled by sedan chair. Ordinarily, since it was not winter and the weather wasn't really cold, our sedan chairs (hired ahead of time) would have been the open kind, bamboo and wicker. But it was a dark, wet day; and when we climbed into the roofed-over box-like 'chairs' that had come for us, the front panels had to be hooked on against an active drizzle.

I was riding with Mother. I remember the good strong wet oilcloth smell of the front curtain. There was a space at eye level for an adult passenger to look out of. Mother could see where we were going. Sitting by her far below, I felt as if we were being carried along through the air in a small, completely closed-in room—except for slits that opened now and then at the sides of the curtain where I could catch glimpses of walls or shop fronts and of shiny wet cobblestones down below.

I couldn't have been very old that first time we went to see the Bore . . . I remember crowds. I remember my father hoisting me up and perching me on his shoulder so that I could "see" when the Bore came rushing by. I remember wishing after it had passed that it would do it again.

The next time, we were with the Olivers. I remember an early start again but a sunny day . . . and, typically for any outing with the Olivers, a picnic snack after arrival, in a small unadorned rest house at the station where we were to see the Bore. We had the use of a room minimally furnished. It had clean white-washed walls and was bright with sunshine. Our supplies were unpacked from their wicker containers: the thermoses of coffee and cocoa—and hot water for washing our hands. A small enamel basin—washrags, towels. From the picnic basket—crackers, cookies, fruit. (This was a snack, not a meal.) The supplies included a small enamel chamber pot for the convenience of the children—taking turns in some improvised attempt at privacy (circled about by others facing outward— somewhat like the protective wagons on the American westward trail).

Outside in the sunshine on the wide length of paved terrace high above the river were throngs of people waiting. We went out to join them . . . (the only foreigners). The crowd was cheerful and chatty, but not boister- ous. They showed no impatience. Nature follows its own time tables; the tides are not to be hurried.

After a little while there was some calling out and pointing down at the river. Something was going on, and there was a general movement of people towards the balcony at the edge of the sea wall. The crowd pressed close but made way for us children so that we could stand next to the balcony and see what was happening.

A junk and two or three smaller craft had waited too long and were frantically trying to make it to one of the special shelters alongside the river—jetties built out from the sea wall. From far to the east came the faintest muttering sound. The boatmen in the smaller craft were strain- ing at their oars, rowing as hard and fast as possible; while on the junk, figures could be seen scrambling about on the small deck, adjusting the square, patched sails to catch every available breath of wind.

Now we could hear the sound of the approaching Bore distinctly—and growing louder. How far away was it? The smaller boats had reached shelter. The junk—tacking with the wind—seemed not to be getting much closer. Everybody watching from above leaned in sympathy as if to help it move to safety. Everybody cheered when it sailed into its safe mooring.

It was just in time. No one spoke; all heads were turned to listen and watch. The sound increased. It wasn't a watery sound; it wasn't even the roar I'd expected. It was like tons and tons of small rocks and pebbles being tumbled and rolled over and over together.

Now we could see it—first as a line across the river in the distance, moving this way. For some reason I thought that this time (I scarcely remembered it from that other viewing when I was so little) it would be a great glassy wall wearing a curling but never collapsing crest. Instead we saw a turbulent foaming mass stretching across the river and moving rapidly towards us. Here it came and we could see it plain . . . and there it went, not stopping for us to study and admire it. People watched turning their heads to the west until it was out of sight and hearing, then strolled away from where they had been standing—chatted together, commenting and conjecturing on the height: "How high was it?" . . . "About the same as last year?" . . . "—or yesterday?" The consensus seemed to be that, though it didn't rank in the higher brackets, it had been satisfactory and worth coming to see.

I was older now and knew better than to wish it would "do it again," but it still seemed to be over with too soon; and I thought to myself that it had certainly been interesting and it had been exciting to see the boats reach their safe places just in time—and maybe some day I would see the Bore when it towered so high that everyone could say, "There hasn't been one like this since that time a hundred years ago!"

Hangchow College

Going to view the Bore was a rare and memorable occurrence but in a way forgettable. It was not something I thought about very often, though I always felt a twinge of superiority when a grownup foreigner obviously didn't understand what it was and had to have it explained. *I* knew and had seen it. At other times I forgot about it. Going to the College was a different matter.

"The College" began in 1845 as a boys' boarding school in the port city of Ningpo (Chekiang Province). It was founded by American missionaries—Presbyterian. 1844 was the year of the treaty between China and the United States permitting Americans to enter and work in a number of port cities. Actually the missionaries were already there; they hadn't waited—believing that their call to evangelism was more compelling than edicts of government or emperor. There were 18 boys in the original school. Their lodging, board, material needs, medical care—all were provided free of charge—in addition of course to their education. Education in China was still—as it had been for millennia—the study of the Chinese classics. Some of the boys in the school turned out *not* to be students. (Not surprising, considering the courses of study. *Chinese Classics* alone would be formidable!) The non-students were trained in certain trades: tailoring, shoe-making, printing, hospital skills.

The story of what grew out of this earnest, unpretentious little school for boys makes quite an impressive success story in itself. When the details are filled in, it also appears as part of the story of China the nation, from the mid 1800s on when it was forced to deal with the modern world.

The school moved from Ningpo to Hangchow, the provincial capital, in 1867—and from the city out to the campus overlooking the River, in 1911. By then it was a college; it was to be a university by the time of the Japanese war.

When the property for the College was found and purchased, it was (approximately) sixty-seven acres of hilly land, mostly brush and a scattering of abandoned graves and coffins. The land was cleared and leveled as necessary for construction of the first buildings. In one area of the property there was a small bamboo grove. Tea bushes were planted on a sunny plot to be tended by tenant farmers and earn income for the College. A fruit orchard was started in another area for the same purpose, but apparently it didn't do too well. (I don't remember seeing fruit trees anywhere on the place.)

My earliest memories of the College come from when I was a very small child. What I remember from the earliest times are the first three college buildings: Severance Hall (administration-cum-classrooms) and two dormitories—and farther back and high up alongside a very steep path, three foreign faculty residences, occupied by the Mattoxes (assigned to the "Hangchow Boys' School" in 1893), the Marches, and the Wilsons—and, still farther up and to one side, the Observatory—and to the other side, the Reservoir.

I can still see the raw, new look of the campus—the buildings still few and far apart—a lonely open space leveled off for a basketball court— narrow paths. And I remember how steep and hard to climb the pathway was for me; and I remember the students we encountered on our way, in small groups of three or four. Their voices rang out when they were near enough to hail us. They bounded, light as air; their feet seemed not to touch the ground—or just barely.

For the educated young people of Hangchow (not knowing what lay ahead), it was a time of almost giddy optimism and expectations for the future of their country, China—which, because it had become captive of its past, had been subjected to shame and humiliation and held in contempt by the rest of the world. But now the Manchus—and the old imperial system of government—had been overthrown. The old ways were obsolete . . . And breaking away into new ways was heady business.

My father used to say that these years in China—Hangchow, at least— were like the eye of a typhoon, that deceptive interval of sunshine and calm in a spot surrounded by violence and fury. A ship could pass from the battering of winds and waves into this haven of peace but it was not for long: wherever the ship might go—or even if it tried to stay—it would once more be enveloped in the storm.

The building continued. The children who lived at the College always had a building project where they could go and stand and watch and check on how it was all progressing, and they often took us to a particularly active construction site. I remember seeing the Chapel at about the halfway stage. It was being built of stone (not brick like the others); there were discussions as to what it was to be called. I also remember seeing the Science Building when it was going up. It was fascinating, because it would have *modern laboratories* where all kinds of mysterious and exciting *experiments* would be performed.

From that earliest time, I remember a Thanksgiving Day which the Hangchow Americans had decided to celebrate together out at the College.

It was gray and overcast—a typical November day. We children were still too young to roam and so we watched with the mothers and the other ladies while the men played an unusual game of basketball. They had a referee and there were the two teams, but the players were wearing dresses over their regular clothes—also their wives' wide-brimmed hats.

213

It must have been hilarious for the ladies, seeing the gentlemen leaping about awkwardly in skirts and holding on to feathered, flowered, and fruited hats that were about to fly off. Mr. Van Evera, who was somewhat shorter than Mrs. Van, was continually tripping up on her long skirts and drew much attention. I worried a bit about his falling down and about her dress being ruined and I wondered (as I sometimes did) about the grownups—the men choosing to play basketball in this ridiculous way and the ladies apparently finding it so funny.

The communal Thanksgiving dinner was held in one of the still-few college buildings—in a large plain room with tables fitted together down the center and plain wooden classroom chairs alongside. (I can't remember about us children—were we perched on books?)

Perhaps I was getting tired by then—but I can't recall anything exciting about the food or festive about the occasion. In my memory it is—not *depressing* but gray and almost spartan, like the November weather outside.

A Train Ride

Sometime after the College had moved outside the city, a little spur railroad line which had ended at the River at the traditional ferry crossing, was extended to Zakow—only about a mile from the campus.

The excitement of going to the College began for us in anticipation during our rickshaw rides to the Hangchow Railway Station to catch the train for Zakow.

Any kind of motorized vehicle seemed like a work of magic to me. We had few chances to experience the wonder of the magic—not in Hangchow. In Shanghai, where we went every couple of years or so (to catch up on such matters as going to the dentist), we saw motor cars and street cars ("trams") and probably had a chance to ride them—though rickshaws or horse-drawn carriages were still preferred for getting around. We always had a chance to travel in the fascinating little cage—the elevator or "lift"— that went up and down between the floors of a British department store like *Whiteaway Laidlaw.*

But best of all was the train trip—five hours between Hangchow and Shanghai—to be anticipated with eager impatience, enjoyed throughout the journey, and remembered with relish. I wonder now why we didn't become bored or fretful. If we did, I don't remember it. We were fully involved all the way—with the rhythmic clickety-clack of the wheels, the horizon swinging slowly around in the far distance as we sped through the landscape, the changing sights—rice paddies and water buffalo, irrigation canals and water wheels, turned by a pedaling farmer or a blindfolded donkey going round and round—fruit trees on gentle hillsides and bamboo groves in valleys—clusters of farm huts—children waving to us from pathways along the railroad tracks. The busyness at the station platforms where the train made its stops—the hullabaloo of passengers piling off or crowding on, all with their baskets and bundles and assorted paraphernalia—the milling about on the platform in excited confusion and food vendors pushing their way through and calling out the local specialties for sale. There was a wonderful candy we always acquired at Kashing (halfway between Hangchow and Shanghai) to add to the edibles brought with us: for us as for our fellow passengers, the trip was a perpetual picnic or series of picnics ....The most wonderful part of it all, though, was the feeling of motion and power as we were carried along—and the sound of the whistle from the engine ahead—and sometimes catching sight of it as it rounded a slow curve with a dark cloud streaming out behind from the smokestack.

Going to Zakow was different. The Hangchow Railway Station was quiet: it was between the scheduled stops of the mainline trains (of the Shanghai-Hangchow-Ningpo Railway). We had the platform almost to ourselves and would have a clear view of the giant engine as it approached to where we stood waiting. We heard the hooting of the whistle and then the increasing roar and rhythmic rumble of wheels on tracks; we heard the slowing of the rhythm and the grinding of brakes as the engine appeared and came close to where we were standing. We could see the pistons that drove the huge wheels moving more and more slowly and coming to a halt. There was a sudden prolonged hiss of white steam and we jumped back out of its way.

There were two passenger cars—second class and fourth class. We rode fourth class to save money. The ride to Zakow—with two stops on the way—took half an hour. (Going to Shanghai we enjoyed greater comfort and traveled second class.) The fourth class car—which we had almost to ourselves—had an aisle down the center and on either side beneath the windows a continuous hardwood bench—no cushions, no matting—just wood polished smooth by use.

We immediately chose the farther side, which we believed afforded the more interesting view, and sat down waiting for the train to move—with the accompanying sounds of whistle, steam, clanging of metal and a few violent jerks.

As soon as it was properly on its way, we climbed to our knees to look out the window. We saw the breach in the old city wall as we passed through it and then we were out of the city.

It was mostly a kind of nondescript scene—of stubbly unused fields, untidy with a scattering of litter, that rose farther out into mounds and low brushy hills.

These were not without interest. One regularly shaped hill or mound was pointed out to us as "where our ice comes from"—which made it extremely important to us, since our ice was what made possible our favorite dessert and party treat, ice-cream made in a hand-cranked freezer. The ice was bought and brought to the house wrapped in burlap and then (bits of straw and pebbles and all) packed in layers, interspersed with large amounts of coarse salt, around the canister. It was intriguing to think of our ice coming from out of a hollow place in that mound—and to imagine it being collected from rarely-frozen canals in winter to be stored away in a dark cave for use through the year—even in the most sweltering summertime . . . Actually—as I've since learned—the ice was gathered every winter from up north and floated down in barges by canal—wrapped in straw for insulation and stored away in the recesses of the hill. Also—this was not done to please us foreigners and satisfy our love of ice-cream but had been practised for centuries. In the Sung period, there were at least two famous shops that specialized in iced delicacies. Perhaps Marco Polo himself when he was in Hangchow in the late 1200s passed by this very place or was refreshed by a beverage chilled by ice that had been stored here.

Past the ice storage mound were other low brushy or bare risings. Mounted on the slopes of several of these were enormous billboards (a novel sight for us) advertising cigarettes—produced in China under the tutelage of the B.A.T., British American Tobacco Company (its company compound was outside the city wall nearby). For Hatamen cigarettes, there was an impressive depiction of a massive gate and portion of wall (representing a well-known landmark up north in the city of Peking) with the name HATAMEN in large English lettering (horizontal) and also in large Chinese characters (vertical). Ruby Queen Cigarettes presented—against a pink background—the somewhat stylized picture (head and shoulders) of a young woman of modern China, holding aloft a lighted cigarette, white smoke rising from the farther end . . . Smoking cigarettes apparently was never a male prerogative in China.

The train chugged along, making two brief stops, and then we were at Zakow Station . . . "*Already?*" we exclaimed, though our knees were already sore.

The Standard Oil Company had its compound for foreign personnel close to Zakow. (Alice Tisdale Hobart, the wife of one of the staff, authored the novel "Oil for the Lamps of China"; and her sister, Mary Nourse, who came to visit and was a teacher in China for a number of years, later wrote an excellent brief history of China, "The Four Hundred Million.") Sometimes we were treated to a ride in the Standard Oil motor launch from its mooring near Zakow to a dock below the College campus.

In the small waiting room, before boarding the launch, we had another unaccustomed treat—also courtesy of Standard Oil: each of us was offered a bottle of American soda pop taken out of wooden crates standing on the floor against a wall. There were two choices—lemon soda pop and sarsaparilla (pronounced *sass*parilla). The fascination of seeing the burst of fizz when the bottle cap was pried off!—the taste and the tingle!—the bubbles up the nose! Someone referred to a marvelous-sounding concoction—*ice-cream soda*—which some day we would experience; for now, this was enough.

We clambered down into the launch. It was small and bobbly. We could see the engineer-pilot tugging at the starter—hear the motor sputter and catch and roar—and off we sped, close to the water, feeling the spray, smelling the good smell of gasoline mixed with wetness . . . The American child of that era in Hangchow could never forget in adulthood that exciting voyage in the Standard Oil Company launch.

The usual way, however, to go to the College from Zakow was on foot. The roadway wound along with the river below it on one side and steep bluffs above it on the other. On one of these bluffs, part way up, was the famous Liu Ho T'a (Six Harmonies Pagoda), which we could see from the roadway—except that in those earliest years it was covered over with

217

bamboo scaffolding while undergoing repairs and renovation (a procedure that had taken place in various ways—even to complete rebuilding ,
down through the centuries of the pagoda's existence) . . . When the scaffolding came down later, it was a pleasure to see the pagoda, calm and
dignified, above us—overlooking the wide sweep of the Ch'ien-t'ang River.

Soon we came to a small stream flowing from the hills down into the
river; and just after that, we left the roadway for a narrow steep pathway.
We were at the College.

Explorations

It is impossible to untangle my recollections of all the different days
spent at the College or to fit them into a reliable chronology.

What was always the same for us city children was all that wonderful
natural space to roam—the paths to explore, the steep hills to climb—the
openness and heady sense of freedom . . . and always the river flowing
below, wide and serene.

As in our visits to the T'ienh Sway Gyao compound, we children were
given the hours to spend as we liked—only *there* it was in the constriction
of a city neighborhood and here it was in the world of nature, seemingly
boundless.

Our special comrades at the College were Elizabeth and Nancy Wilson, daughters of "Uncle Morrie" and "Aunt Martha" (who had come to
China soon after our parents and were among their closest and most
congenial friends)—and Bobby and Paul March, sons of Professor and
Mrs. Arthur March.

There were younger children in both families (Jimmy Wilson, who
was DeWitt's age—and Sherman and Amy March), and there were (from
late 1919 on) the children, Edward and Betty, of the Clarance Days; but
age and its prerogatives were finely defined and seem to have been terribly important as to who our childhood companions were. Perhaps the
younger ones joined us at least sometimes on our wanderings, but it was
Elizabeth and Nancy and Bobby and Paul whom I remember as our co-
adventurers at the College. More precisely, they were our leaders. Anywhere else, Robert as the eldest (Bobby March was next and I was after
him) would have taken the lead. Not here, where the outdoor experience
and self-reliance of the College kids took precedence over age-differ-

ences. We who were from the city admired their knowledge of the terrain and where all the little paths led to in their windings. We were particularly impressed by their leg muscles, hard as rocks, acquired from daily climbing of steep hillsides. We compared them enviously with our own. (At least our arm muscles were just as good—maybe lumpier and better because of our tennis practise and Robert's hours of sports at the Y.)

What varied in our visits to the College was partly in how we spent those hours of freedom; but, more than that it was the College itself—the campus as it developed and as buildings and athletic facilities and plantings were added—and, in a more subtle way, the students and the current mood.

Probably when we city children spent the day, the College children were advised not to take us too far afield. (I wonder if their parents knew how far afield they sometimes went.) But we were regaled with accounts of interesting events—such as the discovery of a cobra (eight . . . ten . . . twelve feet long?) up at the Reservoir—another in a laboratory of the Science building—and still another (later) in the servants' quarters of the Wilsons' new home . . .

Our rovings could take us many places. We trekked sometimes to the tea farm and played hide-and-seek. The tea bushes were large and dense and fairly close together—ideal for dodging from one to another and being fully hidden from the sight of whoever was "It."

One day we were led to the bamboo grove where a sapling, sturdy but still flexible, leaned over a shallow ditch. We took turns: one of us caught hold of the top end of the sapling, pulled down and held by the others and then let go so that the tree sprang up, carrying its rider skyward in an exhilarating swoop.

Severance Hall was a kind of center where we could stop for a bit to look at the River and feel the breeze before deciding where to go next. The view was wonderful. The area in front of the building had been terraced and landscaped. We used to roll down the steep, grassy slopes to the lowest level and sit up with heads reeling and the sky and earth and river slowly revolving about in a delightful way.

Our most serious adventure was in a part of the campus not too far from here, where a very large and venerable tree stood by itself. We were passing by and admiring it, when Nancy Wilson—the most daring and agile of our small troop of rovers—proposed to climb it. We stood below and watched intently as she pulled herself higher and higher. We should have warned her to stop; more probably we cheered her on. Close to the top where the tree was thinning out, the branch supporting her snapped with her weight and down she plummeted. We stared in horror, holding our breaths and expecting to hear the thud when her small body struck the solid earth. But at the very last instant we saw her arms reaching and her hands catch and hold onto the lowest branch. She hung there briefly before dropping the rest of the way to the ground, landing safely on her feet. None of us said much, but Nancy was a heroine ever after.

In the busier parts of the campus, we saw the students on their way to and from classrooms. Sports facilities were being developed; and we could watch the young men engaged in basketball, track, and other athletic games and activity imported from the West.

One noontime when we had been wandering and probably beginning to feel the pangs of hunger, we met with a large group of students coming up the pathway from the college dining hall (in one of the dormitories). They were joyfully singing—in English—at the tops of their voices:

"There is a boarding house not far away
Where they have scrambled eggs—three times a day.
Oh, how the boys do yell
When they hear the dinner bell!
Oh how the eggs do smell
Three times a day!"

And oh, how the 'boys' enjoyed singing this rude and happy little song!—in their newly-mastered English, in which certain consonants were pronounced in the local dialect. The Western 'l's and 'r's were difficult to manage and often were somehow reversed, so that the rhyming in this song came out in a quaint fashion:
"Oh, how the boys do *yehr*
When they hea(h) the dinnuh *behr* . . ." (and so on)
It wouldn't have taken a great detective to deduce that the students had learned this American college ditty from Aunt Martha Wilson (mother of Elizabeth and Nancy and little Jimmy) who taught classes in both English and Music and obviously couldn't resist sharing this probably all-too-accu-

rate song—and perhaps others—with her appreciative students.

Later Times

We continued our visits (at least one a year) after we had moved to Shanghai—and the scenes and adventures of those times are mingled with those recalled from earlier on . . . Some are easy for me to recognize as being from teenage visits or even later, when I was back in China after college.

We learned to roller skate on the family furlough in America,1923-24. When we were back in China, we were advised to bring our skates with us on our springtime visit to Hangchow. Our College friends—now old enough to go beyond the campus grounds—had discovered an ideal place to roller skate. And so, when we were out at the College this time, we trooped down to the River road carrying our skates and making sure that *someone* had a skate key. We walked alongside the river a little way, and then climbed the path up the bluff to the Six Harmonies Pagoda. No one else was there except for two or three grey-robed priests who came from the attendant temple to see who we were and stayed to watch.

The ample-proportioned octagonal pagoda rose from a wide, stone-paved base, edged by a low balustrade all around. The paving stones were large and almost satiny smooth and fitted together very nearly perfectly—a wonderful surface for skating. We swooped—we flew—we pivoted and twirled. The priests stood by at an unobtrusive distance, smiling indulgently—and, I think, in enjoyment.

Strolling back along the river, we saw below us a large, heavy wooden barge beginning to unload its cargo of water buffalo. We stopped to watch. The barge rocked with the shifting weight of the reluctant animals as one by one they were shouted at and prodded and pushed over the side to splash into the shallow water and stagger to firm ground. The operation had just been successfully completed when I caught sight of something curious farther east on the river . . . a thin, wavering but continuous line—perhaps a few inches high (it was hard to tell at the distance) stretched clear across the river from shore to far-off shore and hurrying along in our direction. A smooth, strange little wave or wavelet—modest and non-threatening but determined.

"Oh look!" I called out in excitement.

"Oh yes—that's the Bore," Lib explained, kindly and without conde-

221

scension for my ignorance.

"But it's just a *baby*!" I said (or thought) in wonder.

Lib added matter-of-factly, "It comes by every day" . . . as of course it would, according to the tides. And to think it could be seen here every day by anyone who knew just when to look.

This was my third viewing of the famous Hangchow Bore.

Somehow here, far away from the Bay and the China Sea—overlooked by the old Pagoda which had been built to tame the tides, and by the College looking into a new and unknown future—the baby Bore seemed more mysterious and evocative of wonder than the turbulences I had seen before. In my recollection, it is my favorite viewing.

I remember being at the College when anti-foreign feeling was running high and the mood was tense and strained—and I would wonder which of the sober-faced students we saw on the campus might be "Communist infiltraters" said to be working underground to spread poison against the foreigners in China, the "running dogs of imperialism"—particularly the Christians . . . .There was one Easter season when the group of vacationers from the Shanghai American School were staying with friends in the city and rented bicycles for our day at the College. Riding through a small country village, we were set upon by barking, snarling dogs while the villagers (friendly in the past) stood silent in their doorways stony-faced and grim.

And then there was another, later time when it was all very different. The College had become coeducational—and at springtime romance was in the air. The Pagoda was a favorite trysting place . . . It was possible now to climb the steep spiral stone stair-way in the pagoda up to levels where there were openings from which the River could be viewed in all its grandeur. It was shadowy inside with only the light that came from the openings—barely enough to show niches in the inner walls in which ancient Buddhist images could be seen dimly. On the walls also, both inside and out, were much more recent graffiti—such as names linked by the romancing couples from the College in Chinese characters or their adopted Western names (*John Lee* and *Celia Wang*). Or there might be a few lines of prose or poetry in either language. I found a verse that I liked so much (this was in an after-college-in-America visit) that I copied it down from memory as soon as I had something to write on:

The River Beyond the City

"The tower stands highly on the hill
The Chientang river stretch surrounding
The scene is beauty and serene
It makes my heart to sweet and glee"

My heart was often made to "sweet and glee" by the viewing of the River, whether from the "tower" (the Pagoda) or from any of the heights at the College or near by. I remember climbing the path above the faculty homes one year when the wild azaleas were in bloom in lavish profusion, making the hillsides glow rose-pink. Seen closer to, after a recent springtime shower, the flowers were fresh—almost translucent as if they shone from within. I climbed higher and higher the rounded risings that were said to be the undulating back of a sleeping dragon. The air was clear and sweet. Down below the whole panorama spread far and wide—of plains reaching to distant horizons, of hills to the west and southwest and the river appearing from out of the hills in an arc and proceeding straight and free and untroubled through the landscape towards the Bay . . . I picked a great armload of azaleas to take down with me and no one could have seen the slightest difference where I had gathered.

The Year and Its Seasons

In those days of childhood, time was very nearly timeless. This is probably true in any early childhood but was more so for us I think, because we had no electronic reminders like radio and television counting off days and hours before this or that event or program. We didn't even have a permanently-fixed clock against which to check our activities. My father had a beautiful gold watch on a fob by which to pull it out of the watch pocket at his waist. Mother's beautiful little gold watch was (like his) on a black grosgrain ribbon; it was pinned to the shoulder of her dress or blouse. If and when these time-pieces were consulted, it was done gently and without anxiety or any "Hurry! Hurry! Hurry! . . . We're late!" Our only clock was a Westclox Big Ben (with alarm), which moved about from an upstairs bedroom down (usually) to the kitchen—not where *we* could keep glancing . . . Our days were orderly, but did not seem to be arbitrarily separated into blocks of time for us to fit into; they seemed simply to flow.

As for those large swatches of time—the *seasons* . . . although they were predicted and talked about, each was a surprise when it came, and then seemed permanent. Summer—usually spent up at Mokanshan, the mountain resort for missionary and other 'foreign' families in this region—was (we hoped) eternal; winter, with its chill creeping into our bones and lodging there, was forever; spring and fall were seasons in motion but not too swift to seem at their height the endless reality.

In our household, every season (even at its worst) was a matter of wonder; at its best each was relished and celebrated. The natural world in its changes had an excitement that my parents had not known growing up in Florida where there was little differentiation during the year. My father noted and commented on each seasonal change with interest and enthusiasm and cheerfully made the necessary adjustments. And Mother had songs for every time of year; we sang in salute to the burgeoning of spring, the opulence of summer, the color and fruitfulness of autumn, the cold of winter. There were songs, also, honoring seasonal occasions and remembrances and religious observances, but more of our singing had to do with flowers, creatures, autumn leaves, sun and rain—wind—snowflakes.

All of these were a part of reality for us; we were actually very close to nature living there so near lake and hills and rice paddies and at the edge of a city which, though populous and crowded and long settled, was always conscious of its affinity with nature. And we, in our flimsily built house, were barely protected from the outdoors; but by the same token we were privileged to hear the sounds of nature: roosters crowing at dawn, orioles singing in the garden of a wealthy Chinese neighbor, cats yowling on our enclosing high walls, stray dogs barking in nearby alleys. We smelled spring-time in the flower scents and the powerful, biting odor of earth freshly turned over with ripened human manure in the fields not too far away (a wonderful smell like trumpet sounds heralding a new beginning of life and growing). We smelled fall in crisp air scented with woodsmoke from burning brush on the hillsides. In summer, when we were still in the city, there was the stench of human waste and rotting debris—and also, at the right time and place, the intoxicating fragrance, blown from the Lake, of lotus flowers in full bloom. In winter, sounds and smells were more of human origin. We were mostly aware of the penetrating cold, sometimes more palpable in the house than outdoors. One of the stories about early missionary days in Hangchow is how, in the dead of winter, Mrs. John Stuart would welcome her bundled-up, shivering visitors on the open front porch of the Stuart home in the mission compound and say, "Let's sit out here and visit where it's warm." (Warmer than inside.)

All year round, in our comings and goings and our walks and our larger excursions—as well as in our not-very-comfortable home—we knew ourselves as part of the natural world and its seasons. And woven into this experience were the festivals and celebrations called for by lunar and Western calendar—by the customs and traditions and religious beliefs of China and those brought here from the other side of the world. The timeless progression of time in early childhood was amazingly full of riches.

225

Winter

Christmas was the pinnacle. It was the season, the celebration—the Day towards which the rest of the year moved, beginning again not *quite* on the day after December 25th, but early in the new year—perhaps when an itinerant peddler stopped by with curios and knickknacks from which Mother might acquire the first of a store of presents for the folks back home *next* Christmas . . . In the spring was the arrival of the new Montgomery Ward catalog ("Monkey Ward" in missionary parlance and much studied by wives and mothers)—with its reminders and suggestions of what we children might want and even *get* for Christmas. In the fall, there was shopping in the Hangchow Bazaar near West Lake for more gifts—all locally made—to send to America—and then the wrapping and the packing and the mailing at least six weeks ahead. Our own celebrations began just after Thanksgiving with singing Christmas songs and continued from then on in all the traditional 'back-home' ways plus some that we borrowed and shared with our Hangchow British friends— some that we adapted to our Chinese friends (in church or otherwise) and some that were invented or simply sprang up of themselves because of where we were. As for the weather—although Thanksgiving Day was often cold and bleak, Christmas Day (in my memory) was clement and benign.

Chinese New Year's Day—weeks later—was a great celebration—setting off a succession of other special celebrations, all of which were part of the Season. They were ours in a once-removed way—not wholly and utterly ours as was Christmas. We participated in much of the festivity that took over daily life at this season and enjoyed the scene and the spirit, but we were only at the edge—lookers-on. *We* had Christmas; the children of Hangchow had Chinese New Year. I hoped it evened out, although in my heart I believed we had the better of it.

The festive season that followed Chinese New Year's Day traditionally lasted six weeks. A long time for celebration! And yet our preparations and occasions leading up to Christmas Day were nearly as long and eventful.

Chinese New Year's Day marked the end of one lunar year and the beginning of another. It also was a promise that the weather would ease— that the penetrating chill and damp of the season of the Big Cold would be over—not immediately, but soon.

One February, the first day of the new Lunar Year coincided with a joint family birthday—my father's and mine. We stood out in the front yard, marveling at the sunshine—still pale but almost comforting; and I felt as proud as if I'd helped in bringing about the conquering of the Great Cold.

No more flannel nightcaps to cover our ears. No more flannel pajamas with 'feet' to keep us warm in our unheated high-ceilinged room at night. No more glazed pottery hot water bottle that lost its warmth long before morning and might come uncorked or spring a leak so that sheets down at the foot of the bed were wet and more miserably cold than anything ever should be. (Mother and Amah to the rescue. It must have been an ordeal for them.) No more dressing in the morning huddled against the 'drum' that was faintly warm from hot air rising from the pot-bellied coal stove in the dining room below. No more tugging on long-legged union suits and, over them, thick cotton stockings—two pairs sometimes—then struggling with button-up shoes, before hurrying out into a frigid hall-way and downstairs into one of the three rooms that had been partitioned off from each other. A portable kerosene stove was in the parlor if we were to be there. There was always, in the daytime, the stove in the dining room—red hot when fresh coals were added and fanned—which made the room *look* warmer. . . . But nowhere was Hangchow a Heaven Below during those interminable weeks.

But even then there were wonders. When it snowed, the air seemed to be softer and gentler—and the world was transformed. The beauty of the Lake, with its causeways and bridges—and of its hills with their temples and pagodas, was outlined and accented by the fall of snow. Artists through the centuries had loved to paint West Lake after a snowfall. In the city, grubbiness was covered over; snow lay lightly on the tops of high walls and on the curving rooftiles and upturned roof corners of low-lying close-together buildings. The sounds of the city were muffled; there was a kind of hush and sense of peace.

One late afternoon when, to our delight, it had snowed through much of the day and we were bundled up outdoors rolling up snow to make a snowman, our father came home and hailed us with his "I-have-a-sur-prise-for-you!" look and voice.

"Come on, everybody! We're going to take a walk." By this time, it was already dusk and rapidly growing darker. To be going out like this when it was almost night time was exciting in itself.

To this day I can't figure out exactly where we went, though it couldn't have been far. Everything looked different and unfamiliar. I know that somewhere after walking out of our alley, we turned back into the narrow, cobbled streets of the real city (Chinese, not modernized 'Manchu').

Almost immediately, we caught sight of a figure made of snow alongside the street—and another and then another in varying sizes, at random on either side. They were not snow *men* like ours, but replicas of figures in temples or monasteries. ("Snow buddhas," I named them—maybe only to myself.) They looked either serene or stern on their snow pedestals. On the ledges of several were lighted red candles in a row. The head of one figure reached all the way up to the eaves of the one-story building below which he was seated—a Buddha, massive and calm—the candles flickering light and shadows on his face.

The most wonderful sight of all, that evening, was the little snow pagoda which we saw, both when we set out on our expedition and on our way back. It might have been in our own alleyway. It was perhaps five feet high—symmetrical and graceful and perfect, with its tiers of little up-curved roofs encircling it (an odd number, I'm sure, as was proper for pagodas). The most wonderful thing about it was that it was partially hollowed out and a candle placed inside at every level. The candles were lit so that the pagoda shone from within—radiant in the darkness. It was magic.

Festival Season

The first day of the Lunar year, the day that we called *China* (not 'Chinese') New Year, was the only time when we had our little compound entirely to ourselves—that is, to family and house guests, if any. All the servants, (even Amah), dressed in their best, left for the day; and it seemed lonely—not natural—and I secretly wondered how we would cope with the necessities of everyday life—like meals, for instance.

The day passed and normal life was resumed, though the holiday mood continued, with more dressing up and comings and goings and visiting and socializing. And out in the city the pace was leisurely and the look of the streets was different, with families walking together to pay calls on other families—stopping to gather near street entertainers: story tellers, puppet shows, traveling animal acts, acrobats.

Like other Hangchow householders, we had our own private entertainments when one or another of the small troupes appearing at the gate was invited in to present a show in our front yard. I liked the monkey show. I liked it when the monkey scampered confidently to each one of us holding out a cup for copper coins. Sometimes there was a goat that trotted around in a circle with the monkey on its back. I was troubled, on occasion, however, when the monkey in the visiting troupe came down from having perched on a high pole and showed a red bottom. Poor thing! I didn't know that this kind of monkey was naturally that way. I was relieved when someone thought to explain it to me, but was never quite sure and I always enjoyed the show more completely when the monkey was not one I had to worry about.

The puppet shows were the best. 'Chinese Punch and Judy' we called them; and even though the characters did not include a 'Punch' or a 'Judy' and some of the sound effects were different (squeaky voices spoken through a bamboo reed and the clanging of tiny brass cymbals), the plots were understandable and the slapstick universal. There was always a fight, with the hero and villain whacking each other loudly on their wooden heads. The most suspenseful episode was when one of the characters was attacked and devoured—almost—by a tiger . . . and then just before disappearing completely, was rescued by the hero after much hauling and tugging.

We were visited also at this season by vendors selling special toys—whirligigs and others whose names I don't know, made of bamboo and string and paper. Some of these toys appeared only at this time of year; some required a large measure of dexterity: we had to learn how and practise.

About two weeks into the new Lunar Year was the Lantern Festival; and this gave us another night-time outing—a family walk to the Great Street to see the Lantern Parade. Lanterns of all sizes and shapes were carried single-file the length of the Great Street for people to see and admire. Many were elaborately designed and decorated, but the rabbit lanterns, made of bamboo and paper, pleased me the most. There were quite a few of these—in different sizes and some pulled along the street on little wooden wheels. After all, this was the festival to celebrate the moon and the immortal rabbit in the moon.

The New Year was fire cracker time—especially in the first festive days and nights of the season. We heard the crackling and the popping and the booming and smelled that sulfurous pungence of the smoke. Like everyone else, we had our own variety show of sound and light, from double-blasters on the ground and rockets exploding in the air to strings of little poppers . . . and the biggest (and most expensive) of all which were also propped upright on the ground and made no sound at all, but sent up fountains of lights that showered down again like falling stars or incandescent flower petals . . . and our own hand-held sparklers, which waved about in the darkness as we pranced around the front yard or tried to make letters or designs in the air.

Fire

Every China New Year season, fires were started by the festive fire-crackers.

One night, word came of a fire raging out of control in a crowded slum section of the city, spreading rapidly through narrow streets of flimsy, one-story wooden structures—devouring them—trapping people.

From the balcony of the upstairs porch, we could see a huge ugly glow in the sky over a distant part of the city and we could hear the eerie sound of a thin, continuing wail—cries of pain and panic fused together at this distance. Someone—a YMCA colleague of my father's—was let in at our gate and came to join us at the balcony. I looked to see if he and my father were going to go and *do* something—help rescue people caught in the fire. But they stood there quietly talking—and planning how to organize and deliver relief to the homeless and hurt which we would begin to hear about the next day.

When we had our own fire the following year—to the envy of our young Hangchow missionary friends—it was also in the holiday season. Our servants had all gone visiting for the evening and the cook's wife had left the charcoal-filled iron still hot on a table next to an inner wall of a room in the servants' quarters building, which was attached by a roofed-over walk to the main building . . . The wall caught fire. My parents, already asleep on the eastern side of the upstairs porch, were awakened by the excited cries of the neighbors which seemed to be directed towards the rear of our big house. Hurrying to look out a window at the back, they saw flames leaping through the roof of the servants' quarters. My father and my Uncle Henry (a holiday visitor), joined by Yienh San (just returned from his outing) and then by our gateman-gardener, formed a bucket brigade, hauling water from the well in the back yard and passing the bucket to be emptied on the blazing roof. I have a vague recollection of Yienh San tossing the water from the top of a ladder propped against the outer wall of the two-story building.

After the fire was put out, there was a clamor at the front gate, and in came the newly-inaugurated city fire brigade in their uniforms and helmets. They were drawing along with them a flat, open vehicle on which was coiled a large hose. Probably there was some device to pump water from well or handy canal. Without a city water supply and hydrants, the Hangchow Fire Department was limited in its ability to serve.

From the upstairs porch balcony, I watched a long palaver between my father and the chief of the Brigade. The next morning at breakfast, my father reported that he was being asked to respond to a lengthy list of questions, obviously for the official records and mostly having to do with such data as my father's age and where he was born—*his* father's age and birthplace—and his father's father's . . . and other such bits of information seemingly having no bearing on the events of our fire.

But perhaps this kind of record-taking was relevant and important in former times. Marco Polo in his account of how the city was organized in the 13th century wrote about the strategically situated guardhouses and what happened when there was a fire: "As soon as the guards see that a fire has broken out in some house, they give warning of it by beating the drum, and the guards from other bridges (each with its own guardhouse) come running to extinguish it and rescue the goods of the merchant or whoever it may be by storing them in the towers of which I have spoken or by loading them on barges and taking them out to islands in the lake . . ."*There was a ready supply of firefighters in a city said to have 12,000 bridges and plenty of water on hand. It was necessary to keep records of property that had

---

* From *The Travels of Marco Polo : New Translation* by R.E. Lathan. 1958 Penguin Books, Inc. [p.192]

been saved and of family members who would reclaim it.

Our New Year fire was not only a triumphant show-and-tell story for us to share with our little friends when they came for Sunday School the following Sunday; it became a favorite family story—the punch line being that at the successful extinguishing of the fire, my father realized that he and his sensitive and dignified younger brother and poet, Henry, were in their pajamas (no bathrobes) and were *barefooted* . . . and the next morning, a few hours later, my father had to break the ice in the ten-gallon tin can before up-turning it for his morning shower. (There was also a supposedly amusing postscript about how eight-year-old daughter was found, at the end of all the excitement, curled up in a chair in an upstairs bedroom reading "Under the Lilacs" by Louisa May Alcott—which I've always thought was a sensible thing to do after I'd had a terrifying look at the blazing servants quarters building and knew that there wasn't anything I could do about it except not to panic or pester. I've never understood what was funny about it.)

Spring and the Pilgrim Season

Springtime brought pilgrims, holiday-seeking tourists, lovers of nature and romance—and beggars.

The beggars were the horror of my childhood—and were the stuff of my worst nightmares—much worse than the one about fire, which I still remember.

In my nightmare about fire, Hangchow was burning up and we were fleeing to Shanghai for refuge. As we stood together on a hillside, looking back sadly at the city which was totally ablaze and which (in my dream) I knew we would never see again, a messenger came running. "No use going to Shanghai!" he told us. "Shanghai is on fire! The whole world is on fire." Somehow, with Hangchow gone it didn't matter. This dream had no pain and no real terror—only sadness.

The most dreadful of my beggar nightmares began with the sound of dogs barking (a common enough sound) and a voice intoning the beginning of a familiar Mother Goose rhyme: "Hark! Hark! The dogs do bark . . . Beggars are coming to town"—and in my dream I saw them coming down from the nearby hills and approaching the city in an endless line. They were all dressed alike in faded gray, nondescript garments. They

232

were crippled, all of them on the same side so that they limped in a horrid kind of unison; and as they came closer I knew that they were all blind. They were on Law Court Street now—never pausing—inexorable, and we were hurrying in that slow motion way of nightmares toward the Wu San Church, where we could find safety behind its iron gate.

What was the terror? Not of violence from those creatures. Was it of being taken over and becoming one of them—no longer ourselves—no longer being fully human?

The beggars we saw on the street throughout the year were pitiful and hard to look at, but they were individuals—real persons. It helped somehow to know that some of them were not impoverished and that in many cases the disabilities were cleverly faked. We could recall how Miss Boardman, that fastidious, tender-hearted stalwart little lady from Virginia, caught sight one day of a beggar groaning in pain by the roadside—a horribly suppurating sore on his leg. She got out of her rickshaw and insisted that the poor fellow (protesting loudly but in vain) get in. She walked him in the rickshaw to the nearest mission hospital clinic, where the sore was washed away, leaving a clear and healthy leg and a greatly embarrassed beggar.

I saw the so-called King of the Hangchow Beggars once when he was on one of his ceremonial journeys down the length of the Great Street—everybody standing politely at the side, giving him the right of way. His legs were gone from below the knees, and he was kneeling on a small board and pushing himself forward on the center paving. Each time he pushed ahead, he struck his head on the paving stone just in front of him; and, since he had what looked like a flat bamboo plaque bound to his forehead, the sound was sharp and shocking. Everyone looked on, silent and impressed, as he continued on his way . . . It was common knowledge that, as head of the Hangchow Beggars' Guild, he was a personage of some wealth—which seemed generally accepted as due him for his role in the guild and maybe for the drama of his periodic public appearances.

To Ling Yin Monastery

The floods of springtime visitors were at a peak at the time of the Ch'ing Ming Festival, the third day of the third moon. This was the time of the annual sweeping of the ancestral tombs, when the family grave sites were properly tended to and special respects were paid to the ancestors. Members of the family gathered from near by or elsewhere in the province or from farther away for the traditional duties and rituals and festivities. Picnicking at the gravesites was part of the tradition.

These visitors—most of them—joined the hundreds and hundreds of others who made pilgrimages at this time to the temples, shrines, and monasteries in the region, chief of which was Ling Yin Ssu (Monastery of the Spirits' Retreat), the most important Buddhist center in this part of China and one of the oldest and most beautiful.

The monastery grounds were about ten miles from the center of the city (and roughly six miles from where we lived)—in a wild little wooded natural valley west of the lake. It was a pilgrimage site throughout the year; at Ch'ing Ming travelers streamed along the ways leading from city, hills and countryside to Ling Yin. A few were in sedan chairs; most traveled on foot. The more devout wore, hanging from their waists, large pouches of coarse yellow cotton carrying coins to give as alms . . . or long strings of cash, the older and cheaper brass coins, round with square centers, to be dispensed by the less affluent of the followers of the Buddhist Way.

Like practically everybody else, we were having friends from out of town visiting us; and since they had never been to Hangchow before, we were taking them first of all to Ling Yin Monastery. This was an excursion that could include several stops on the way: Emperors' Island with its famous pavilions and the Imperial Library, the Sacred Fish pond, and the Tomb of Yo Fei, the great hero-patriot-martyr of the Sung dynasty. This time it was to be only Ling Yin, because it was the height of the pilgrim season and the ways would be congested and there would be much going on at the monastery itself.

It was a fresh and sparkling April morning. We had breakfast, and the sedan chairs, ordered the day before, had come and were waiting inside our front gate.

I was happy and excited. I loved going to Ling Yin—perhaps more than anywhere else. And then suddenly I remembered "pilgrim season" and my heart plummeted and I felt a little sick. "Will there be beggars?" I nearly asked, but didn't, because if the answer had been 'yes', I might have said, "I can't go!"—and how could I bear not going? Maybe this year would be different. If not, I would just close my eyes tight.

As soon as we left the city, we found ourselves joining a trickle of travelers going our way; it wasn't till we had taken a wide, rustic path in a valley out of sight of the Lake that we became part of a larger procession all moving in the same direction.

My father as excursion leader called out facts of interest about Buddhism in China and particularly about the Mahayana Buddhism practised at Ling Yin; and he compared what we were seeing with the variety of persons and the pace of travel of the pilgrimages to Canterbury Cathedral in the England of Chaucer's time. These comments meant nothing to me then, though I remembered them later . . . I was tightening up to shut out the sights and sounds I was afraid were coming.

Then from ahead of us, we heard a sound that shivered my spine—a deep, despairing sound, something between a wail and a groan, and we saw the beggar by the roadside on his knees, bowing his head to the earth and raising it again, crying out with a long indrawn sobbing breath. The saddest sound in the world.

There were more and more beggars as we went on—and the most of all as we came to a village where several valley roadways and hillside paths converged. Here the beggars crowded the sides of the unpaved street through the center of the village. There were the crippled and maimed, the blind with staring rheumy eyes, the mothers and infants in filthy rags, the bodies with putrefying sores and—the most horrifying of all: a human shape in a burlap sack thrashing about at the intersection of the street with another narrower one. Was it armless?—legless?—*headless*? What kind of human creature was it? It haunted me ever after.

Beyond this village, there was relief. I began to enjoy my perch in the gently swaying sedan chair. We left the noise behind us and entered the springtime freshness of a bamboo grove. There were only the travelers now on the well-worn flagstone and cobbled roadway—until we came to a small clearing on one side of the way and standing in it some distance back, as if reluctant to be seen was a beggar woman. She simply stood there all by herself in her shapeless faded clothes. Her nose had been completely eaten away, probably by leprosy, so that it looked like an open mouth in the center of her face rounded into a perpetual soundless cry of woe. I could never forget her either.

The Monastery at Pilgrim Season

The first glimpse of Ling Yin were flashes of the vermilion of the outer monastery walls seen through dense wild shrubbery and trees. We came to a small huddle of buildings—hardly a village . . . a single, uneven little street of rickety, two-storied tea shops, restaurants, inns to serve travelers and visitors to the monastery. It was bustling with activity today.

Outside the entrance to the grounds, the sedan chairs were let down for us to proceed on foot. Other visitors were gathering to go through the gateway. The mood was festive. At this season the great scowling guardian gods in the entrance building lost their power to strike awe. A holiday atmosphere prevailed inside the grounds. Travelers strolled and chatted; they rested in the pavilions overlooking the mountain stream, beyond which rises the Peak That Flew from India. Water flowed fresh and free from spring rains, and to cross over to see the grottos and caves on the other side, it was necessary to pick one's way carefully on stepping stones that were almost covered with water.

Alongside the way were small temporary booths, where vendors sold their specialties: bundles of incense sticks and packets of red candles to be offered in reverence and worship; strings of dark-colored wooden prayer beads for the truly pious to count as they walked under the shade of old trees, saying over and over, "0-mi-to-fo," the affirmation of belief in Amitabha. There were booths hung with colorful toys for children like the miniature wooden fish drums with knockers and paper whirligigs—and others offering holiday souvenirs for adults.

People stopped to stare up in appreciation at the enormous Protectors of the Temple—two on each side—in the entrance to the monastery itself. My father explained why one carried a sword, another a mandolin; one held a folded umbrella and another a serpent—to keep away any kind of danger or evil that might threaten this holy place.

The Laughing Buddha facing the entrance seemed even more affable than usual, as worshippers lit their incense sticks for containers on the altar before him and bowed respectfully. The ample bare belly obviously bothered new visitors to China; so my father told them that to be fat meant good fortune and happiness. It seemed quite natural to me, who saw prosperous, well-fed shopkeepers fanning themselves—cooling off in hot weather, stomachs bare.

The holiday mood was changed now to a kind of attentive, yet relaxed and unhurried quiet. The approach to the Main Hall, the Worship Temple with its three tiers of roofs, was long and leisurely, shaded by lofty old trees and flanked by one-story halls for meditation or other priestly uses.

The air was wonderfully pungent with incense. In the huge bronze urn on the terrace of the Main hall, hundreds of sticks of incense burned, dwindling down to a fine, pale ash. The urn brimmed with the ashes.

A bell tolled the beginning of worship. Instead of entering the building to walk around inside as we ordinarily would have done, we stood at one side of the open entrance. Someone helped me step over the very high wooden threshold so that I could stand just inside and see.

From doorways at either side gray-robed priests paced in slowly, hands pressed together in prayer, eyes downcast, chanting as they came. Each one bowed at the altar before taking his place and kneeling on a round prayer cushion on the floor. At measured intervals, a priest standing next to the great bronze bell in a front corner struck it with a wooden mallet wrapped in cloth and the sound rang out deep and mellow. It was said that the noonday tolling of the Ling Yin monastery bell could be heard on the Great Street of Hangchow ten miles away if there happened to be an instant or so when the noises of the city were stilled. The chanting continued, low-pitched and rhythmic. Flames of the tall red candles on the altar table wavered and smoked; and the Great Buddha himself (Sakyamuni . . . or Gautama) looked down through half-closed eyes with an enigmatic expression of remote and infinite calm.

We were quiet and respectful. I almost wanted to kneel like the priests, but I remembered what the Bible said about graven images and "thou shalt have no other God . . . " All the same, I was awed. And I didn't have to be reminded that this was a place of worship.

After a while, someone helped me back over the threshold and we left still not speaking until we were well out on the paving stones of the portico.

"You'll be interested in the Hall of the Five Hundred Lohan," my father told our visitors, as he led us around to the rear of the Main Hall and then off to one side of the grounds. In an off season this could be a spooky place with its rows and rows of dusty images, larger than life, looming over us on either side as we walked the silent aisles. Now with other viewers besides ourselves, the atmosphere was subdued but more sociable than scary and the figures non-threatening in spite of exaggerated poses and expressions and grotesqueries of appearance such as earlobes hanging down to shoulders, extra arms fanning out from the body, little hands reaching out from the ears, bulging eyes—symbolic representations of the character and story of each of these noted disciples and followers of Buddha. Not all of them were holy personages, however; a few might simply be important supporters or admirers of the faith. My father always pointed out the figure of Marco Polo, who had apparently won his place of honor in this Buddhist Hall of Fame as an illustrious admirer of Hangchow (known to him as Quinsay). Years later it was learned by us Hangchow foreigners that this was not our 'Marco' but someone else with a name like Po-Lo—a convert or patron, perhaps one of the many foreigners here during the time of the Mongol occupation.

Our sedan chairs were waiting for us at the outer gate to the monastery—the bearers nearby chatting or taking their ease in the shade, probably after having been refreshed in a tea shop and having something to eat from food bar or vendor . . .

I was dreading the journey back; but alms had been entreated from pilgrims on their way to worship and had been received. And the beggars had vanished.

Later in the spring, after the special religious celebrations were over, Ling Yin continued to be filled with visitors—springtime in Hangchow being a season of freshness and flowers and romance that attracted travelers and holiday-goers of all kinds.

In the outer grounds of Ling Yin, the portable booths still lined the walkway overlooking the mountain stream, and among them for a matter of days were the vendors of newly harvested sugar cane. For a while the broad roadway and also the courtyard and grounds of the monastery itself were strewn with pieces of the chewed pulp.

We always had fresh sugar cane when we picnicked as a family or with the Olivers (our fellow picnic-lovers), somewhere in the spacious courtyard, sitting on the ground under the lofty and elderly trees.

Our very careful mothers believed it was safe, even though raw and unsterilized. Hot water from thermoses was poured over the stalks, which were then carefully peeled and cut into chewable chunks and divided out, piece by piece. It was delicious—like clear, not-too-sweet nectar.

One time after we had delighted in the treat, Robert who'd had a loose tooth exclaimed, "It's gone!"—and we never knew whether he'd swallowed it with the juice or discarded it with the pulp.

In the dead of winter it was a long chilly journey to Ling Yin—not frequently taken; but I saw it once after a snowfall when it was particularly serene and beautiful—belonging to nature and to the resident monks—most of whom were indoors studying or meditating—and to the Abbot in charge (a youngish man, chosen from a family of the provincial gentry—able, well-educated, thoughtful—a friend of my father's).

The only worshiper we saw was carried in a private sedan chair into the temple grounds almost to the Main Hall—an elderly woman, dressed soberly but sumptuously in silk and brocade—obviously wealthy, obviously troubled. She stepped carefully out of the sedan chair and walked, all alone, slowly and carefully on her bound feet into the great Hall to make her personal prayers and petitions to Buddha and probably even more directly to Kuan Yin, the Goddess of Mercy, in her special booth at the rear of the Hall.

Autumn at Ling Yin

The best time of all for Ling Yin was in the fall when only the random traveler shared the valley roadways and the villages were quiet and the smoke from the burning dried brush gathered on the hillsides blended with incense from small shrines along the way growing more fragrant as we neared the monastery.

Autumn with its mellow sunshine and clean, crisp air was a time of recharged energy and also a time that invited reflection and the telling of old stories. So, as we roamed the grounds of Ying Lin, we heard again in scattered snatches the legends attached to the place and the story of the priest from India who had founded the monestary. He had traveled all the long way with his pet monkey and, coming to the Hangchow region, decided to settle here. One day while he and his small companion were wandering in the hills north west of the Lake, they came into a quiet little wooded valley, whereupon the monkey became wildly excited, scampering about in great joy as if he'd found himself back in his forest home in

India. Therefore Hui Li (the Chinese name given the Indian priest) chose this place for a monastery. The rocky cliff rising up at one side of the valley was named The Peak That Flew from India and has been so-called ever since . . . The monastery was founded in the year 326 A.D.—which didn't mean much to me as a child, except that it was spoken of with respect and I knew it was long ago. As far as I was concerned, Ling Yin had always been there.

There were legends and superstitions and tales told about the Buddhist carvings on the rocky face of The Peak That Flew. One recent story, oft retold, was about the time that our young parents-to-be were taken by missionary friends for their first visit to Ling Yin. Someone pointed out to them a famous carving high up on the cliff. It was said that if a person threw a pebble and it landed on the ledge and stayed there, there would be a son in the family within a year. The young husband took up the challenge. It was a long throw high up and across the wide stream, but on the third try he was successful. And Robert was born in the November of that year. Firstborn and a son.

At this season we could cross the nearly-dry stream bed to the caves at the base of The Peak That Flew. There were figures of Buddhist deities and disciples carved out of the stone in the walls of the grottos—some with lighted candles on the ledges before them. On one wall was a famous fresco carved in relief of the sacred sutras being brought to the Hangchow region, carried by eight horses (a story common to other ancient temples in China).

A gray-robed priest was in attendance. He directed us to a small dark cave opening off from a larger one, where (we were told) the pure in heart might be afforded a glimpse of Paradise—or perhaps of Kuan Yin, Goddess of Mercy . . . or of Hui Li's white monkey. We took turns. The priest carried a long slender bamboo pole. He directed the seeker to stand in the center of the dark little cubicle and he pointed upward at the apparently solid rock above. Unless your heart was pure, you would only see darkness. Peering earnestly up along the line of the pointer, I saw a small circle of brightness—a crevice with the sky showing through?—or was it a tiny view of heaven? It would have been exciting—though really not expected—to see Kuan Yin or, better still, Hui Li's white monkey, but I had been able to see that spot of light in the

240

darkness and I was satisfied.

In the large courtyard of the inner grounds, the sun slanted golden through the tops of the giant shade trees. Pale yellow leaves were beginning to fall—drifting gently down.

The wooden fish head drum up ahead was struck, signaling mealtime for the resident priests, most of whom gathered and entered the dining hall, one of the long, low buildings flanking the approach to the Main Hall. Two or three priests were in attendance in the worship hall to assist worshippers or other visitors like ourselves. We were made welcome by one of them, who after we had gazed upward for a while at the great Buddha, led us over for a closer look at the huge bronze temple bell hanging from a beam or scaffolding in the front corner. He asked if we would like to try ringing it and the invitation was made especially to the children. We took turns here too—holding the wooden handle of the mallet with both hands—swinging and striking—and that wonderful sound seemed to reverberate through us and then spin out of the temple door on and on into the autumn air. Could they hear it on the Great Street in the city? . . . (He wasn't asked, but my father unobtrusively dropped a few coins into the shallow wooden platform under the giant bell where others had done the same, and, bowing slightly, the priest indicated a thank-you.)

We heard more stories as we walked, past the figures of the Lohan lining the side walls, to the rear of the temple building—and then gazed up at the fresco in plaster-of-Paris relief, graphically depicting all over its surface Buddhist lore and Buddhist doctrine, from birth to after death. Many were stories of Kuan Yin and her acts of compassion. The largest and most beautiful figure, to my eyes, was of Kuan Yin borne lightly on the back of a leaping dolphin. Another scene that always held my attention was of a nearly-naked baby lying in the center of a small wooden craft being rowed through tossing waves by an elderly boatman. A soul about to be born crossing the waters into life in the everyday world. (In later years, there came into my mind a picture of Charon ferrying a soul the other way across the River Styx into Hades.)

In describing "The Monastery of Ling Yin (Soul's Retreat)," Robert Fitch (author of *Hangchow Itineraries*—1919) wrote: "Facing the entrance on the outside is an inscription signifying that this spot is but a foot from

Heaven—thus marking the sacred character of the place."

At any time of year—even in the bustling pilgrim and tourist season—a spirit of other-worldly tranquillity prevailed at Ling Yin, along with the awareness of the beauty of the natural world . . . most fully to be sensed in autumn when the fragrance of incense and of woodsmoke were almost indistinguishable.

Autumn Closer By

In the fall during persimmon season, the peddler came regularly to our home with the lovely red sweet fruit from somewhere to the south.

In the fall, we were visited by the date peddler with the jujubes from the north—and Mother chose the medium size for desserts and cookies and the large ones for eating and stuffing with walnuts at Christmas time. Yienh San bounded to the kitchen with some of these to be steamed, then eaten almost immediately—still sticky on the outside.

We were visited by the peddler of walnuts (also from the north)—large and pale with sweet meats.

The transactions all took place in the front yard—on the pathway or on the lawn. The peddlers carried their wares in baskets or containers hung from the ends of bamboo carrying poles—set them down—showed what they had to offer. The purchases were heaped on a brass pan, hanging from a slender bamboo rod held by a string from its center and the weights measured by metal disks hanging from the other end and added or taken away till the two ends were in balance . . . always interesting to watch.

In the fall, our garden was bright with chrysanthemums; and chrysanthemums were in bloom in homes and courtyards—on balconies all over the city. At the peak of their blooming, there was the annual Chrysanthemum Show on Emperor's Island. We walked to the lakeshore, hailed a sampan and were rowed the brief distance to the Island. Just beyond the stone-paved landing and to one side stood a temporary ceremonial archway made of bamboo and festooned with fresh chrysanthemums. We passed through to stroll with others and admire the chrysanthemums in bloom on either side of the walkway. They were in pots set on the ground, on long wooden benches—perched on stools. All colors and shapes (and all with their special names). Sunshiny yellow, crystalline white, mauve,

plum, bronze, gold, burgundy—spidery, rounded or spread out, spectacu-
larly large and satiny, dainty and tight as buttons—all smelling of spice.

There was no judging—no awards—no competition. These were the
favorites of private owners brought here for the pleasure and delight of
the public—and all for free. Everybody was happy; no one was in a hurry.
Singly or severally or in family groups, they walked along slowly (as did
we), pausing to admire, leaning over to examine or sniff, exchanging appreciative comments with each other . . . as if storing up the color and
scent and beneficent autumn sunshine against the somberness and chill
of winter.

In the fall, the moon was at its brightest. The curving tiles of rooftops
were burnished at night with silver. Moonlight flowed into narrow streets
and alleys, disclosing pale walls and dark doorways usually invisible at
night.

On the ninth day of the ninth moon by the lunar calendar (some time
in October by ours), the Moon Festival was celebrated all over China. In
Hangchow people took to favorite spots in the hills overlooking the Lake,
where they picnicked on special foods like fresh crab—and, in legendary
times, drank chrysanthemum wine.

We never went on one of these outings, but someone always brought
us moon cakes, which were part of the celebration. They were round and
thick and substantial—made of rich flaky pastry with a dark sweet filling
of bean paste or maybe a mixture of dates (jujubes) and ground nuts. A
single moon cake went a long way, divided amongst us. I relished my
share—the more so knowing that this was a treat that came only once a
year.

The Lake and the River lent themselves to the celebration and the
enjoyment of the autumn moon. On the shore of Emperor's Island, there
was the Smooth Lake and Autumn Moon Pavilion first built more than a
thousand years before, in the T'ang dynasty (618-907).

There were legends and stories about the autumn moon like those connected with the three stone lanterns imbedded in the lake offshore from
the island created by the poet Su Tung-p'o (1036-1101) in the Sung dynasty—and how these lanterns were mysteriously lit up as if from within
on a certain night each year when the moon was full.

There were poems written. There were paintings. One painting from

243

the Sung dynasty is of a splendid but airy pavilion on a bluff over-looking the Ch'ien-t'ang River entitled "Viewing the Bore in the Moonlight."

Most of my life I assumed that the T'ang dynasty poet Li Po had drowned by drunkenly trying to embrace the reflection of the moon in West Lake. It seemed an appropriate ending for one so free-spirited—a true romantic; but Li Po never saw West Lake, although he had adventured in the wild and lonely mountains and valleys to the southwest of the province.

Always—even now—I see the Rabbit in the Moon grinding powder for the Elixir of Immortality. Only if I try very hard can I see the face of the Man in the Moon.

One night, bright and clear, there was to be a total lunar eclipse: the Heavenly Dog was going to swallow the full moon. There were sounds of great excitement in the neighborhood—shouts and cries and the banging of gongs and cymbals. The din increased as we saw the bright edge of the moon grow dark and the darkness getting larger. The heavenly dog was eating the moon. If he couldn't be stopped and swallowed it all, he would have to be frightened into disgorging it.

We wanted to help. Yienh San ran into the house to collect noisemak-ers—enamel basins and pots and pans and kitchen spoons to beat with. We sat on the steps in front of the Flowery Pavilion and joined in the tumult. By this time, a large part of the moon had already disappeared. When it vanished completely, the noise crescendoed all about us outside our walls and we beat furiously on our noisemakers, watching—watching.

And it worked. A small sliver of white moon appeared and gradually grew larger and larger as the heavenly dog was forced to choke it out. And finally the precious moon was whole and free—not lost forever. Triumph. And the night was quiet and at peace.

We were told, of course, the why's and wherefore's of an eclipse and what had actually been happening, and the explanation was interesting; but we still could believe that along with all those others near by we had helped save the moon. It was a gratifying feeling to have been part of the rescue—the triumph.

Summer

When Dr. Duncan Main came from Scotland to Hangchow in 1881 with his bride (neé Florence Nightingale Smith—a nurse who had worked in the slums of Edinburgh), he was taken on a tour of the city which included the worst quarters. "The streets were a revelation to him . . . with their seething crowds . . . the revolting smells and sights . . . Men with yokes fitted to their shoulders were carrying sewage from dwelling houses and sewage pits uncovered through the streets; open cesspools stood at the corners; unsightly lepers and maimed beggars in all states of decay rubbed shoulders with the throng . . ." The senior missionary (according to this account) glanced at the young doctor expecting a look of disgust but saw instead a merry twinkle—and "a distinctly shut mouth." The young doctor himself was saying to himself, "And this is the city of 'Heaven Below'. How vastly below!"*

This was in the winter. It was worse in the summer when heat lay heavy and menacing on the city and diseases were rampant.

Dr. Main became a prime booster of Hangchow—as well as the healer of countless individuals and the founder of hospitals, a medical training College, pharmacy training college, nursing training schools (men's and women's), a children's home, convalescent sanatoria, a consumptive hospital, fresh air homes, Alms House, Ragged School (whatever exactly that was) . . . to name only a part of the list. Always he was aware of the unwholesomeness and threat of the city with its crowds and lack of sanitation; and one of his frequent prescriptions for cure or recuperation was to send the patient up into the hills where the air was pure.

In the summer months of the early years, missionary families took refuge in one or another of the Buddhist monasteries in the hills, where they rented lodgings in the simple one-story hostels customarily providing shelter to pilgrims and other travelers. There they more or less camped out in the cooler, cleaner air—the mothers doing the necessary chores, the children playing in the shade of venerable trees on the monastery grounds.

By our day, Western foreigners in our part of China had discovered, acquired, and developed a mountain resort where they could go for their allotted vacations and where their children could spend all summer away

* From *"Dr. Apricot of 'Heaven Below,'"* the life story of Dr. Duncan Main of Hangchow, taken from *"Heroes of the Cross,"* Series Eight.

from the health hazards of the crowded cities. The name of the resort was Mokanshan. It was in Chekiang province and could be reached for much of the way by the Grand Canal.

Most of us were not aware that it had been the site of a Buddhist monastery, which had been totally destroyed by the T'ai P'ing Rebels (in about 1862). For the Western children in Chekiang and nearby provinces, it was (as the parents put it) a paradise on earth throughout the summer months. It belonged to us.

Because of Mokanshan, we Barnett children never experienced an entire summer in Hangchow and were never there in midsummer. But I remember a time—or maybe times—when we were delayed, perhaps by the presence of house guests or by an important YMCA event, and didn't leave for the mountain until well past the departure of the other families. And twice we came back early—both times when a new sibling was to be born and we stopped off in Hangchow on the way to doctor and medical facilities in Shanghai.

When we were late in going to Mokanshan and summer had taken over in the city, we drooped in the heat. We fretted in our shoes and stockings and thought of our little friends running barefoot on the mountain paths. We would never dare going barefoot here in the city, having seen what might happen to us: elephantiasis and a leg as gross and huge as a log; or maybe we would pick up hookworm, which we didn't dread quite so much, not being sure what it would *do* to us.

We thought with longing of going swimming—scampering down the path through the bamboo grove to the Mokanshan pool (built—full-size—by the earlier generation of missionaries and their teen-age sons), where like our little friends—we had learned to swim, most of us graduating from water-wings in the shallow end at about age four.

We thought of the spring just above the tennis courts and the pure cold water that we could drink unboiled—with its lovely taste of the bamboo spout that carried it out of the mountainside.

Here in the city our drinking water was never cooler than lukewarm, and sometimes it had tiny creatures in it—"wiggle-tails" we called them. I would watch them with interest busily darting about in my glass of water on the dining room table. "Don't drink the water," Mother would say—and the glasses were removed to be emptied for other use or to be re-boiled. Sometimes a cooked vegetable would have a slightly off taste and Mother would say, "Don't eat any more!"—and it was tossed out.

The only refrigeration for food was provided by cages of bamboo and mesh hung outside to catch any stirring of the air—or by the interior of the well, where a tin of Australian butter or jars of boiled milk or drinking water would be held in the bucket let down to hang just over the surface. In reasonably warm weather, this would be cooling; in real summer it was a lost cause; and the butter ran.

Our beds were moved out onto the upstairs porch. The mosquito nets, which at first had provided intriguing little private houses or boats in which to sail through the nights now seemed to cut off any freshness. Inside the net the air was still and stuffy. The whine of a mosquito that had somehow made its way into the enclosure was shrill and persistent, growing louder and angrier on attack.

I don't know how we passed those days as we waited to go to Mokanshan. Maybe we sulked and complained. Mostly, I think, we slowed down to near-stop and waited.

One time, I remember, we heard that Dr. Barlow and his family were making a brief visit to Hangchow—professional for him—and the girls had gone swimming in West Lake. I was struck open-mouthed with surprise mixed with envy—but on second thought wondered where the lake was deep enough. What about all that soft mire turned up by the oars when we were out boating—said (poetically) to be ashes of incense fallen from the hundreds of shrines and temples and monasteries on the shores and the hillsides overlooking the lake . . . And what about germs?

We went boating on West Lake one full-fledged summer night. It was moonless and sultry. No breeze; no starlight. The air pressed down around and about us. It was infused with the perfume of lotus blossoms. Our sampan pushed its way through full-grown lotus pads. Darkness surrounded us until we heard muffled voices and saw others in their pleasure boats near by, leaning out to gather lotus seeds in the pods from which the petals had fallen.

A Canal Trip

In the Sui dynasty (A.D. 589-618), the Grand Canal was completed by joining together many existing canals and waterways and extending it north to the Yellow River and south to Hangchow.

It was at the southern terminus, just north of the city, that we boarded our rented houseboat to go to Mokanshan.

There was pandemonium at the landing place when we arrived with our assortment of belongings needed for the summer and our picnic supplies and bedrolls and mosquito nets and other overnight necessities for the journey. It seemed as we made our way through the jostling crowds in our sedan chairs or rickshaws that we saw more than usual of the sores and skin diseases that thrived in summer—of shaved heads with patches of ringworm treated with medicinal powder—of eyes streaming from trachoma. I tried hard to avoid looking at these half-blind people. I had the feeling that if our eyes met, they would quickly be connected by invisible threads across which thousands of tiny trachoma carriers would come scurrying.

It was not just fancy that there were so many with this eye disease there. Trachoma was rife among the boat people. The intrepid lady missionary evangelists who spent weeks traveling by houseboat through the countryside with them treated their eyes and advised them on sanitation as well as preaching the gospel.

I seem to remember locks in the canal close to its terminus and boats being dragged over a mud bank from one level to another by men at the sides pulling on ropes.

Once we were on our way, it was a floating picnic that continued delightfully on and on—never in a hurry—always with something for us to do or to see. We had our cabin to climb down into; we had our deck from which to watch the slowly passing scene on either side. The older children could clamber up on the wooden roof of the cabin and view the whole visible world fore and aft. When we passed through a city or town, there would be cries of warning as we were nearing a stone bridge that might be barely high enough for the houseboat to pass under; anyone on the roof might be scraped right off into the water.

We saw mulberry trees in small groves or neat rows on the banks. We saw green rice paddies and farm plots squared off by irrigation ditches and narrow raised footpaths; we saw the farmers at work and every now and then a water buffalo or sometimes a little blind-folded donkey going round and round turning the water wheel. We saw, set at random somewhere out in the midst of the fields. tiny villages with clusters of farm buildings or lone gravemounds—each of these shaded by old trees. We saw flotillas of ducks rounding the corner from other smaller canals. We were surprised every now and then to catch sight of the brown sail of a junk seemingly traveling on dry land—actually on a canal too small to be seen at a distance.

This was a region of canals interconnecting in a bewildering maze which could be followed to intersect finally with the Grand Canal. (The Mongols in the 13th century, accustomed to fight on horseback, had a hard time conquering this part of China.)

In the late afternoon, we had our picnic supper on the rear deck. The countryside lay quiet and deserted. We sang songs as night came on. By nightfall, any city we passed through was boarded up and silent—a ghost town.

Down in the cabin, bedrolls were spread out; mosquito nets were rigged up . . . Through the night, if we wakened we heard the creaking of the oars up front—the splashing of water—maybe the whine of a mosquito.

And in the morning, there was sorting out to do and getting ourselves and our belongings ready for the end of the voyage and for the rest of the Journey. After unloading at the landing, we set out in sedan chairs or on foot across level rice fields to the foot of the mountain and then on upward to the summertime we had been waiting for.

A New Baby

It is odd—or maybe not—that I have no clear recollections of the reverse journeys—back from Mokanshan or, for that matter from other memorable trips, excursions, or occasions. There was too much of what had just gone by still filling my mind.

And so I don't remember the boat trip back, that second time we left the mountain early in order to go on to Shanghai for the arrival of a new baby.

But I do remember that the city, still held in thrall by the summer heat, seemed normal and unchanged. The alley off Law Court Street was just the same as ever.

Our house, however, seemed a little strange; it seemed to have gotten used to our absence and had a half-neglected, almost uncaring look. Our quarrelsome little dog, Brownie—never a lovable friend and companion like Zip (forever lost)—was studiedly indifferent to our return. Our pet canary, left in the care of the servants who had stayed on to look after the place, was alive and well in its cage, but was silent—failing to respond in joyful song to our greetings.

We were not there long before going on to Shanghai. A few days and nights only . . . I remember the heaviness of the air—and how uncomfortable it was to crowd our feet into stockings and shoes again—and how hard it was to sleep at night where there was no freshness or motion in the air. I remember listening for the periodic chorusing of cicadas rising into the darkness and falling into silence—and hearing instead the sound of a lone musician playing the two-string fiddle (*erh-hu*) from somewhere near by—on a doorstep in the alley or in a neighboring courtyard. On and on into the night—variations on a simple air . . . brave, persistent . . . that seemed to sing to life while knowing of its chanciness and brevity. This is the way I have remembered it.

In Shanghai, we waited for the new baby. Days passed. Schools opened for fall sessions, and Robert and I were entered into the fifth grade of the Shanghai American School in its original premises in the Hongkew section of the city. For a while Robert and I stayed with our friends the Joel Blacks, in the French Concession and every morning rode across the city to school in a taxi with Ruth Black and a couple of other American children who lived in the vicinity.

One day, when we arrived back from school, Aunt Lucy Black told us that we had a new brother. (*Brother?*—I'd expected a little sister!). Dr. Fearn (as we knew) was away in America on a furlough; Mother and the baby were in a hospital on Range Road, over in the Hongkew district. We wouldn't be seeing the baby right away—and (we were told gently) our mother was very sick.

Mother nearly died. No one at the hospital could stop the hemorrhaging. A friend, Dr. Hiltner—flouting medical etiquette and procedures— stormed the hospital and took over. He saved my mother's life—to my father's eternal gratitude . . . and ours when we knew of it later.

When Mother recovered all of us, with our new brother Doak, settled for the time being in a row house on Dixwell Road in walking distance of the school.

It was "for the time being." But we never went back home to Hangchow. Also we never really left it.

‖Epilogue

From a letter of my mother's to "Dear Friends" in America, dated March 5, 1922:

> *When I wrote last we were in our quiet peaceful home of "Heaven Below" as the Chinese call Hangchow. Many of you will be surprised to know that we are now living in Shanghai, the metropolis and "Gateway" of China. The suggestion of a change came to us as a great surprise . . . Eugene was asked to take up the National student work in the absence of Mr. Rugh who is necessarily kept in America . . . [The] World's Student Conference meets in Peking in April . . .*
>
> *The children and I were in Shanghai when the decision was made so Eugene went to Hangchow and moved up our household things . . . [W]e do miss dear old Hangchow with its beautiful hills and West Lake and all of our dear friends, both Chinese and foreign. That has been home to us now for eleven years and they have been wonderful years. It is pretty hard to pull up roots when they are so deep. I hardly feel like I am in China here in Shanghai . . . it isn't like real China.*

Going Back

Every year—except for the 12-month family furlough (early 1923 to early 1924)—we had at least one visit "back home" severally or as a family.

Robert and I had our visit even in the spring of 1927 when the violence of political upheaval and anti-foreign sentiment had forced Americans to evacuate their inland posts and stations for safety in Shanghai.

The Olivers stayed with us in our house in the YMCA compound in the French Concession. For a while we were a household of thirteen.

For some, the 1927 exodus was permanent: they left China, never to return. Others lingered on in Shanghai for varying lengths of time. The Olivers took their chances (according to some) and went back to their work in Hangchow rather soon, leaving Lillian and John in Shanghai to continue at the Shanghai American School.

As Easter vacation approached, there was uncertainty about their going home for the holidays. There was much discussion (by mail) between their parents and ours, and it was decided that the four of us, Lillian and John and Robert and I (as slightly older escorts) could safely make the journey by train—by ourselves.

There was not the usual holiday mood anywhere. It was one of those tense, uneasy times when no one was sure what was happening or going to happen, but our parents were sure we would be all right—and the four of us, who had been doing a lot of prodding, were overjoyed.

The station, when we left Shanghai, was a-swarm with anxious-looking travelers. The passenger cars were crowded. We saw no other foreigners except for a black-robed Catholic priest (probably French Lazarist) who after one look at the four American school children dived out of sight—probably into another train car. He seemed frightened of us. We didn't know why, but we felt very independent and confident of ourselves.

Hangchow when we got there was quieter than usual, but otherwise comfortable and normal—the right place for us to be.

For most of our last visits before college in America, Robert and I were included in the traditional Easter vacation "house parties." Ever since the Shanghai American School had been in existence, it had been customary for the boarding students from Hangchow to take home with them at Eastertime some of their fellow-boarders who were from cities too far away to allow the journey there and back. The Hangchow "house parties" were famous, and Robert and I were delighted when we were old enough to be participants. Co-hosts were what we considered ourselves.

We usually stayed at T'ienh Sway Gyao—the girls in one of the mission homes, the boys in another—and we sallied forth every day on foot or rented bicycles for all-day outings to the hills—the Lake—the College—Ling Yin.

Those wonderful visits. In all of them, whether with family or our own contemporaries, I cannot remember a single unhappy moment.

252

A Visit to the Old House

Only once did we see our place off Law Court Street again.

I don't know if it was impromptu or planned by someone like Uncle Jay Oliver, who might have said, "How would you like to drop by and see where you used to live?"

It was all very polite and proper.

We were greeted at the familiar entrance by a gateman, not the one who had worked for us.

Someone explained to him who we were and why we were there. He gave a small welcoming bow and invited us in.

We paused for a look at the Eastern Flowery Pavilion facing us, and then the gateman waved us on along the pathway into the rest of the premises.

Apparently none of the current household were at home.

There it all was—the main building and the wing beyond. I suppose the moon door into the connecting courtyard was still there; I'd have noticed if it hadn't been. Oddly, the compound walls seemed higher than before and the space within more constricted. In fact, everything seemed slightly shrunken.

It was curious to think that we'd lived in that rather plain-looking grey brick house—and that once I'd been a child playing in the front yard where we were standing.

We didn't go around to the back and didn't presume to go into the house—not even up to the front porch.

We came; we saw; we left—thanking our guide, the gateman, as he ushered us out.

I was glad to see "our house" again, even though my larger, older self didn't seem to have much connection with the child who had lived there. It never occurred to me to imagine living there again now—or ever in the future, for that matter.

In Exile

College in America was a painful parting and separation from their children for the parents, who nevertheless spoke of it as our "going home" to school to continue our education. They knew that we wouldn't be seeing each other for years and that communications would be slow (a back-and-forth exchange of letters took about eight weeks), but we would be 'home' in America. They didn't know about "culture shock"—a concept not recognized or identified as such at that time even when experienced, and they didn't conceive of it anyway as something that would happen to us.

But it *was* culture shock—a sense of being alien and unconnected to this America where I was supposed to feel like an American. I was homesick for my family, never having lived away from them; I was homesick for China . . . for a long time. China was reality for me—not America.

Gradually I accustomed myself to Randolph-Macon Woman's College and the reality of China became dimmer, in spite of letters from Shanghai and news reports of dire happenings in that part of the world. In college I wrote papers and stories and even a little play about China— mostly with Hangchow in mind—and dutifully sent them back to Shanghai for the family to read. My mother saved them all. I'm surprised now to see what time and distance had done to change the truth of China into an idea—sometimes embarrassingly sentimentalized.

After Four Years

At the depth of the Great Depression, graduates of Randolph-Macon (called by its admirers the Vassar of the South) found their jobs (if any) back in their home towns where they were known and had connections.

I felt uneasy about leaving America without knowing more about it than I'd experienced in my four years in a well-protected woman's college, with summers spent working in a girls' camp, and vacations as a perennial visitor—always warmly welcomed but still a visitor. But I had no home town in this country where I might have a chance at a job. I had a major in English, and in China there was always a market for teachers or tutors in English. And my parents and two little brothers (not so little by now!) were there.

And so in August after graduation, I crossed the continent by train and the Pacific Ocean by ship—and when the S.S. President McKinley had turned into the yellow-brown waters of the Whangpoo River and I saw Shanghai, I felt (as I wrote later) that a piece that had been missing had been restored to me.

I also realized very soon that now that I was grown up—and at age twenty I felt wiser and more grown-up than I ever have since—China wasn't really my home. I was one of the 'foreigners' now—and I had left America still a stranger. I was conscious of being uneasily though not unhappily adrift and floating on the surface of things—a sort of vagrant water weed. But life was too exciting for me to brood unduly over this, and I expected when I saw Hangchow again, here I would have a sense of belonging and being in a place where I still had roots.

It didn't happen—except in brief snatches—either on my first trip back which was some time in the fall, or on subsequent visits. Hangchow in becoming more convenient and up-to-date had changed more than I had expected. Streets had been widened and paved. Outside the city there were motor roads everywhere it seemed—even on the Su Causeway, where the ancient stone bridges had been done away with and cars were enabled to cross the Lake at unseemly speeds . . . The Needle Pagoda on its rocky peak had been 'repaired' by encasing it in concrete. Long ago it had been compared to a 'girl' and the Thunder Pagoda across the Lake to an 'aged monk'. They had both seemed alive. The slender, graceful Needle Pagoda was like a mummy now. The Thunder Pagoda had collapsed a decade before and was gone from its bluff. (There were rumors that a Hangchow family, descendants from princes from way, way back, wanted to rebuild it, but events of history have obviously made it impossible.) Pleasure-seekers boating on West Lake seemed mostly to be young Chinese sophisticates from Shanghai who had brought their portable radios with them. Popular Western songs of the day blared out from sampans full of vacationers. A favorite was Bing Crosby singing "Under a Blanket of Blue" . . . This was *not* my Hangchow.

Yet there were glimpses of an older Hangchow than 'mine' on visits to the Olivers who had studied old maps and had searched for and discovered visible reminders of its glorious and just plain fascinating past. In our rovings we saw remnants of the Sung dynasty imperial gardens on the southern hillsides overlooking the Lake . . . And farther, on another ridge, were the seven ancient iron cauldrons (waist-high) which for many centuries had served as fire prevention insurance for the city. Open to the sky, they were filled and replenished by rain; if they ever became dry, Hangchow would be destroyed by fire . . . I wondered if in times of drought did people haul water from down below to pour into the cauldrons and avoid disaster.

There was the visit in the summer of 1934 with an elderly English bachelor affectionately known to his friends as the "Hermit of Hangchow." George T. Moule, born in Hangchow, son of Bishop Moule, founder of the first Protestant mission in the city, had upon retiring from the Chinese Customs Service (which was under the management of the British) shut himself away behind the walls of his modest and gently bedraggled Chinese-style residence, because he could not bear to see the encroachments of the 20th century on his beloved city.

'Uncle Jay' Oliver took me and my brother Robert (back in China before going on to a Rhodes Scholarship in England) to call on the 'Hermit'. He hurried out to meet us at the gate and led us across a narrow little courtyard to the one-story building which was obviously his all-purpose daytime quarters—with his study at the front end. The desk was piled with papers and Chinese dictionaries and writing materials. The walls were lined with shelves full of books; and there were family pictures hanging on one part of the wall and, (incongruously), personally signed photographs of buxom London Music Hall beauties from his Cambridge University days back in England.

Our host could not have been more delighted with his callers. The conversation was lively and touched on all sorts of subjects of common interest. Before we left, he presented Robert with a porcelain vase decorated with the leaping carp motif, symbol of the striving and successful scholar.

After I was back in Shanghai, there came in the mail a small book and a note written in a beautiful old-fashioned Victorian hand:

> *Dear Miss Barnett,*
> *When you and your noble Brother so kindly visited me, I meant to offer you a copy of my father's Notes on Hangchow, but in the joyful sight of you and your Brother, the little book was forgotten.*
> *Now I send it . . .*
> *Most cordial greetings to you and your Parents and Brothers from G. T. Moule*

This little book is one of my treasures, with its notes and footnotes on historical facts and data about Hangchow gathered from journals and the local gazetteers and other sources and translated with the help of his Chinese "secretary" by the scholarly Bishop Moule. I wonder how his son, the friendly, loquacious recluse, knew that this was the gift for me.

The Bamboo Curtain and Separation

After Mao Tse-tung and the Communist Party took control of all the country in 1949 and founded the People's Republic of China, it became forbidden territory for U.S. citizens. Also (I found) it seemed to have become a distasteful, if not forbidden, subject of ordinary conversation, here in the U.S. It was almost as if, now that 'we' had 'lost China', we were willing it not to exist—and that the whole ancient land and its people had sunk like Atlantis into the sea.

It was strange at this time of total severance to try to retrieve on paper the life and look of the China I had known as a child, and along with that, to learn (which seemed important) as much as I could about the story and character of *my* city from its beginnings. This was with my husband's help. Often, both the Hangchow of history and the Hangchow of my childhood seemed impossibly far away.

(Written some time in 1965 in Arlington, Virginia):

I have not been back to Hangchow for more than thirty years . . . It is quite likely that I shall never see it again   and once in a long while, something . . . usually a chance combination of sounds and scents . . . reminds me of Hangchow with a sudden stab of longing that seems for an instant almost unbearable. But Hangchow was a happy place to live in . . . and except for these brief unreasonable moments, it is a happy place to remember.

At Long Last—Return

In May 1980—not too long after the end of the Cultural Revolution and the "reopening" of China—I was there again, thanks to my dear friends Jim and Joan Wilson and their older sister Lib, who had heard of a tour which included Hangchow. It was my first time to be in China as a *tourist.* I took notes and wrote a detailed account of our "Twelve Days in China" when back in Virginia.

In the account of our stay in Hangchow I wrote of how the Wilsons and I had arranged to take off on our own for a morning of finding our "old places." So much had changed—even the hills, covered now with trees, beautiful but different.

Meeting us [at noon] at the bus, our tour group friends wanted to hear about our morning adventures and whether we had succeeded in finding our old places. Lib and Jim answered first and said we'd been back to the College and seen their old home and other familiar buildings. Then I was asked if I'd found my old home in the city . . . I suppose I hadn't realized how much I'd counted on re-discovering certain sites and buildings both on the Great Street and in our own neighborhood, or how the many small disappointments had accumulated. When I began to say something about them, I was astonished and mortified to feel myself choking up and on the verge of tears. I was able to get hold of myself and report on the visit to the [former] YMCA and our welcome there.

[But then] Before boarding the bus, I stood for a moment looking about me— hearing the cheerful noontime bustle—aware of the Lake barely out of sight. And then suddenly, quite unexpectedly, I felt wholly at home. No time to ana- lyze—but for all the modernization and change, this could be nowhere else but Hangchow.

━━━━━

From my Impressions and Comments—China Trip (September 24 - October 24, 1987 . . . the last ten days in Hangchow):

I had thought before this trip that I was finally an American and that thirty three years of living in Arlington, Virginia had made it home. Now I realize that China is where I feel truly unselfconscious and most natural and comfort- able in my identity. This is surprising, even ironic, considering that in China I am obviously a foreigner among the myriads of true Chinese. In my heart, I feel that I am one of them; and when I tell them (in Chinese) that I was born in China and add that I am a "Hangchow person," something happens—an in- stant connection—that convinces me that in their minds as well as mine, we are kin—we are all in the same family . . .

Of all the places in China [where we visited], it was Hangchow where I felt most attuned to the rhythm—the pace—the way of life. The people were busy but not too hurried or harried . . . The air was softer there.

Epilogue

In early summer 1989 I took my granddaughter Alexandra on a China tour as her gift upon her graduation from Brown University. Because of the student demonstrations, centered in Tienanmen Square in Peking (Beijing) and the tensions rising and falling in China, there were doubts as to whether or not our tour might—like many others—be canceled. It wasn't. We left Seattle May 30 and arrived 9:30 pm May 31 in Shanghai (the plane we had changed to in Narita Airport, Japan was almost empty.)

After the scheduled stay in Shanghai, we traveled by train to Hangchow, arriving in the early evening.

From my notes of the trip:

Next morning I was down in the [hotel] lobby at 6:30 and decided to cross the street to a path leading up towards the Needle Pagoda Hill, hoping to reach the top in time to see West Lake in the early morning sun. The stone pathway was sylvan and steep. I had to stop often to catch my breath. Paths led off to either side, winding and disappearing around the curves . . . In the freshness of the summer morning people were strolling, some climbing upwards, others coming down individuals lone and reflective, couples holding hands. Looking along a narrow path to one side, I caught sight of a gentleman seated on a small level clearing, gazing off perhaps at the Lake—a bird cage set on the ground beside him. The bird in the cage was joyously singing its heart out and wild birds in nearby trees were singing back . . . Lovely.

That evening was 'free'—no entertainment offered, presumably because we had a full day of sightseeing and would be having an early start in the morning for travel by bus to our next stop, Wuxi.

Close to midnight, there was what seemed an impromptu demonstration on the wide amber-lit roadway outside the hotel . . . a procession, somewhat haphazard, mostly of young people (students?) carrying placards, singing patriotic songs. They came from the west and were met later by another procession approaching from the east. There was a brief period of talk and singing. At about 1:00 am, the gathering dispersed. Puzzling. In the middle of the night.

Next morning we heard rumors that word had come from somewhere to university students that the Chinese Army had been ordered to move in on the demonstrators holding out in Tienanmen Square . . . No more news was available.

At 8:30 we boarded the bus for our overland journey—with a stop only a few minutes later for our final 'Hangchow' sightseeing—at the Golden Dragon Cave on the hillside not too far from the hotel.

A brief stop; we didn't have time to explore all of the glens and courtyards. It was a soft fresh morning—light rain. Few other visitors. Fewer entertainments (music and drama) than [when I'd been there] before—perhaps because it was early. The Chinese classical musicians in their pavilion were unsmiling; I didn't feel drawn to speak to them as I had last time (when they had been so delighted to hear that I was a 'Hangchow person'). Having the place mostly to ourselves was a gift. It is a lush and beautiful place—like something out of a Chinese fairy tale.

It was not until the following afternoon June 5 after a night and no news in Wuxi and our cruise on the Grand Canal, that we arrived in Soochow and were told of the shocking and tragic happenings in Beijing on June 4. Our city guide, haggard and pale from sleeplessness, had been with the demonstrators in Soochow all the night before. Our bus skirted the continuing demonstrations on the way to our hotel (the same, with a different name that our 1980 tour group had stayed in). Our China tour was suddenly over. Problem: what to do now—how to leave Soochow—and China?

But that, as they say, is another story.

China Trip—1991 (September 26–October 27).

This was a re-visiting of our part of China with my lifelong friend Ruth (Black) Running. We were in Shanghai (her childhood home), in Soochow briefly, and in Hangchow for nearly three weeks. We were returning sojourners, not tourists.

Epilogue

1993 (May 10–June 2)

Alexandra and I took another China tour—this one even more inclusive and farflung in its itinerary than the one in 1989 that had been cut short. It included Kunming in Yunnan Province, where my husband (her grandfather-to-be) had served on General Chennault's staff in World War Two. Hangchow was on the itinerary—a couple of nights only. We were determined to see West Lake at dawn. The first morning it was pouring rain. The second, we walked along the shore and saw West Lake in the early morning mist—which (according to my diary) "made our whole trip worth while", even at this early stage of our tour.

═══════

I have friends now in the rehabilitated, reactivated Hangchow YMCA. In the building, which has been restored to its original layout and look (with added construction of new facilities), there is a "Barnett Room" honoring Eugene Barnett, my father, and another room dedicated to Leighton Stuart—Educator, Ambassador, true son of Hangchow.

I have friends in the lively YWCA in its new building not far away from the YMCA. We keep in touch.

I have been to Sunday morning services in a church that was filled to the brim. I was the only Westerner and was given a seat in the front row reserved for guests. The church (*Ssu Ch'eng T'ang*) is on the old *Fong Leh Gyao* (Abounding Joy Bridge) site. The bridge is gone—the canal itself and the narrow streets are gone, and any recognizable buildings; but here in this geographic spot was my very first home and near by the kindergarten where Robert and I went to our very first school.

All of this should be enough perhaps—and on each trip back, I've thought, "This will probably be the last time." But as I've left again, I'm not so sure.

In one of my collections of Chinese verse (in translation) I came across a poem—quite by accident—that made me nod my head and smile. In spite of differences in age, race, gender, and the time it was written—

1792 (which is not really so long ago in China), the poem struck home. I quote from it.

The poet: *Yuan Mei*—From *Hangchow visiting Su-sung, P'i-ling, and Ching-kou and staying the night with friends on the way.**

> *Seventy-seven, such an old fellow!*
> *In three years I get one look at the West Lake rains;*
> *Back I come, place after place for a short visit . . .*
> *My friends, forbear to ask the date of my next coming,*
> *For this is an uncertain thing not for my ordering;*
> *I keep saying I will never return and then returning . . .*

---

* From: *The Penguin Book of Chinese Verse.* Translated by Robert Kotewall and Norman L. Smithe. Edited by A.R.Davis. 1962